OVERNIGHT
SUCCESS

OVERNIGHT SUCCESS

FEDERAL EXPRESS AND FREDERICK SMITH, ITS RENEGADE CREATOR

VANCE H. TRIMBLE

Crown Publishers, Inc.
New York

Excerpt from "Overnight Flier" by Dan Dorfman August 15, 1978, *Esquire* magazine. Reprinted courtesy of the Hearst Corporation.

Published by Crown Publishers, Inc., 201 East 50th Street, New York, New York, 10022.
Member of the Crown Publishing Group.
Random House, Inc. New York, Toronto, London, Sydney, Auckland
CROWN is a trademark of Crown Publishers, Inc.

Manufactured in the United States of America

Library of Congress Cataloging-in-Publication Data

Trimble, Vance H.
    Overnight Success : Federal Express and Frederick Smith, Its Renegade Creator /
by Vance H. Trimble. — 1st ed.
        p.   cm.
    1. Smith, Frederick, 1944–   . 2. Businessmen—United States—
Biography.   3. Federal Express Corporation—History.   4. Express
service—United States—History.   I. Title.
HE5896.S65T75   1993
388'.044'06573—dc20   92-17333
                                                                          CIP
ISBN 0-517-58510-3

10 9 8 7 6 5 4 3 2 1

First Edition

For Josie and Guy L., and Flora and Jake, and Cliff for the honorable lifetime heritage they gave Elzene and me.

CONTENTS

OVERNIGHT SUCCESS

AN HOUR MOST DESPERATE

At age thirty Frederick Wallace Smith was in deep trouble. His dream of creating Federal Express had become too expensive and was fast fizzling out. He had exhausted his father's Greyhound Bus millions, outraging his two sisters. He was in hock for 15 or 20 million more. He appeared in danger of losing his cargo jet planes, and also his wife. His own board of directors had fired him as CEO. Now the FBI accused him of forging papers to get a $2 million bank loan and was trying to send him to prison.

He thought of suicide.

In his then hometown of Little Rock, Arkansas, he rode the elevator to the seventeenth floor of the Union National Bank on Wednesday morning, May 15, 1974, took his bearings from a six-by-eight-foot painting of dark trees hanging on a far wall, turned left into the first corridor, and went seven or eight steps across a bright Oriental runner to a massive unmarked door.

Inside he gave his name to the secretary and asked to see Herbert Hall McAdams II, the bank's chairman.

"Someone is with him now," said the secretary. "Do you have an appointment?"

"No."

When the secretary told him Fred Smith was waiting to see him, McAdams, a World War II survivor and no coward, nonetheless became alarmed. "There was bad blood," McAdams says. "He could

1

have considered me his enemy. He forged documents and stole two million dollars from the bank. We were suing to get it back."

McAdams at once ushered his visitor out the back door, making gracious southern apologies. Then he phoned his attorney, Griffin Smith, who had offices on the bank building's nineteenth floor.

"Rush down here. Come in the back way. Fred Smith's waiting to see me. I've no idea what he wants. Maybe he's going to shoot me!"

McAdams and his attorney saw the secretary open the door and admit Fred Smith. His appearance stunned them.

"He looked like a scarecrow," says McAdams. "He wore a long black overcoat that was flapping around his ankles. He just looked awful. Looked like he didn't weigh a hundred pounds. He was as low emotionally as I've ever seen a man. And I really felt for him."

Griffin Smith was surprised to see Fred Smith wearing no tie, but some sort of sweater. "He looked like a bum!"

The bank chairman was relieved to see no weapon. Fred Smith stood with his arms dangling and said in a vague way that he had come to apologize for "the trouble."

"He began telling me he was very upset about the whole thing. He said he was going to commit suicide . . . he was going to jump out a window!"

McAdams established immediate eye contact and tried to soothe his visitor.

"No, Fred, don't think that way! You've got to think positively! Read the Scriptures. Read Mark nine: twenty-three!"

In the bank chairman's elaborate, book-lined twenty-by-forty-foot office, the two men stared at each other uncertainly, separated as they were by a couple of generations in age and Union National's two million "stolen" dollars that had vanished in Smith's so far futile pursuit of his entrepreneurial brainchild.

Smith's agitated countenance alarmed McAdams. In thirty or so years as a lawyer and banker he had been confronted by a number of people who said they were going to commit suicide. McAdams says: "I always told them to go right ahead. I'll open the window for you. Or if you really want to do it, I know where you can get a sharp knife. I didn't believe 'em. They weren't going to do anything foolish. This was different. I believed Fred. I believed because of the look on his face—and his body language."

McAdams considered himself something of an expert in interpreting body language. "In questioning a juror or a witness, you learn that body language means a whole lot—as much as the spoken word. And it is usually so subtle. What he was saying—'I'm going to take my life by jumping out the window!'—and his body language . . . everything added up. This was the first time I ever believed anyone!"

Griffin Smith apparently did not share that belief so strongly. "But remember," says McAdams, "we had direct eye contact, Fred and I. I got a visual picture as he walked toward me. We looked directly at each other. He looked so bad when he walked in, I knew something was wrong . . . and saying this . . . the movement of his body. He looked terrible. He was serious, dead serious. I think he meant it. He had no place to turn. No place to go. I really felt for the man. . . . You know, I felt like his coming to see me—well, I felt like he was sort of directed . . . I mean, why did he wander in, come to my office on that specific day?"

The bank chairman managed to get Fred Smith to sit down and then began a gentle conversation—virtually preaching a sermon. McAdams, at that time sixty-nine, slender, and handsome, knew the Bible thoroughly. He had taken a strong interest in religion as a direct result of his own close brush with death in World War II when he was a twenty-nine-year-old ensign. Two Jap bombs hit his ship, the USS *Gamble*, off Iwo Jima, killing five sailors and wounding him and seven others. He suffered head, neck, and back wounds, including three broken vertebrae, and 60 percent of his skin was burned off.

"I wasn't supposed to live," says McAdams, "but I did. I wasn't supposed to walk, but I did. I spent six months in Washington, D.C., and heard some Peter Marshall sermons. But the man who got me most interested in the Bible was Norman Vincent Peale. I was in New York and went to hear him preach. I heard him a number of times, and still get his printed sermons. Mark nine: twenty-three was one of the verses he preached on. That's the one verse of the Bible I've tried to live by."

Fred Smith was squirming on his chair, rubbing his hands together, fidgeting in obvious embarrassment. He muttered that he had made a mistake and was ready to take his punishment. "Or words to that effect," McAdams testified later.

Beyond the windows of the banker's office hovered dark clouds. It was gloomy and unseasonably chilly weather for an Arkansas spring.

McAdams was struck by the fact that this was only the second time he'd seen Fred Smith. He had not been personally involved when the loan was made, and it had been close to four years since their other meeting, which had been very brief.

That meeting had occurred about a week after October 19, 1970, when McAdams had been persuaded to come in from Jonesboro, Arkansas, as a white knight and purchase control of the Union National Bank to save it from going under.

McAdams's first decision was to sweep out the bank's old officers and start fresh. Among those to be fired were three members of an advisory board, one of whom was Fred Smith. "I had to do this," said McAdams, "even though the people I met all considered Fred to be a rising star in Little Rock business. He had a tremendous family background in Memphis. He's a very bright man, tremendous mind."

Anticipating the change, Fred Smith had come to McAdams's old fourth-floor office within the week and stayed just a few moments to hand over his letter of resignation.

Now he slumped on a chair in the bank chief's $500,000 suite, breaking in occasionally to interrupt the stream of vocal encouragement that flowed steadily across the polished desk. He kept trying to apologize and said he "had been very distraught and very upset." McAdams later testified that Fred Smith asserted there had been a family squabble, "leaving him out on a limb," and he was alienated from his two sisters and had separated from his wife, "voluntarily isolating himself."

It had been only a few weeks earlier that the bank had made the stunning discovery it held no genuine collateral to secure the $2 million personal loan to Fred Smith. Documents he had presented pledging three hundred shares of stock from his family trust were fictitious, describing a board meeting that never took place and bearing forged signatures. The bank promptly alerted officials of the Smith family trust of the fraud and started suit to recover the $2 million and interest, which had run up to $500,000.

Fred Smith now was trying to explain to McAdams that he wanted to make payments on the loan. "In a few days I'm going to sell a four-hundred-thousand-dollar airplane and give you the proceeds. Then I have a nine-hundred-thousand-dollar note and mortgage that I intend to assign to your bank."

Strangely, the banker at that moment was feeling compassion for an intruder whom only two or three minutes before he had felt might be invading his office to do him harm.

He didn't feel the Union National's loan officer had been negligent in accepting the spurious collateral documents for the $2 million loan. "The bank was dealing with a reputable businessman. You have to trust at some point in time in a business. If you don't, you'll never complete a transaction. At some point you've got to believe that the certificates they bring in as collateral are not fraudulent, not fictitious. Anyone could go down to a printer and get certificates right now that look just like A T and T stock. All you need do is get one share of it. . . . I've seen that done."

In an interview for this book, McAdams said: "He made minutes of a fictitious board meeting and signed the secretary's name to it. But, you know, I got to thinking the poor fellow probably didn't realize what he was doing. And he didn't break the bank. Losing two million dollars wouldn't have helped us; it would have hurt us badly. But fortunately my reputation and credibility were good enough in banking and in Little Rock business; it wouldn't have broken the bank. . . . And I wanted to help him. I found out a long time ago the most important thing in life is helping people. Material things don't amount to very much. The older you get, the less they amount to."

That 1974 meeting in the bank chairman's office lasted at least forty-five minutes. Griffin Smith sat at one side, watching and listening but participating little in the conversation. Most of the talking was done by McAdams. The banker took off his glasses a time or two and rubbed the back of his neck to ease little twinges that kept him from ever forgetting the battle for Iwo Jima. Three or four times he brought up Mark 9:23.

Fred Smith listened attentively and respectfully and made only occasional comment. The banker could detect little change in his expression, though he did seem somewhat less tense than when he'd come in.

The "suicide" threat was first revealed publicly—and not disputed—when McAdams later testified about it in federal court in 1975; but any talk of suicide was uncharacteristic of Fred Smith. "It is ridiculous to think of Fred ever contemplating such a thing," says a former close Federal Express colleague. "Jump out a window? More likely he might say he would throw somebody out a window. Fred's a fighter! He's cut out of the same cloth as his dad. And his grandfather."

Friends and colleagues say Fred Smith, usually taciturn about personal matters, never talked about this difficult period, perhaps the lowest point in his life. His infant Federal Express became a ravenous money-eating ogre. To keep his planes flying, Fred had to beg, borrow—and, as McAdams testified, steal. At any risk, at any cost, he refused to let his Federal Express dream die.

The situation confronting him on this May morning in 1974 was dismal, at a dangerous ebb. Not only was Federal Express teetering on bankruptcy, but its founder, with the FBI and the U.S. district attorney hard on his heels, could possibly go to prison for bank fraud.

Now after sitting at least three-quarters of an hour in the office of the chairman of the Union National Bank, Fred Smith finally lifted himself from his chair. He extended his hand to the banker and Griffin Smith and said good-bye. He turned and slowly walked across the vast carpet past the row of picture windows that presented a sweeping panoramic vista—the cluster of downtown buildings, the bend in the sluggish Arkansas River, and the green hills beyond. His scarecrow overcoat flapped at his ankles. At the door, he paused and looked back. The expression on his drawn face was still enigmatic.

McAdams, watching him, reached up and once again began to massage the back of his neck.

He noticed Fred Smith flick a little glance toward the high windows, perhaps the view beyond, and then he went out abruptly. McAdams watched the door open and close and suddenly felt sad and empty. Softly he recited to himself the verse Mark 9:23: "Jesus said unto him, If thou canst believe, all things *are* possible to him that believeth."

CAP'N JIM BUCK'S STEAMBOAT LIFE

In the early evening of Friday, February 17, 1911, the pilot of the steamboat *Chancy Lamb* refused to pull away from the wharf at Ashland City, Tennessee, twenty miles northwest of Nashville. Smoke rose from the twin stacks; her boilers had been fired up for two hours. Up in the wheelhouse, Captain James Buchanan Smith glared at his subordinate.

"Cap'n, it's too dark," said J. B. Winfrey, the pilot. "We got a mean river tonight. Currents look plum crazy. Stirring up snags. That's damn sure. I ain't leaving till the moon comes up!"

"Cap'n Jim Buck" Smith, fifty-four years old and a steamboater for more than a quarter century, looked alternately at the merciless Cumberland River and the inky sky. Rules made him defer to the pilot. Though anxious to get under way, he was keenly aware of his responsibility for the fifteen others aboard—among them his new wife and his sixteen-year-old son, James Frederick. Tonight he, too, felt vague misgivings about the downriver run and the tricky bridge at Clarksville.

It was ten P.M. before the moon broke through the clouds and the *Chancy Lamb*, a one-hundred-thirty-six-foot wood-hulled packet-towboat cast off her mooring lines and departed for Paducah, Kentucky, pushing a single barge loaded with two thousand bushels of coal.

This was still the heyday of steamboating on the mighty Mississippi and Ohio rivers and tributaries like the Tennessee and the Cumberland. Lumber, iron, coal, livestock, grain, groceries, and cotton bales moved among Pittsburgh, Cincinnati, Dubuque, St. Louis, Nashville, Memphis, New Orleans, and hundreds of lesser river cities. For a round-trip cabin ticket from Memphis to St. Louis, a five-day voyage, passengers paid as little as seven dollars, hearty meals included. Fare for deck passengers was one dollar, regardless of destination.

The *Chancy Lamb,* built at Dubuque in 1872, was one of probably four thousand steamboats then still carrying passengers and freight and towing barges. Since before the Civil War, the paddle wheelers had been the cheapest means of transport, but now they were beginning to lose out to the burgeoning railroads.

Jim Buck's concern tonight for the dark river was almost equaled by worry about his son. The boy—who hated "James" and insisted on being called "Fred"—had already run away from home once, recklessly signing on as cabin boy aboard a banana boat bound for South America. His unhappiness stemmed from the untimely death in 1908 of his mother, Laura Ann, whom he idolized. Captain Smith had soon remarried, and Fred despised his stepmother. But after landing penniless in New York, being thrown off the banana boat, and having to sleep in empty crates on the waterfront and beg at a bakery for stale bread, he had slunk home. Back in Paducah, for a time he hawked on the streets the newspaper edited by the famous Irvin S. Cobb. Then his father hired him as clerk aboard his steamboat.

Fred was an exceptional young man, as Captain Jim Buck already knew—a hard worker who readily made friends and was, in his father's words, "as quick and sharp as a sawmill!"

For the first hour or two the *Chancy Lamb*'s journey was uneventful. Two searchlights stabbed the darkness ahead of the coal barge, alerting Pilot Winfrey to bends clotted with overhanging brush, half-submerged, broken-tree "snags," and other hazards.

At midnight the watch changed in the pilothouse. Winfrey turned the wheel over to the second pilot, John Newman of Paducah, and went below to his bunk. Newman, though now in his eighties, was one of the most respected pilots on Ohio and Mississippi river steamers. He also worked the Cumberland, but this was his first voyage aboard the *Chancy Lamb*.

Jim Buck took a last turn around the stern-wheeler's deck. He checked the boiler room, where two engineers and two Negro firemen were keeping up steam. First Mate Briggs Hinton of Paducah was on watch in the pilothouse. Everybody else—Mrs. Smith, Fred, five deckhands, and Mollie Britton, Buck's steamboat cook for the last ten years—had turned in.

In his own bed, the skipper wondered about potential hazards that lay ahead, especially the railroad bridge across the Cumberland at Clarksville. It was a tight squeeze between the piers—really too narrow for a long tow. He knew of some captains who cut their barges loose above the bridge, let the current carry them through, and caught them downstream and hooked up again. The bridge's center pier supported a giant turntable on which the middle span of the structure rotated. When the bridge was open for river traffic, boats could go through on either the east or west side. Each gap was the same width—one hundred eighteen feet. The pilot's option depended on how he gauged the prevailing tide and current.

A little after one o'clock Saturday morning Pilot Newman whistled for a landing as they approached Clarksville. Smith woke up, climbed up to the wheelhouse, and studied the river.

"Mighty strong cross-current," he said. "Better pass through the west gap."

"I know my business," retorted Newman, steering east of the middle pier. "Tows always go through this side."

Within one hundred yards of the bridge, Smith could see the barge was in danger of rubbing the main pier. So did the pilot. He spun the wheel frantically, but it was too late. One corner of the barge struck and crumbled away, deflecting the course of both craft toward the west bank. The barge hit again on the side and broke loose. Now the steamboat was headed straight for the massive west pier, bearing down at ten knots. Captain Smith yanked the whistle lanyard, giving five short blasts, the distress signal.

In graphic detail, the Saturday afternoon *Clarksville Leaf-Chronical* reported:

When she struck, her head crumbled like ice and the massive stone pier had plowed back nearly to her boilers. Hanging there, her stern swung on downstream until the wheel struck the middle pier. In this position the boat lay for about ten minutes, gradually turning upstream.

When at an angle about forty-five degrees, the head broke loose and the boat drifted out, beginning to list until she was almost flat on her side. At that point the boilers were loosened from their foundation and rolled off. This broke the main steam pipe, resulting in a loud explosion that awakened several persons blocks away.

The *Chancy Lamb* was doomed, and all aboard knew it. The two firemen leaped into the water and swam for shore. Smith managed to get his wife, his son, two deckhands, and the second engineer into a lifeboat and row to the west bank. As the overturned steamboat drifted on, the skipper and two deckhands rowed back to rescue crewmen floundering in the water, clinging to floating timbers, or hanging on to the steamboat's hog chains.

Pilot Newman, who grabbed his valise and heavy overcoat before leaping overboard, was drifting away along with the chief engineer and a deckhand, all hollering for help. Smith and his helpers made three trips and rescued all but three of the crew; Mollie Britton was trapped in her bunk when the galley was crushed, and the two firemen drowned.

Meanwhile the boat drifted one hundred yards, hit a sandbar, righted herself, and settled squarely on her keel in twenty-five feet of water, leaving the hurricane deck and pilothouse visible. Townspeople took the bedraggled survivors to the Franklin House and fed and consoled them. One thinly clad deckhand lamented the loss of his hat. A merchant took off his own fedora and handed it to him; another gave him a blue serge suit.

Captain Jim Buck sent a wire to Nashville notifying the owners, the Ryman Line, that the $10,000 boat had been wrecked but might be salvaged. Pilot Newman took the morning train for Paducah after showing the *Chronicle-Leaf* reporter his vest pocket watch, which had filled with water and stopped at 1:34. "I am getting too old for the river," he said. "I had a fine record, but I made one trip too many and have ruined it all."

The *Chancy Lamb,* named after the Iowa lumberman who built her, sat helpless on the river bottom for three weeks while her owners debated how to raise and restore her. Suddenly the Cumberland rose and powerful cross-currents assaulted the wreck, crushing and splintering her weakened superstructure. The debris floated downstream, littering the riverbanks for miles with boards and scraps of machinery. And the proud little stern-wheeler, after thirty-nine valiant years afloat, was forever gone.

America's westward migration brought Captain Smith's ancestors from the Atlantic coast to middle Tennessee in the early 1800s. They may have come from England aboard James Edward Oglethorpe's "prison ship," which brought one hundred twenty debtors in 1733 to help found the colony of Georgia. At any rate, the steamboat captain's grandfather was Joshua R. Smith, a farmer, listed in the 1830 census at Trenton, Gibson County, Tennessee.

This particular Smith clan, mainly farmers and a few black-smiths, moved on through Salem, Kentucky, into the lower southern tip of Illinois, settling in Massac County, across the Ohio River from Paducah. There on March 4, 1857, James Buchanan Smith was born. His father, William A. Smith, raised three girls and two boys, eking out a living on 320 poor acres that sold for $450 when he died at the age sixty-three November 15, 1880. His next most valuable asset was a bay horse that brought $40 at the estate auction, where his bedstead went for $.25, a spinning wheel for $1, and one lot of plows for $.45. William A. Smith's caretaker billed the estate $12.50 for nursing him his final five days, plus $10 for "damage to the feather bed and pillows," $14.90 for horse feed, and $40 for boarding wife, Mary, and daughter "Gilly." The body was ferried across the river for $5 to Warren's Mill, Kentucky, clad in a new $16.50 suit and buried in a $12 coffin.

By then Jim Buck, with no desire to emulate his father's hardscrabble life-style, had already quit the farm at Brookport. As a youngster he was enthralled watching steamboats plying the nearby Ohio River with their fancy gingerbread decks, brass bands, gaiety, and seeming opulence. His ambition took a new bent, drawing him to the Paducah waterfront, where he signed on as a deckhand. He set a single-minded goal: to work hard and learn everything there was to know about steamboating. In a few years he climbed first to clerk, then mate, and was gaining the know-how to be a captain. Meanwhile he fell in love with Laura Ann Windland in Mississippi County, Missouri. She was a niece of General George Custer, according to family legend. They were married December 31, 1883, at Bird's Point, Missouri, when Laura Ann was only sixteen, which required her nearest relative, C. S. Clark, another uncle, to sign his consent.

They had a house at rustic little Anniston, Missouri, but Laura Ann often went on the steamboats with her husband. They had five children. Their first, Ethel Mae, was born in 1889; then came another daughter, Olive [nicknamed Polly], in 1892. James Frederick was born at Anniston on February 6, 1895, followed by Earl William in 1897 and John Byrd in 1900.

The year James Frederick turned thirteen, 1908, his sister Ethel Mae, wife of a farmer named Thomas, died February 26 in childbirth at only nineteen years of age. Four months later, he was stunned by the unexpected sudden death at age forty-one of his mother. Both are buried in Paducah's Oak Grove Cemetery, where Captain Smith erected a central "Smith" headstone in a large family plot, leaving a space for himself. In this one-hundred-acre cemetery are many Paducah notables, including Irvin S. Cobb.

In 1891 when he was thirty-four years old, Captain Jim Buck had got his first command—the *Ora Lee,* a one-hundred-forty-foot stern-wheeler, built that year for the wealthy Lee Lines of Memphis, which operated thirty-five steamboats.

Captain Smith remained master of the *Ora Lee* until the vessel was sold in 1900 to an Arkansas steamboat line plying the White River. (Renamed the *Orlando,* the boat hit a snag in 1901 and was lost.) Smith then switched to the famous Thomas Ryman Lines of Nashville to run packets on a three-hundred-mile stretch of the Tennessee River between Paducah and Waterloo, Alabama.

The high regard and trust the Ryman Lines had in Jim Buck is shown by the fact that immediately after the *Chancy Lamb* disaster he was placed in command of the pride of the Cumberland River fleet, the *R. Dunbar,* a one-hundred-sixty-foot stern-wheeler named for Reuben Dunbar, the storekeeper at Greasy Creek, Kentucky.

The very first time he took the *Dunbar* through Clarksville, one month after the wreck, Jim Buck stopped long enough to express his gratitude. The *Clarksville Leaf-Chronicle* noted his brief visit in its Marsh 25, 1911, issue, adding:

> Capt. Smith is now master of the steamer *R. Dunbar,* of the Ryman Line, and had the boat here today en route to Paducah, where she is to go into a new trade. This is the first time Capt. Smith has been in Clarksville since the fateful event. He stopped the *Dunbar* here today long enough to come uptown and shake hands and again thank those who extended him courtesies on the night of the accident.

Jim Buck was conscious of the hazards on the rivers but also deeply impressed by their beauty. As he wrote daughter Olive: "The scenery down and up stream is varied and beautiful. The shores seem so far away. . . . The great width of the river often looks like a lake and is very beautiful—especially at sunset when we gather favored passengers in the pilothouse. . . . They always get a kick out of hearing the mate shouting at the roustabouts, and our whistle and bell—when we signal passing boats or hail plantations, and smelling the odor of the cool swampland." He calculated that in addition to the sheltered wharves at a dozen or so towns along the Tennessee River, there were at least two hundred listed steamboat landings, usually run by country merchants, not accessible to railroads. "Today," he wrote, "we loaded hickory lumber that goes to Metropolis

Bow Bending Company, where it will be made into buggy frames for the Banner Buggy Company in St. Louis. In a few weeks we'll carry some of those finished buggies back upriver."

In another letter: "I'll save you some of the Tennessee Red peanuts. We carry tons of them out. They are lightweight and some days we have them stacked in five-pound bags man-high all over the first and second decks. Of course, we carry passengers, cotton, cattle, sheep, hogs . . ." Returning upriver, the packet would often be carrying farm machinery, wagons, cooking stoves, plow lines, harness, chewing tobacco, lamp chimneys, washboards, and all the odds and ends needed to run homes and farms. Smith told his children that a mecca for early travelers was Shiloh battlefield, which was opened as a national military park in 1894, and he promised to take them sight-seeing there.

In the summer of 1912 when steamboat business on the Cumberland began a serious decline, Captain Smith returned to Memphis and rejoined the Lee Lines as master of the *Ferd Herold,* taking along his ex-runaway son, now almost seventeen, to serve as clerk.

In a cubbyhole "office" on the texas deck, James Frederick "Fred" Smith found he had to master and juggle myriad duties, not the least of which was to maintain fuel for the boilers. Going upstream, the boats burned coal; on the way down, cordwood. Sometimes snakes infested the stacks of wood and struck unwary firemen. "I had to make sure we had an eight-gallon jug of whiskey in the boiler room," Smith told his children years later, "to keep the victims alive until we could get them to the hospital in Memphis." His children detected a sly grin on his face.

Fred Smith was an energetic and serious student of steamboat races. They still occurred, especially along the Mississippi and usually on the spur of the moment. He even heard the Lee Lines patriarch, three-hundred-pound Captain Tom, quoted as having said he had been "blowed up in twenty-two states and several territories" when too much pressure was put on boilers in an effort to cross the finish line first. He became so curious for details about one race in particular—the grand-daddy of them all—that he spent a few hours in the Memphis Public Library reading up on the *Natchez* and the *Rob't E. Lee.*

A feud and a fistfight between the rival captain-owners, Thomas P. Leathers and John W. Cannon, over competition for the Vicksburg trade, triggered the unofficial race. Captain Leathers, a six-foot giant who wore a ruffled shirt and diamond stickpin, was a die-hard Rebel and always wore Confederate gray. Captain Cannon, although a Kentuckian, was mild-mannered and accepted the South's defeat. Both were in their mid-fifties.

The steamboats were massive side-wheelers, at least two hundred eighty-five feet long, each with eight boilers that allowed 120 pounds of steam. Captain Cannon's *Rob't E. Lee* was built in 1866, the Leathers boat in 1869. An item in a Cincinnati newspaper praised the *Natchez* for speed and snidely reported that the *Lee* was so slow, she seemed propelled by mules on a treadmill. This was an insult that called for revenge.

On June 30, 1870, both steamboats were advertised to depart New Orleans upriver at precisely the same hour, five P.M. The owners denied they intended to race, but U.S. inspectors sealed safety valves on both side-wheelers to discourage tampering. Deck cannons were fired, and hundreds of spectators on the levees and harbor boats watched the *Rob't E. Lee* get off with a three-minute headstart. St. Louis was the finish line.

The first night out, the *Lee* sprung a boiler leak so bad it doused the fires. The *Natchez*, still behind, started gaining. How to find the leak inside a blazing firebox? That boiler was shut down, the grate cooled with a water hose, and assistant engineer John Wiest pulled on old overalls, tied a bandanna around his head, put on heavy gloves, and crawled inside with a hammer and a chisel to search. He spent a minute or two prying and banging around before Captain Cannon and two other steamboat captains pulled him out. When Wiest recovered his speech, he announced that the leak was around the mud guard flange seam. Still under way, they tried cutting hemp packing into tiny pieces and putting it in through the cold-water suction valve to clog the leaky seam. It worked.

Tugs at several ports brought out barges of coal and lashed them alongside. The steamboats didn't even slow down while roustabouts furiously shoveled the coal aboard, then cut loose the barges to be picked up by the tugs. Several miles below Cairo, the side-wheeler *Idlewild* came alongside and quickly transferred some daring passengers to the *Lee*. At Cairo the *Natchez* was an hour behind, but with 180 miles to go it was still anybody's race. That night the *Rob't E. Lee* was hampered by fog, running on slow bell, but she managed to "break through" by two A.M. and ran on to St. Louis with no further delay. The *Natchez* had no such luck and was forced to tie at shore twice, losing four hours forty-five minutes. Thus the victorious *Rob't E. Lee* steamed into the harbor late on the morning of July 4, 1870, three days, eighteen hours, and fourteen minutes out of New Orleans, the all-time record for a commercial steamboat. The *Natchez* limped in later that evening.

Chatting with his father, Fred Smith suddenly offered: "I've been thinking about that race. You know, someday I may try to beat the record of the *Rob't E. Lee*."

Captain Jim Buck blinked, stared at the youngster, and then guffawed.

"Don't laugh, Dad. I'm serious. It's kind of a dream I have!"

3 ► HOW TO MAKE $17,000,000

At age twenty James Frederick Smith started his climb to fame and fortune. His ambition was dead on, aggressively supported by un-limited energy, a quick mind, and open and honest friendliness—plus a certain amount of gambler's luck. (He now had totally abandoned his given name and henceforth would be "Frederick" in legal papers and "Fred" in conversation.)

Both he and his father had quit the river. The great days of the steamboats were ending. Railroads, of course, had cut in on the trade. One hard blow was death of the "combine" formed in 1899 by Andrew W. Mellon's syndicate, linking 36,000 acres of coal fields to eighty towboats and tugs and six thousand barges. In September 1909, a hurricane swept the lower Mississippi, devastating hundreds of river craft, costing the Mellon people $709,000. In going out of business, the combine fired hundreds of captains, pilots, engineers, and mates—the biggest mass layoff in river history.

Captain Jim Buck and Fred came ashore in Memphis and found work with a wholesale grocer, Clarence Saunders, who was to make and lose a fortune as founder of the Piggly Wiggly grocery chain. The grocer built Memphis's fabulous Pink Palace when his income was $3,500 a day. But neither father nor son took much to storekeep-ing. "Saunders was smart," Fred Smith said later, "but he was hard to work for. Very demanding. He worked you like a horse."

At that point he had the good fortune to meet John T. Fisher. An

18

ex-Yankee from Ohio, Fisher had studied law until an accident at twenty had cost him one eye. He'd learned the sales game peddling liver pills on horseback. By fifty he had acquired a small fortune as southern manager for a national tobacco company and was making a name as a Memphis philanthropist and religious leader, while branching out into a sideline—automobiles. He sought out young men he could help but demanded blind faith and commitment.

"I'm looking for a young fellow to go out to the Texas oil fields and sell trucks." That was Fisher's opening when he summoned Fred Smith in 1914 to his auto agency in downtown Memphis. "Think you can do it?" His tone was gruff and intimidating, as Smith later recalled.

"Well, I—"

"Listen, young fellow. Here's what you need to be a successful salesman: integrity, sincerity, industry, sobriety, self-culture, cheerfulness, self-reliance, good temper, stick-to-itiveness, confidence, concentration, steadfastness, loyalty, ambition, optimism, and politeness. Do you think you have those qualities?"

Apparently Fred Smith had quite a few of them. In the Texas oil boom towns, he got out of bed before dawn and worked into the night. By letter and telegram from Memphis, Fisher prodded him with ideas and encouragement.

"This was a matter of salesmanship—as all things are," Fred Smith said when he relived those early days. "In this instance it was a matter of making others see through my eyes, of influencing them to adopt my viewpoint. Some salesmen put the proposition to the customer on the ground of charity, others beg assistance to make up their quota, and some actually talk hard luck at home. This system is all wrong. Any fellow who talks like that is no salesman. The man who gets the business is an honest, sincere, intelligent, modest man who knows when to stop talking to his prospect as well as when to begin."

From Fisher he learned to "know at a glance" how to approach potential customers. "A salesman must learn to know without being told what his prospect really desires. A cordial, free, and open greeting will often soften up the exterior and lead the customer to 'warm up' and offer suggestions that will enable you to place him at the very first. But there are some people who will endeavor to keep you from knowing what they really want, and you have to use your wits to learn what you want to know without letting them know your design."

Beyond any doubt, Smith learned his trade. "In less than twelve months, I had sold a truck to every oil field operator who needed one. I had, in fact, worked myself out of a job."

Not really. Fisher brought him back to Memphis as his protégé. His Memphis Motor Company on Union Avenue was agent for a variety of automobiles, from Reos, Marmons, and Hupmobiles to the Starter-Dayton, the Mercer-Holmes air-cooled, and the Jordan. Fred was not only salesman, but also mechanic, apparently having gained much skill with machinery from observing repairs made by steamboat engineers.

As a pal of the boss, Fred went to Southern League baseball games, where Fisher was among the loudest rooters in the park for the Memphis Chickasaws. Deeply religious, Fisher almost single-handedly funded the new St. Luke's Methodist Church and confided to Fred that he intended to give away all but $100,000 of his wealth. He could not abide pretense or carelessness. Fisher's wife, writing in a 1930 *Memphis Press-Scimitar* series, said he "comes close to knowing the Bible by heart," liked to help boys get through school, didn't smoke and hated cigarettes, and hogged the radio when baseball results were broadcast. She said he was fair-minded and had a sense of humor—and was quite a nice husband, but different from any man she had known. She quoted Fisher as saying: "I know I'm odd, but I don't mind."

Nor did Fred Smith mind the fact that his eccentric boss kept encouraging him to think entrepreneurially and look for opportunities to branch out.

The First World War diverted him, but only slightly. Because of his expertise in motor transport, Fred Smith was recruited as an inspector into the government's military truck procurement program for a couple of years. Following the Armistice, he was southeastern sales manager for Bethlehem Motor Truck Company, making $4,000 a year. Ideas for what Fisher called "branching out" were germinating in his head. Observing a taxicab that operated across the state, he convinced the owner that a modern comfortable bus would not only increase the volume of business, but would be more economical.

Then Fred Smith figuratively kicked himself for giving away a million-dollar idea. It struck him abruptly that he could—and should—go into the bus business himself!

"I've got a big idea," he told John T. Fisher, and explained that he wanted to start daily bus service from Memphis to some of the nearby small towns. He had a problem—no bus. Fisher solved that; he gave Fred Smith a used truck and loaned him one thousand dollars. With his own tools and hands, Fred built a bus body on the old truck chassis that seated a dozen passengers. His first route was thirty miles to Rosemark in northern Shelby County. Soon he tackled an all-day round-trip fifty miles east on State Highway 64 to Bolivar, with stops at Cordova, Eads, Oakland, Somerville, and Whiteville.

"I must have been working twenty hours a day," Fred Smith recalled. "I was ticket agent, conductor, driver—I did it all, even changing the oil and spark plugs and making repairs overnight. But I loved it."

Others, however, did not share Smith's enthusiasm or his optimistic conclusion that the infant venture warranted immediate expansion. "All the time I was trying to sell the idea to my bankers that with more coaches and equipment, the line could be developed into a handsome business, but they were not so easily sold at that time."

Eventually he persuaded two men to invest five thousand dollars each and promptly began buying motor coaches and opening new runs. He gave fast, courteous service, and business boomed. By the end of the second year he was running twenty-five highly profitable buses; sixty by the end of his third year.

Just before this new enterprise began its fast growth, Jim Buck became desperately ill. He had suffered for some time from Bright's disease. In July 1920 he was struck by acute nephritis, and his Memphis physicians sent him to specialists at Deaconness Hospital in St. Louis. But it was too late; he lived less than forty-eight hours, dying July 11 at age sixty-three. Fred Smith and his sister and two brothers escorted his coffin to Paducah's Oak Grove Cemetery for burial in the family plot next to Laura Ann and their daughter Ethel Mae. Jim Buck's pallbearers included two river captains and a judge. "He was a man of splendid qualities and had many friends here," said the *Paducah Evening Sun*.

Fred Smith was wise enough to engage as legal counsel two adroit Memphis attorneys, Walter Chandler and James H. Shepherd. They knew their way around not only the courthouses, but Tennessee politics as well, and especially with the mayoral administration of "Boss" Ed Crump, who ruled Memphis with an efficient hand. In no time at all the bus company chief was learning to play the game, especially in the state legislature at Nashville. Perhaps his biggest coup was to get passed in 1929 a law making intercity bus lines a public utility. This gave the state the power to award exclusive routes to bus lines. Fred Smith was usually present when choice routes were given out. His charm easily won friendships in high places. When he started his "Governor's Special" coach, making a daily four-hundred-fifty-mile round trip from Memphis to the state capital, Governor Henry H. Horton was on hand to give his personal best wishes for the inaugural run. One reporter quoted the governor: "Fred Smith is a fine fellow; he could sell the king a side-saddle; what isn't right, he will make right."

In the formative years, all the Memphis public could see of the Smith bus line was a little ticket office on Front Street, south of the auditorium. As the number of routes and passengers grew, the company's office expanded into the second floor at 146 Union Avenue. Various terminals were used until a large "union" bus passenger depot was opened at 161 Monroe Avenue, at that time the largest bus station in the South. Smith extended his routes to connect Memphis with Nashville and Chattanooga, Little Rock and Fort Smith, Paducah and St. Louis, and eventually Chicago. The Smith bus left Memphis at noon and arrived in Chicago next morning at eight o'clock. The fare was ten dollars. By dint of mergers, acquisitions, and rough competition, where Smith cut fares to discourage rivals, the Smith Motor Coach Company began to dominate highway passenger transportation through a large portion of the mid-South. New ideas for improving service seemed to sprout every day. Smith bought "sleeper" coaches, inaugurated overnight runs, built a $100,000 plant in Memphis to construct his own bus bodies, and erected his own terminals in Nashville, Chattanooga, Evansville, Indiana, and several other cities. One of his admitted "pet ideas" was to train his carefully picked drivers in salesmanship—by which he meant courtesy to riders. He schooled them in the machinery of their bus, dressed them in smart military uniforms, and encouraged safety and pride by mounting in their bus a personal "Gold Star Club" plaque when they drove twelve months without an accident.

"The placing of responsibility on the employee and inculcating in him a feeling that a share of the success that is attained will be a credit to him, generally will produce a loyal follower," Smith said. "A lot depends upon the character of the man employed. A rascal will never be loyal to anyone except through force and necessity. Only buccaneers and pirate chiefs can intimidate thieves into pseudo-loyalty, and their day is passed.

"The point is that better results may often be obtained by show-ing confidence in good intentions, allowing more freedom of action, and should it be necessary to control the meaner spirits, resort to education, elimination, and the spirit and example of their comrades. Fitness of a leader is proven by ability to arouse a spirit that makes the men want to give 100 percent results."

By 1930 Fred Smith was head of a $3 million concern and so successful that he was profiled in the book *World Leaders* by Hazel Manley, along with Sir Arthur Conan Doyle, J. C. Penney, Clarence Saunders, Will Hayes, Powel Crosley, Jr., A. Atwater Kent, and sixteen other notables.

"I believe," Fred Smith told the author, "that a man who expects to win out in business without self-denial and self-improvement stands about as much chance as a prizefighter would stand if he started a hard ring battle without having gone through intensive training. Natural ability, even when accompanied by the spirit to win, is never sufficient. I have never believed that there was such a thing as 'secret of success.' It is no secret, in my opinion. It is the magical common denominator—work, intelligent effort, to be more specific."

Within a few years Fred Smith's own ideas of unremitting "intelligent effort" attracted admirable and respectful attention from the motor coach industry executives who were creating the merger that would establish a national network of Greyhound Bus Lines.

The ex–steamboat clerk who had started with a single handmade bus would become chairman and controlling stockholder of the Dixie Greyhound Lines out of Memphis. It was an achievement that would enable him to build up a fortune estimated at $17 million.

At the time his business was burgeoning, tragedy again struck the family. His brother John Byrd Smith, a traveling salesman for a Minneapolis flour mill, was killed in an automobile collision near Brownsville, Tennessee, on September 9, 1930. He lived at Paris, Tennessee, and left a widow, Laura Frances. He was buried in the family plot at Paducah.

To honor his thirty-year-old brother, Fred Smith ordered all Smith Motor Coach Company buses to stop for five minutes at eleven o'clock the morning of the funeral. It saddened him to realize that his parents were gone, as was one sister and now his youngest brother. He had brought his other siblings into his Memphis business. His brother Earl William, two years his junior, had worked as a manager for the Harvey House railway restaurants in Missouri and Oklahoma and had married a waitress named Estelle. They had a son, Earl junior, born in Sapulpa, Oklahoma. Smith had prevailed on Earl to take a managerial position with the motor coach company. He also provided a supervisory job for Felix C. Barron, who had married his older sister, Olive (known as "Polly"). His belief in holding family together was so strong that he induced John Byrd's widow to move to Memphis.

▶ ▶ ▶

Fred Smith was well built, lively and handsome, easy and glib. He had a powerful libido, and over the years he gave close attention—as well as flattery, flowers, candy, and perfume—to many women. But the success he found in highway transportation did not readily follow him into the boudoir. His first wife, Bessie, whom he married January 13, 1917, in Memphis, found their romance souring after about ten years. The story is told in the family that he came back from a trip to Nashville to find that Bessie had packed his suitcase and left it sitting on the front porch. There seems to be more to it than that.

Beginning in 1928, he habitually was in a "bad humor with her, gruff and grum," said the divorce petition she filed June 16, 1931, and was "cruel and inhumane" by criticizing her personal appearance and speaking to her "abusively and profanely." In their home on November 27, 1930, he used "physical violence" against her and also beat her up on the street three weeks later, she alleged.

After a six-month separation, Fred Smith agreed to give Bessie title to their apartment at 216 Hawthorne Street, plus furniture, her Cadillac, and five thousand dollars a year for five years. In turn she surrendered her interest in their fifty-five-acre tract on North Second Street Road in suburban Frayser and agreed to pay any debts she had incurred since they separated. The divorce was granted in Shelby County Circuit Court on July 10, 1931.

As a retread bachelor, Fred Smith kept searching out attractive women—and they captured his attention much more quickly if they were young and naive enough to be impressed by his sophistication and wealth.

He was destined to make three more well-publicized marriages, any or all of which would have provided enough melodrama for a B movie in Hollywood. But it was the river that had the most visible and unbreakable lock on his heart; he would always be passionate about boats and the Mississippi.

The juvenile boast he had made to his father that he dreamed of beating the *Rob't E. Lee*'s record came back to him when he discovered that a Memphis physician had been scheming since 1913 to get a boat that would break the New Orleans–St. Louis time.

Dr. Louis Leroy, chief of staff at General Hospital, who sported a stylish mustache and goatee, collected rare books, and was married to a concert pianist, tried to break the record in 1927, but his motor gave way. He started anew with another engine, but it was too weak to make time against the current. On the third challenge, Dr. Leroy got all the way up to Chester, Illinois, before a drifting log stopped him.

Fred Smith, envious, read in the *Memphis Commercial Appeal* that Leroy sent abroad for some mahogany lumber and in the backyard of his Poplar Avenue home was building a hull for a twenty-six-foot speedboat he named *Bogie,* using a six-cylinder 150-horsepower Scripps engine. On July 21, 1929, Leroy left New Orleans on his fourth run. For relief at the wheel, he took along two Mississippi River pilots, Captains J. Hervey Brown and Bob Hunter. Near Greenville, Mississippi, the *Bogie* had some trouble with an underwater log, but the crew repaired the damage and pushed on.

Leroy, at that time fifty-five, was creating a sensation. *The New York Times* and other papers coast to coast reported the race on page one, noting the *Bogie*'s daily position, comparing her time and distance with the *Lee*'s. After four nights with little sleep, living on buttermilk and orange juice, Leroy and the two pilots thundered into the St. Louis harbor. They stepped ashore eighty-seven hours and thirty-one minutes out of New Orleans, knocking two hours and forty-three minutes off the record that had stood for fifty-nine years. As a symbol of his triumph, the St. Louis Yacht Club presented Leroy with a silver loving cup engraved with his record time.

"That won't stand," Fred Smith told his brother-in-law Felix Barron. "I'm going to beat the *Bogie*'s time! Just wait!"

The waiting took a long time. Smith kept grumbling that he ached for a chance to break the record. "I want to go with you," Felix Barron said. Smith thought it over and agreed.

Nothing happened until May 1931, when Fred Smith attended a boat show in New Orleans. Visitors were admiring a new twenty-three-foot speedboat built by Higgins Industries of New Orleans. The forward cockpit was protected by a streamlined canopy, and she had a powerful 130-horsepower engine, an eight-cylinder Gray. Fred Smith was captivated. This black-and-gold-trimmed speedboat was the answer to his dream.

"How much?" he asked A. J. Higgins, the builder who had her for sale.

"Why do you want her?" said Higgins.

"Set a new record to St. Louis."

"You mean with a stiff boat that hasn't been tested? Well, the price is ten thousand—with, ah, one condition: You take my boy Eddie along!"

"Okay—and I, too, have conditions. Get her name painted on tonight. *Greyhound*—spelled with 'e,' and copy that picture of the racing dog you see on all our buses."

"What's the rush?" Higgins asked.

"I want to go tomorrow!"

Summoned by telegrams, overnight to New Orleans came Felix Barron and Captain J. Hervey Brown, owner-master of the Memphis tug *H. H. Colle,* who had piloted Dr. Leroy's successful *Bogie.* The race was on.

"Fred Smith said nothing to anybody," the *Memphis Commercial Appeal* said later. "He just lit out."

The speedboat embarked from the wharf at the foot of Canal Street at 12:59 P.M., Thursday, May 7, 1931. Higgins was at the throttle until they reached Baton Rouge at 6:39 P.M. that day. Then Smith took the helm to Vicksburg, arriving at 7:25 A.M. Friday; the other men kept watch for dangerous water hazards. The *Greyhound* behaved beautifully; as a precaution, mechanic Brady Lyle went along. Night and day the speedboat roared upstream, with a new man at the controls every three or four hours. There was no moon; they had to navigate at times in the night by shore lights and by guess. But they charged ahead, eagerly and happily. Once in the darkness with Fred Smith at the wheel, the boat crashed dead center into a floating log and flew ten or twenty feet through the air before slamming back onto the water. "I thought for a moment," Smith said later, "that would finish us!"

They passed Caruthersville, Missouri, at 6:40 P.M. Saturday and stopped during the night at Cairo, Illinois, to take on pilot Tony McHale; then they sped on. On Sunday afternoon the *Greyhound* crew sighted the tall buildings of St. Louis, and docked at two minutes after three o'clock, an elapsed time of seventy-four hours and three minutes. Smith had beaten Leroy's time by thirteen hours and twenty-eight minutes; and he was staggered to realize he had eclipsed the best time in the *Rob't E. Lee–Natchez* contest by sixteen hours and eleven minutes!

In one way it was a hollow victory. Though Fred Smith had the fastest time ever over this 1,153-mile course, he could not claim the cup from the *Bogie*. He had not followed protocol by giving the requisite ninety days' notice that he would challenge the record. The commodore of the St. Louis Yacht Club, however, was so impressed that he decided to award the *Greyhound* a silver "time cup" trophy.

As his wealth accumulated, Fred Smith would move steadily ahead to become a yachtsman, buying several expensive oceangoing vessels on which he would take friends on Caribbean cruises. But daily he was exposed to the sight and sound of the Mississippi lapping at the old steamboat landing on Front Street, and nostalgia invigorated his senses. Missing his days on the river with Jim Buck, he made inquiries about old steamboats for sale. He found two he wanted.

He bought a one-hundred-forty-seven-foot stern-wheel towboat built originally as the *Alabama* in 1895 in Pine Barren, Florida. It had been twice remodeled as the *John Mills* and again as the *Capital* and run in the Black Warrior River trade. To honor his father, Smith renamed her the *J. B. Smith* and made her earn her keep by hauling beer down to Memphis from Evansville, Indiana, returning with a cargo of cottonwood beer cases.

For present-day fun, Smith bought a ninety-foot craft with a steel hull built in Charleston, West Virginia, in 1901. She had been owned as the *Etta J.* for twenty-five years by the U.S. Corps of Engineers at Memphis before being converted at Paducah to a 100-horsepower diesel-engined yacht and renamed *Unique*. On the practical side, he also ferried loads of beer from Evansville for Memphians' thirst, but mainly the *Unique* was Fred Smith's party boat. Over the years she carried hundreds of family, friends, and business associates on excursions to some pleasant sandbar for fishing, swimming, or barbecue picnics. His political and business cronies held many an all-night poker game aboard. (The *Unique* was sold and in 1942 sank near Cape Girardeau, Missouri.)

In the fall of 1933 Fred Smith was stricken by a mysterious and savage illness that brought him to the point of death.

It was a blood disorder that caused a high fever. His physician found only a few cases in the medical literature where such symptoms had been reported—all fatal. In Smith's penthouse apartment atop Memphis's Wm. Len Hotel, his doctor sat at his bedside night after night and gave several blood transfusions. The *Commercial Appeal* reported Smith's condition as "very grave." He was moved to a secluded room at Baptist Hospital. On October 25 the *Press Scimitar*'s story was captioned: FRED SMITH NOW FIGHTING FOR LIFE. His case was critical for several days. In his hushed hospital room, doctors and nurses administered more transfusions. As a last resort, Smith's doctor consulted a Philadelphia hematologic specialist, who suggested that a serum just developed might save the dying man. The bottle was rushed to Memphis—and it worked! The treatment was so unusual, it was written up in a medical journal.

Finally able to be up and around again, the patient got dire news from his physician: because of the long siege of high fever, Smith had become sterile. He wanted children, especially sons, but his doctor said he would be unable to father any.

His most pressing business at the moment was to keep in mind John T. Fisher's advice and look for ways to branch out—start new enterprises with his growing wealth. Thus he had his lawyers draw up a charter for a holding company, the Frederick Smith Enterprise Company. He had in mind going into cotton planting by buying a couple of plantations just across the line in Mississippi, acquiring a registered bull and raising pedigreed beef, expanding his river barge business. Perhaps his wildest idea was to go into the airline business. In 1929 the *Press-Scimitar* had carried this dispatch on page one:

NASHVILLE, Sept. 11—Plans for establishment of air lines operating between Memphis, Nashville, Chattanooga, and Knoxville were announced today by Fred Smith, president of the Smith Motor Coach Co.

Announcement was made after Smith and Walter Chandler, his attorney, conferred with state railroad commissioners and decided to make application to the commission for writs of convenience and necessity permitting operation of the lines. They will be established as the "Golden Eagle Airlines," Smith said.

As soon as necessary approval is obtained from the state commission, the company will buy from the Ryan-Mahony airplane manufacturers of St. Louis two six-passenger cabin planes. Fare from Memphis to Nashville is expected to be $20 one way, and $30 for a round trip, with rates to other cities figured from the same base. The Memphis-to-Nashville service will be the first opened, with planes operating each way once a day.

This was one scheme that literally didn't fly. The Memphis papers carried a few more squibs about seeking a permit. Then not another line. However, Fred Smith did eventually name his express bus from Memphis to the state capital the *Golden Eagle*.

He was more successful when he realized that bus passengers needed a place to eat. As a subsidiary under the umbrella Frederick Smith Enterprise Company, he opened in bus stations several sandwich shops called the Post House, using the valuable experience his brother Earl had gained in Harvey House cafés. These were fairly successful. But by mere chance a real fast-food business plum fell into his lap.

It was the Toddle House chain.

Started in Houston in 1929, the Toddle House restaurant was the brainchild of a lumberyard owner, J. C. Stedman, whose business was being dried up by the nationwide Depression. An amateur architect, he designed a little twelve-foot by twenty-four-foot Dutch colonial cottage that made an excellent small office, laundry substation, florist shop, or souvenir store. Perhaps its best feature was that it could be jacked up, loaded on a truck, and moved from site to site. He sold quite a few.

But Stedman realized that the little house—which he described as a building that would toddle down the road—would be ideal for a sandwich shop. He created a slender, standardized menu of coffee, milk, scrambled eggs, waffles, chili, steak, and a "super-deluxe" ten-cent hamburger—a gamble, because during the Depression hamburgers were going for a nickel. Stedman had room only for one counter and ten stools. One cook handled everything, and customers were on an honor system, dropping the bill and coins in a glass box as they exited. The name Stedman chose for his shops was "One's a Meal"—referring to his extravagant hamburger. He knew he had hit on something good and wanted to expand. He joined forces with an investor, and together they opened a few of the sandwich shops in Memphis; but subsequently they quarreled and broke up the partnership.

By chance Stedman found his way to Fred Smith, and they joined as partners. They picked a new name—Toddle House—and with new capital from Greyhound profits expanded the café chain rapidly, opening as many as fifty new outlets a year. They formed the National Toddle House Corporation, with Fred Smith as president and J. C. Stedman, vice-president.

The Toddle Houses quickly became a major bulwark of Fred Smith's growing financial strength, and he was happy with his success. But he was finding life as a bachelor stale and humdrum. "I've about decided," he told his sister Polly, "to think about getting married again."

4 ▶ A PERFECT BABY!

It was springtime 1934 in Memphis. Charlotte Clark, twenty-two, started across Poplar Avenue to the golf course. A Cadillac drove by; the driver started blowing his horn. Charlotte jumped and whirled to glare at him, but instead she smiled. Obviously it was a tease— admiring toots. "Everybody said I resembled Gene Tierney," she said.

Two weeks later she went dancing at the Peabody Hotel's roof-top Skyways ballroom. Her date, Lincoln dealer Jimmy Colbett, saw a friend come in with two blondes on his arms and called him over to their table. It was Fred Smith with two reporters from Paducah in town to interview him. Charlotte Clark smiled. She recognized Fred Smith as the driver who had honked.

"It was very romantic," she recalled. "He stuck out his hand— and never turned loose of mine until we were married."

Their hand holding lasted until after Christmas. She went dining and dancing, to movies and concerts, and was frequently aboard the *Unique* when Fred Smith cruised the Mississippi River with family and business friends. "We'd go swimming, and one time I got caught in a current. I thought I was a goner and would wind up in New Orleans. Fred got a long boat hook and hooked my suit and dragged me back onto the boat. That was quite dramatic."

Though he was seventeen years her senior, they had in common that both had run away from a stepmother. Charlotte was three when her mother, sister, and brother died in Pine Bluff, Arkansas, in an epidemic. Upset when her father remarried, she fled to Memphis at sixteen and lived with an uncle while training at Methodist Hospital to become an operating room nurse.

"I was gorgeous—I hate to say it, but I was. Men would come out of the stores to watch me walk down the street. I was medium size, dark hair, and eyes sort of greenish—you know, real southern looking. I was real pretty."

It became a serious romance. "I adored Fred," she said. "He had that Clark Gable look. I was proud of his success." Charlotte was an accomplished equestrienne, so Fred took her to Mexico, Missouri, and bought her a fine saddle horse. He had just built a distinctive cabin on his Frayser acreage on Highway 51 north of the Wolf River, five miles from his office. It was a totally modern two-floor country lodge with four baths, poker room and bar, fireplaces, and a separate apartment on the lower level. Oak logs were sawed in half to cover the outside walls.

At "Oak Lodge" in August Smith gave Charlotte a large diamond ring and a few days later announced their engagement to be married in December. One of Fred Smith's lawyers asked Frank Ahlgren, editor of the *Memphis Commercial Appeal,* to run Charlotte's picture on page one with a story about the engagement. "I told him we didn't do that—it was society page stuff," said Ahlgren. "Fred was kind of a roughneck. Always wanting something. I tried to avoid him."

They decided to marry in her hometown. Charlotte erred by printing invitations listing him as "James Frederick." He flung them in the ash can. He invited the top Greyhound officials, and the bus line's security chief wired the Pine Bluff chief of police to guard against any "horseplay" with the groom.

The wedding on December 27, 1934, was fine, but the scheduled honeymoon trip to Honolulu aboard the *SS Luraline* fell apart. The new Mrs. Fred Smith came down with flu, and they missed the boat. Still, she dragged herself to Hollywood parties, where they met Glenda Farrell and Howard Hughes, among others. Smith booked them out of San Diego on a seventeen-day cruise, through the Panama Canal to Havana, and they concluded their honeymoon in Miami.

Back in Memphis, Smith took his bride straight to the Tennessee Children's Home Society to confer with the director, Georgia Tann, spinster daughter of a Mississippi judge, about adopting a child. Years later, in 1950, a "black market baby" scandal would erupt, with Miss Tann accused of "selling" babies to Dick Powell and others in the movie colony and wealthy clients in New York. While placing five thousand children, she lived a luxurious secret life, acquiring $200,000 in property and regularly gambling as a high roller in Havana casinos. The IRS was to sue her for $124,000 back taxes, and cancer would end her life just as she was called to testify in the sensational Tennessee legislative investigation.

But on the day Fred Smith took his new wife there, the children's home was popular and respected. "He thought he couldn't have children," said Charlotte Smith in an interview for this book. "His lawyer, Walter Chandler, had adopted a boy from Miss Tann. I told him he'd ruin my reputation! Memphis is such a gossipy town! But Georgia Tann brought out a scrawny little girl.

"I was surprised. I thought he wanted a boy. The child was sick, and so pathetic. I guess she was about nine months old. They said she was born to a Nashville college girl—they always make up stories. Later I thought she may have been Fred's child. I found out that he had tried to get his sister Polly to adopt her, and she'd refused. I think he tried somebody else, too. Anyhow we took her, and named her Laura Ann, after his mother."

Polly Barron and her husband shared Oak Lodge with the newlyweds and their adopted daughter. "Polly was nice to me," said Charlotte Smith, "but, oh, that Estelle! Earl's wife—she was a pretty blonde, with navy eyes. But she hated me. Somebody told me she was related to Ma Barker, the gun moll. At Christmas she'd send me flowers and put in some man's card to try to stir up trouble. Earl was charming, a great chef, but quite a boozer. Fred didn't drink much."

Out in the country while her husband went to his office, Charlotte found Oak Lodge lonely. When a flood knocked out the Highway 51 bridge over Wolf River, isolating him from town, Fred bought a mansion at 527 East Parkway South, and the couple moved into one of Memphis's best residential sections, keeping their riding horses at a fairgrounds stable. But their marriage was in trouble.

"He treated me like a child," Charlotte Smith said. "At times I was afraid of him; he could be rough and violent. He slapped me once; Polly saw it. He'd get tired, and full of stress and take it out on me. He didn't want to take me out—except twice a year, our anniversary and New Year's. All the women were crazy about him. Sparks flew when he came into a room. He took his other women out all the time. Glenda Farrell, the movie star, came to Memphis, and I'm sure they had an affair. I wasn't sophisticated at all; I should have been. He married little people like me. I was sort of the Scarlett O'Hara type, and he was very jealous. He was going to Chicago on Greyhound business, and seeing girls. He was a womanizer—that's what he was."

In Memphis today people who knew Fred Smith confirm his penchant for dalliance. One among several is Walter Chandler's daughter, now Mrs. Lucia Outlan, wife of a physician in suburban Germantown. "You've never known anybody who had as many women as Fred Smith. I got my information by eavesdropping when Charlotte would get in touch with my father. I was just old enough to know you didn't talk about an affair. I had to look it up in the dictionary. I think my daddy didn't like Charlotte. She wore sun-backed dresses, tight clothes. She looked flashy in the 1940s—the way women do now. I was fascinated as a young girl the way she could spend money. She was fun, and she was popular. When Charlotte went to a party, everybody would migrate to her."

Charlotte Smith's own recollection is that for her the marriage became boring and lonely. "Otherwise I just adored him. He was very glamorous, and rich. I don't think I'd have cared so much about him if he hadn't been so rich. He bought me a beautiful Packard limousine, chauffeur and all that. But to give me money, for myself, he was not too good. I almost had to borrow from the cook!"

Smith had plenty of money, with enormous profits rolling in from both his Dixie Greyhound Lines and the expanding national Toddle House chain. And he had no difficulty in finding places to spend or invest his wealth. Situated as he was in the bosom of the cotton country, he could be excused for being envious of the genteel aristocracy of the Old South. He longed to gain acceptance as a constituent of that cultured life-style in the Mississippi Delta—the storied rich cotton land, which in the Memphis vernacular presumed to stretch all the way from the lobby of the Peabody Hotel south to Catfish Row in Vicksburg, Mississippi. However, he would never be looked up to as "Colonel" Smith unless he owned a plantation. So he went out and bought two.

Dealing through his Frederick Smith Enterprise Company, he purchased for a total of $215,000 the Matagorda farm at Jonestown, Mississippi, which had on its 2,000 acres a cotton gin, sawmill, gristmill, store, hall, and seventy-six tenant houses, and the Dodd plantation near Clarksdale, which covered 2,500 acres and contained two manager's homes, a church, a school, and one hundred tenant houses.

Living conditions were deplorable on his plantations, as they were elsewhere in the South, for the Negro tenant families who planted, hoed, and picked the cotton. Fred Smith inspected with disdain the unpainted, leaky shacks that were home to his several hundred plantation laborers. The hovels had no bathrooms, running water, or electricity—and never had since before the Civil War. "That's absolutely miserable, intolerable—inhumane," he told Nowland Van Powell, a Memphis architect who had designed Oak Lodge and some of his Greyhound Bus Line terminals. "Can you come up with a neat little two-bedroom-and-bath house I can build for them on my plantations? . . . And, of course, with something else they don't have, screens on the doors and windows!" The architect could and did.

The *Memphis Press-Scimitar* hailed this experiment in plantation uplift with a page one headline: NEW TENANCY CURE: "MAKE THEM HAPPY." As his farm workers moved into their new bungalows, fresh with green and white paint and indoor plumbing, Smith ordered his manager to burn the rickety old shacks the families had occupied for fifty years.

It was supposed to be further emancipation from old unenlightened slave days. But Smith later concluded that his modernization had come too late. Tenants were not accustomed to upkeep, and the new houses gradually fell into disrepair. "It was a sad situation," recalled a former overseer. To evoke a new mood, Smith also dismantled the huge plantation bell that in antebellum times had summoned the hands to the fields. On a tower he mounted a siren blown by two hundred fifty pounds of air pressure. That didn't make a great difference to the folks on the plantation; the wake-up signal still came at four A.M.

At age twenty-five, Charlotte became pregnant. The doctor had been wrong about her husband's puzzling blood disease; he was not sterile after all. She went into labor on November 9, 1937, at Baptist Hospital in Memphis. It was a difficult accouchement, and her obstetrician took her to surgery.

"When I came to in the hospital," Charlotte Smith recalled, "Polly and Estelle were in my room. One of them said, 'Do you want to see Charlotte Fredette?' I said 'Who's that?' 'Why, your daughter!' They had named her, but that was all right. Fredette is after Fred. I hate people naming their daughters after their mothers. Looks like they could be more original.

"But Fred was happy. He was just wild about having that baby. He adored her!"

His steamer *J. B. Smith* was still plowing the Mississippi and Ohio rivers, bringing cargoes of beer down from Evansville, Indiana. Occasionally the owner made the trip and by that means discovered a bon vivant who was to become his lifelong pal, Walter A. Beckerle, who owned a popular "swinging" tavern at 15 N.W. Third Street in Evansville. Weighing three hundred pounds, bald and looking a lot like politico James A. Farley, Beckerle was a heavy-duty drinker and connoisseur of women. (His only child, Mrs. Elizabeth B. Tolle of Summit, New Jersey, recalled: "You can visualize these two men, who were the same age, becoming sidekicks. They never grew up, I'm assuming—neither one of them. But my father was charming; if you didn't need him as a father, you'd love him. He was a magnificent cook, magnificent! He could drink anybody under any table any time anywhere. I never saw anybody with the capacity for alcohol he had, and I never knew the man to be drunk. He'd start drinking when he got up at noon, and he wouldn't stop until he went to bed at four o'clock the next morning. He just carried it. He was an enormous man, but he wasn't fat; he was hard as a rock. He was married three times—he kept on till he got it right.")

The yacht fever had by now really taken hold of Fred Smith.

Former secretary of the treasury Ogden L. Mills had died, and in the fall of 1939 the executor of his estate put on the market his 180-foot steel-hulled yacht, *Avalon.* Built at a cost of $550,000, she was air-conditioned; had a library, six staterooms, and five baths; and carried a crew of twenty. Smith bought her.

He selected Miami as his winter port, since he already had a $40,000 house in Miami Beach at 4853 Pinetree Drive. For most of January 1940 he cruised the Gulf of Mexico with Charlotte and ten friends. His wife was not an avid sailor. "After two hours on any boat," she said, "I always want to get off." This was one cruise on which she wished more than ever she was ashore.

On Friday, February 9, 1940, the *Avalon* was heading north across the Gulf of Mexico, destined to dock at Pensacola, Florida, the following day and disembark all passengers. For two days the weather had been sunny, the seas smooth. The New Orleans marine radio operator forecast continuing "fair" weather. He was wrong.

About eight-thirty at night the seas began rolling. Wind struck. "Stronger and stronger it howled," Smith said later. "It whistled through the rigging. Lightning crashed and the waves began pitching. The *Avalon,* a heavy and sturdy ship, was tossed about violently. The waves were two stories high, at least, All night we fought those waves. Our problem was to ride them out, stay on top, slide down and go up with them. If one of them had struck from above, we would have been lost. It was the worst I've ever seen in the Gulf, and I've done a lot of sailing there.

"We were really in danger—because the storm blew us off course, and we didn't know exactly where we were. Lightning had knocked out our radio direction finder. There was no way to take sightings and fix a new course because the storm obscured the stars and even the next day blotted out the sun."

Those aboard the *Avalon* did not know they were caught in the fringes of a hurricane that had raked Albany, Georgia. But by coincidence Earl Smith, at his home in Memphis, did. He often tuned in his ham radio to pick up brother Fred's transmissions from the yacht, and he happened to catch the vain effort to get directions from the Coast Guard.

"It was scary," Earl Smith told the *Commercial Appeal*. "For nearly three hours I listened. The yacht was groping through strange waters. About two miles off a large ship hove into view, and Fred radioed them for a position fix. They must have thought a submarine could be lurking. Anyhow they wouldn't open up, didn't give the least help."

Into Saturday afternoon the yacht kept groping in a northerly direction. Finally, over the radio, Earl Smith heard his brother tell the Coast Guard: "Everything's all right. We've sighted a buoy in the harbor at Pensacola." No one was hurt, but some of the yacht's furnishings were damaged.

"Well, it's all over now," Fred Smith told the *Press-Scimitar* from Pensacola, "but I believe I know how a condemned man must feel. How we got out of it, I don't know."

That experience soured him on the *Avalon*. Two months later he sold her to two Canadian businessmen. Charlotte was delighted.

In Beckerle's tavern in Evansville, Indiana, Smith kept watching a pretty blonde who was having a Scotch and soda—alone. In looks, he told friends later, she could have been the twin of movie star Alice Faye. When she noticed him—well tailored, suave, obviously a man of means, and now, although in his mid-forties turning prematurely gray in a fashion that only enhanced his distinguished air—she pushed aside her drink and flashed him a smile.

"Hello, handsome. What brings you to Evansville?"

Whatever answer he gave didn't really matter a whole lot. They had found each other, sparks flew wildly, and from that moment in the Evansville tavern, wife Charlotte was living on borrowed time, dutifully at home bringing up his two little girls—adopted Laura Ann and Fredette.

The stunning and vivacious lady in the tavern was Dorothy Dickman, twenty-nine years old. Smith was forty-four when they met in the spring of 1940. She had grown up in Detroit; eventually he met her mother, Mrs. Bessie Dickman, who still lived there.

Fred Smith's next move was to go to Florida for a serious discussion with his wife.

"I was down in Miami Beach in our winter home, and he came and said he was going to lose his money," said Charlotte Smith in our interview. "The government was going to sue him for nonpayment of taxes. A big deal back in those days. He wanted me to get a divorce so he could put the money in funds for the children and me.

"I'd do anything for my husband and children. So I said all right. I didn't even get a lawyer. And he just ripped me off good. Didn't give me anything, hardly."

She went through the divorce proceedings in Florida and later went back to Memphis, expecting to be rewarded with a diamond necklace.

"I thought he would be throwing a party for me, because I'd saved his money, you know, and everything. Eddie, our chauffeur, met me at the airport. I said, 'Eddie, where is Mr. Smith?' He says, 'Miss Charlotte, don't you know?' I said, 'No.' Eddie said, 'He's on his honeymoon in Honolulu with Miss Dorothy.' How would you like that? That was terrible! He just lied to me, and conned me out of— I should have had millions, but I didn't!"

For once, the Dixie Greyhound Lines president got his wedding picture on page one in the *Memphis Commercial Appeal* with a two-column head that read: FRED SMITH DIVORCED IN MIAMI; WEDS 3 DAYS LATER IN ST. LOUIS. Smith, in a dark suit and wild-patterned four-in-hand, was shown gazing adoringly at this third bride, honey-colored ringlets visible beneath her cloche hat, wearing three strands of pearls and a pale fur jacket.

The wedding took place May 4, 1940, at St. Louis, performed by a Presbyterian minister, the Reverend Walker E. McClure. The newlyweds registered at the Hotel Park Plaza, accompanied by the bride's mother, Mrs. Bessie Dickman, and the groom's Toddle House partner, J. C. Stedman. They sent out a flurry of telegrams and then began their honeymoon journey by visiting friends in Evansville and Chicago.

In her rage, Charlotte Smith went to their home on East Parkway to collect her thoughts. She intended to stay there until she could find a suitable apartment in Memphis. She collected so much that when she signed a lease at the Parkview Apartments, she needed a moving van. When her ex-husband came back he discovered she had taken "without his knowledge or consent" furniture, rugs, ornaments, paintings, and a grand piano, all valued at $2,500. Fred Smith took her to court. "They belong to me," said Charlotte Smith. On May 23, 1940, the Chancery Court decided otherwise and let him send sheriff's deputies to bring it all back.

Charlotte felt powerless—and bitter. "Memphis is full of intrigue," she said. "Charleston, South Carolina, is the same way. If you belong to a certain clique, you can murder your own mother and nobody cares or will do anything about it. If you're not in that circle, you are in deep trouble."

It was not all easy for Fred Smith, either. Presently he began to realize that a bar was not necessarily the perfect place to discover a future wife. Dorothy Dickman Smith had a drinking problem.

That created a number of problems in the East Parkway home, inasmuch as the Florida court had granted him custody of the adopted daughter, Laura Ann, and permitted Charlotte to keep Charlotte Fredette.

His third marriage lasted one year and seven months. He made a settlement and sent Dorothy to Reno, where on November 19, 1941, she was granted a divorce on grounds of cruelty.

But the ex-Mrs. Smith number three did not get out of his life. She showed up periodically in Memphis and on most occasions moved right back into the East Parkway mansion. Fred Smith could not seem to bring himself to evict her. Quite the contrary, his newest girlfriends noted, it took him many months to get over Dorothy.

Her drinking impaired her health, and her life ended abruptly. It was generally believed in Memphis that she committed suicide. "I once met Dorothy Dickman, and I heard she killed herself," recalls Lucia Outlan, the daughter of Smith's chief lawyer. "But I don't know it for a fact. That was hushed up. Daddy [Walter Chandler] didn't mention it." The Memphis newspapers did not publish her obituary.

But while she lived, Dorothy Dickman Smith injected herself as an unstable barrier in the path of Fred Smith's pursuit of his fourth wife.

The next romance was ignited by another chance meeting at a Memphis hotel—in the dining room of the Claridge.

Fred Smith arrived for lunch. At one table he saw a women he knew in business and went over to say hello. She was seated with a middle-aged woman and fresh-faced pretty blonde—the kind of innocent-looking girl who most attracted him.

Introductions were made, and he sat down to join them for a cup of coffee. The girl was Sally Wallace West from Jackson, Tennessee, in Memphis with her aunt on a shopping trip. She was twenty-three years old—half his age.

"I'm just about to leave for Evansville," he told them. "Got to buy a house up there—it's part of my divorce settlement with my wife. She's in Reno right now." He turned his full attention to the young girl. "So you live in Jackson? I get over there a lot on business. Next time I'm going to call you."

Sally murmured that she would be pleased. "He was the most fascinating person," she said. "First of all he had a beautiful voice. Secondly you could see the intelligence there, and he was just so smart that I was in awe of him. But I thought that was it; I'd never see him again."

A few months later, in Jackson with architect Nowland Van Powell to design a bus terminal, he called. "It was the first time anybody had ever brought me candy, flowers, and perfume—all at one time. And for a little country girl that was very, very impressive. I was quite smitten."

Smith took her out to dinner in Jackson, to the movies, and a few times down to Memphis to the Peabody Hotel roof ballroom to dance to the big bands. But the courtship never really caught fire. Sally discovered why Fred Smith was holding back—he was still entangled in his former marriage. Not the memory, but to ex-wife Dorothy herself. She kept coming back to Memphis to see him.

"He was completely infatuated, and thought he was so in love with her," Sally recalled. "He told me all about it later. He called it his middle-age fling."

During their off-and-on courtship. Sally was seeing another man. "I felt obligated to tell this suitor that I was getting pretty serious about Fred, and the fellow got all torn up about it."

Another impediment in their romance was World War II. On July 12, 1942, Secretary of the Navy Frank Knox commissioned Fred Smith a lieutenant commander in the Eighth Naval District at New Orleans. He was anxious to get into uniform and anticipated being on duty in the Gulf of Mexico, waters with which he was quite familiar. Instead he was given a desk job in Washington. It was a hard comedown for a man who craved action. He did his best to get placed on battle duty, but he may have been considered overage. At any rate, after several months he resigned his commission and returned to Memphis.

Sally's life had been marred by tragedy. She was born September 6, 1919. Her mother died when she was young, and her father, a railroad man named Thomas Wallace, raised her so strictly that she eloped at sixteen. Her husband, John Richard West, a railroader's son from New Albany, Tennessee, was young, too. He was a trained bookkeeper, but the hard times forced him to take lesser jobs as an iceman, gas station attendant, and the like. They had two sons, Gary and Tommy. When the second child was three weeks old, her husband, on a new job as taxi driver, crashed into a railroad train in Jackson, killing himself and a passenger.

At nineteen Sally was a widow with two young sons—but still vivacious and pretty enough to catch the eye of an experienced Lothario who had admired scores of women at close range.

Finally Dorothy had at last disappeared, and Sally Wallace West was getting all Smith's attention.

"This all sounds like *Peyton Place* or a soap opera," Sally told me in an interview for this book. "Everybody just wants the good things of life told, and that makes dull reading."

There was nothing dull about the day of their wedding, November 12, 1943.

Aboard a borrowed yacht, the eighty-foot *Atrebor* that he formerly owned, Fred and Sally had been leisurely cruising up the Illinois River. For company they had aboard as guests the Evansville bon vivant Walter Beckerle and the latter's third wife, Emma.

"We had planned to get married, but not that particular day," Sally Smith said. "We were up around Peoria—I really don't remember just where. I'd have to dig out my marriage license and look at it. I remember the mayor's wife got drunk and fell out the window of the boat. She wasn't with us, just a guest.

"After we were married we left the *Atrebor* and went ashore and got on a bus—just Fred and me and the Beckerles—and the driver took us straight through to Memphis. I guess it was sort of a 'honeymoon charter,' as you call it.

"That marriage seems like it happened to someone else because I was so young. . . . I was such a little small-town naive person. As I look back, I can't think of ever being that young, really. You've opened up the floodgates of memories that I had forgotten about."

The honeymooners went straight to a new 3,700-acre plantation called Holly Grove, about fifty miles south of Memphis, which Fred Smith had bought in June 1942, for $178,000.

"I loved it," Sally Smith said. "Happiest times of my life. I love horseback riding, and we had horses. I loved cattle, and Fred was the first in Mississippi to raise black Angus. We had some Tennessee walking horses. He gave me one named Silver, a big white horse, too big for me, really. So I rode his horse, called Sarcasm."

But within a matter of weeks their doctor suggested the bride limit her riding, or at least use great caution. Mrs. Frederick Smith was pregnant.

"Fred was excited and happy about that. Oh, Lord, yes. I was, too. We still had the big house on East Parkway, but we both stayed down there in Mississippi a lot because we liked the plantation. By then we had bought the Salchanick farm of seven hundred acres up on the highway and much closer to Memphis. He wanted to show off his cattle, and no one could see them at Holly Grove, it was so far back off the main road. He planned to sell our home in Memphis and take the children and build a home and live down there."

They had planned to leave Holly Grove and return to Memphis in time for Dr. Blecker to deliver the baby at Methodist Hospital. But as a precautionary move, Mrs. Smith had visited the nearest hospital, located at Marks. It was a twenty-bed infirmary, very well equipped, owned by Dr. James E. Furr, a fifty-two-year-old surgeon and general practitioner.

After breakfast at Holly Grove on the morning of August 11, 1944, Smith went out on the plantation to inspect his cattle. They were leaving the next weekend to return to Memphis.

"All of a sudden—three weeks early—I went into labor," Mrs. Smith said. "Fortunately, our plantation manager's wife lived right across the road. I called her and she loaded me into the backseat of our big Buick and took off over fifteen miles of gravel roads for the hospital in Marks, and Dr. Furr.

"The baby was born about noon. This being my third child, it wasn't a long-drawn-out thing.

"They finally caught up with Fred out on the plantation, and he got to the hospital about an hour after I delivered, and he was so excited. He just couldn't get over that he had a son, you know. He really wanted a boy, but he never said. I knew that he wanted a son. And his son was the very image of him. Of course we named him after his father and my family—Frederick Wallace.

"Freddie weighed eight pounds and had a lot of black hair and a loud voice. He was about twenty inches long. My husband pulled up a chair and took that baby and examined him from stem to stern. And then he looked at me and said: 'A perfect baby!' "

5 ▶ THE HOUSE ON EAST PARKWAY SOUTH

Fred Smith stood before his bathroom mirror, whipping up lather in his shaving mug. Daughter Fredette, a first-grader, appeared impishly in the doorway. She remembers he wore purple-striped pajamas. With a quick thrust of the brush, he daubed her nose with foam. She retreated wildly, with screeches and giggles. It was a daily ritual that made both happy.

Regardless of which wife reigned in the boudoir, the rambling old mansion on East Parkway South echoed in the 1940s to excitement, high jinks, and good times for the children. At the time Freddie was ensconced there in his pristine white bassinet, Laura Ann was almost ten years old, Fredette seven, and stepbrothers Gary and Tommy were eight and five, respectively.

Neither business affairs, extramarital adventures, cotton and cattle raising, nor high-octane yachting kept Smith from being a doting father. He held court for his children in his great bedroom–sitting room. "He had a big carved four-poster bed with pineapples on the posts and a rail between the posts at the bottom, and we used to sit on that rail like birds on a wire," Fredette recalled years later.

They hovered around as he was served breakfast—on a tray, with coffee in a silver thermos—at his desk in an alcove of that room. It fascinated them to see him flip a row of telephone toggle switches to reach secretaries in his downtown office, the Greyhound office, the Toddle House office, or the servants' quarters in the kitchen. Fredette recalled his closets with "beautiful camel-hair double-breasted coats," rows of hats, shoes, white-on-white shirts, and paisley ties. "He would let me pick out his clothes," she said. Then the chauffeur would drive the older children to school, while they usually teased and taunted him over the limousine's intercom.

"Daddy played checkers with us at night," Fredette said. "Taught us how to play gin rummy—on his bed or on the table. We would howl and scream and carry on. But he liked having us under foot. He taught us poker. We would have Monopoly games going on, my stepbrothers and me, for days, and they would be in the corner of the bedroom. And on Sundays he'd pile us all in the car and go check the Toddle House commissary, and let us bring home pies. And he would zoom down the cobblestones along the river, and stop just at the edge. Great fun, wonderful memories!"

At bedtime he would thrill the children with tall tales. "His imagination was superb," Fredette recalled. "They were made-up stories mostly about hunting. Things like black panthers . . . way off in the mountains, or out in the islands. [He] had a Chinese cook, and we'd say, 'Was So-and-so with you?' and he'd say, 'Oh, yeah.' He used to tell about the *Titanic* sinking. 'And the captain was a Smith.' 'One of our family?' 'Oh, yeah.' "

By the time Freddie was two, his father was taking him to his office downtown. The child was outfitted with a Greyhound uniform and cap and photographed for the cover of the house organ, *Dixie Digest*. The three boys got along well, but not the girls. Laura Ann felt "special" because she was adopted and never desired to know who her real parents were, yet even so she later grew to feel like the "black sheep" in the family. She feuded viciously with Fredette. "We had an old chow," Charlotte Smith said, "and the girls would sic him on each other." Fredette knocked Laura Ann unconscious with a Coke bottle. "I think I wanted to kill her," she recalled, "but she only had a concussion." On the other hand, Fredette developed a close relationship with baby brother Freddie that endured lovingly into adulthood.

Sally was "nice" to her two stepdaughters and won them over by making fudge Saturday nights. Ex-wife Charlotte was also present occasionally, having sold her Florida house and moved back to

Memphis. Fredette spent weekends in her mother's apartment in the Kimbrough Towers on Union Avenue. Either the chauffeur or her father would drive her between the two homes. Charlotte was still bitter about her divorce, but she was on friendly terms with Sally, and they occasionally chatted, mainly about matters involving Fredette. ("It took me a lot of Jack Daniel's and champagne to get over my divorce," Charlotte Smith recalled years later. "And I went seven times to Europe.")

Ghosts from the past did not seem to faze little Freddie's mother. Sally was the third Mrs. Frederick Smith to occupy the mansion at 527 East Parkway South, which was bought in Charlotte's time. The three-story house, Georgian style of red brick and white stone, had been built in 1914 by a wealthy lumberman. Awakened one midnight by his barking dog, the lumberman took a fall in the dark and died of his injuries. His widow, who remarried and decided to move to Paris, France, sold the mansion, including all furnishings and two acres of grounds, to Fred Smith. He summoned a Marshall Field decorator and added old master–style paintings to the largely Italianate furnishings.

For the children, he used the stable behind the mansion by buying a Shetland pony and a cart. "Unhappily," recalled Fredette, "that was the meanest pony you ever saw. He never missed a chance to bite you. Daddy was a good horseman, but he wouldn't tolerate that. I remember he took a wrench to that Shetland."

For Christmas he bought a Chickering grand piano, on which the children later took lessons. He installed a self-player attachment and listened to ragtime and waltz music run off on the rolls. Throughout his years, Fred Smith was a "voracious" reader. "He educated himself by reading," Sally Smith recalled. "I mean he just read all the time. Even as a boy, he told me, he did that. He was very interested in history and anything pertaining to navigation. And he always took the Kiplinger letter. He predicted our son would go much farther than he did because he would have the advantage of an education. And he was right about that."

The head of the Dixie Greyhound–Toddle House combine was known in Memphis as a dynamo and a Renaissance man. "He was not a snob," recalled daughter Fredette. "He had friends in all walks of life. He was not one to put on airs. He was truly a man's man, yet women were crazy about him, too. He had a great sense of humor. He was just good company. He had lots of friends who were powerfully connected men in Memphis. What they liked to do was hunt—and he took them often. His idea of relaxing was to build another yacht."

Business leaders, politicians, and his bus and restaurant associates were regularly guests for dinner parties in the mansion. Smith became interested in a bright young minister, the Reverend Alfred Loaring-Clark, whom Fredette described as having "the most beautiful voice you ever heard," and saw to it that one of Memphis's most imposing churches, St. John's Episcopal, was built for him.

How much Fred Smith wanted to be accepted in Memphis "high society" is still debated. The family contends he chose not to join the Memphis Country Club, but Walter Chandler's daughter said he wouldn't have been accepted even though her father worked hard "trying to tame him" and knock off some of the rough edges. "He was too wild for that group of people," said Lucia Outlan. "Daddy was trying to make him a gentleman."

Fred Smith certainly did not always endear himself to the country club set; once at a party at the club, he quarreled with a female companion and was seen to slap her. The distinguished Tennessee Club, which had a noble tradition of good whiskey and fine cigars, and occupied imposing downtown quarters, welcomed him; he and his cronies played poker there every Friday. He also held membership number 536 in the University Club and was a thirty-second-degree Mason. His civic roles grew in pace with his increasing wealth, and he was tapped for important positions such as member of the city harbor commission.

To pioneer, establish, and expand the Dixie Greyhound Lines, Fred Smith had to run his business largely as an autocrat. His direct dealing with his drivers tended on occasion to be tough. Eventually union organizers came in, but Smith wanted nothing to do with them. The National Labor Relations Board and lawyers and courts got involved. In the mid-1940s drivers went on strike for higher pay and a shorter work week. Defying the union, Greyhound hired replacement drivers and kept the buses rolling.

The trouble intensified, and mysterious shots were fired into buses on the highways, wounding a driver and a passenger. On one occasion during this strife, the Fred Smiths with little Freddie were visiting the bus terminal in Jackson. "The manager got a death threat that they were going to try to do something to my husband," Sally Smith said. "We got in the car and went right back to Memphis, a rather wild ride."

In the end Dixie Greyhound signed a union contract granting a 10 percent wage increase and a reduction in hours.

On horseback, aboard a boat, or in a car, Fred Smith was at ease—but not up in the air. "He didn't like airplanes," Sally Smith recalled. "He tried to learn to fly, and hit a hangar. That's what he told me. [Perhaps this was in 1929 during his abortive effort to start the "Golden Eagle" airline between Memphis and Nashville.] I personally know that in 1947 we were down in the West Indies and took a Cuban airliner for Havana. We hit some real bad weather, and Fred turned just as white as a ghost. I don't believe he ever flew again."

In his chain of little restaurants, he tolerated nothing slipshod. One weekend he took Sally and Freddie into a Toddle House for a hamburger. The cook flipped the meat recklessly, and it plopped into sooty grease back of the grill. The boy retrieved it and slapped it on a bun. "He didn't know who Fred was," Sally Smith said. "Besides that, he let two customers walk out without paying. Fred quietly sent me out to the car, locked the place up, phoned his local manager, and told him not to open it again until he found a cook who'd run it right."

Early on a fall morning in Memphis, Earl Smith emerged from a house on a quiet street, went to his car parked out front, and began fumbling with his key to unlock the door. Watching from hiding in nearby bushes were wife, Estelle, and daughter-in-law Joann Manley Smith.

"We got him!" whispered Estelle.

When Earl Smith unlocked the car door, a cascade of tree leaves spurted out. He realized then that his wife had learned of his long-standing trysting place and had gathered leaves off the street and jam-packed them in his car.

"These men had lots and lots of women," said Lindsey "Sissy" Smith Brady of West Palm Beach, Florida, Earl Smith's granddaughter. "Everybody knew it. I don't know how Estelle found out he was cheating. But she spotted his car and had my mother help her pack it so tight with leaves that they could hardly get the door closed."

Earl Smith may have played second fiddle in business to his brother, but for the women in the family the reverse was true. The most aggressive, dominant, and single-minded of women in the clan was Estelle. "She was a beautiful woman, and she had beautiful, almost navy blue eyes," said her granddaughter. "She was a very controlling person, and she always had to be in charge."

Estelle would surmount obvious difficulties—including Earl's persistent boozing—in her marriage, stay with and outlive her husband, and leave their five-million-dollar estate to a lone grandson, who later died young in an auto crash.

Sally Smith got along with Estelle but characterized her thus: "You've seen people who were just eccentric—she was one of those." When Charlotte Smith asked to borrow eggs to make a cake, Estelle sent her a dozen that were hard-boiled. When her grandson, Earl Smith III, was born, Estelle was upset that he didn't have curly hair like his father. When the boy was four she plopped him down in her beauty shop for a permanent wave. The outraged father whisked him the same day to his barber, who snipped off the curls. Estelle flashed big diamond rings and had social pretensions. She wanted the glory and prestige that went with becoming a duchess in the annual Cotton Carnival. But in caste-conscious Memphis society, with her minuscule clout, she didn't stand a chance.

Earl, however, had enough pull when he was arrested for drunken driving to haul the Memphis police judge out of bed at four A.M. and down to the jail to see that he was released on fifty dollars bond. The miscreant told the *Press-Scimitar:*

I had been to dinner at the Tennessee Club with Mrs. Smith. She was returning home in her own car. I was driving east on Jefferson, stopped to watch the tennis matches, then drove on. I was very sleepy and fell asleep and got on the wrong side of the street. I woke up just in time to see another car coming at me. I jammed on the brakes and avoided a collision. The officer was within his rights in arresting me.

For four or five months the arrest made newspaper copy and courthouse gossip. The Shelby County grand jury declined to indict him, but the foreman called the incident "a gross miscarriage of justice." In the end, another grand jury returned an indictment, and on October 24, 1950, Earl Smith was fined $100 and his driver's license was suspended for six months.

The Smith who was a model of decorum and made no waves at all was sister Olive Barron. Fred adored her and was devastated when she died in 1946. Cut from an entirely different cloth, however, was her husband, Felix, a round-faced, pudgy fellow who satisfactorily managed the Toddle House division in New Orleans but usually slept through meetings of the board of directors.

"I remember Uncle Felix very well," said Lindsey Brady. "He did crazy things. When jukeboxes were first popular he got in on the ground floor buying a lot of them and was going to make a killing. He was kind of a drinker himself, and he forgot about them. Ten years later, after the market was saturated, he found them stuck away in a warehouse. He had to sell 'em for nothing.

"Supposedly when Felix died they found desk drawers full of ladies' stockings—which he used to hand out on birthdays. And war bonds he'd stuck back in his desk."

Memphis got a good laugh when he lived in the Parkview Apartments on Poplar Avenue opposite a toy shop he rented to Hugh Sanders. One morning he strolled across the street to get his Cadillac convertible, which he customarily parked on a setback in front of the toy shop. He was stunned to see his car wrapped in a log chain and padlocked. He couldn't open the doors. Felix called the police, and Sanders admitted he'd done the deed.

"I got damned tired of him taking up customers' parking space," said Sanders.

"But, but—I own this place," protested Felix.

The toy man paid a $51 fine for malicious mischief, and Felix found another parking spot.

His most notable gaucherie, perhaps, was a secret he kept from Polly during her lifetime—the fact that he had a "lost" son. He did make amends on his deathbed.

When he became terminally ill in Memphis in September 1958, he summoned his nephew Earl "Billy" Smith, Jr. "I never told anyone. I was married before. I have a son, grown now and married, living somewhere in Arkansas. Please find him."

Billy Smith and his wife, Joann, located Felix's son and brought him to his father in the Memphis hospital. "I'm strapped," the son told Billy Smith. "I hope there's about five hundred dollars in this for me."

There was—and more. Felix Barron's will left him $50,000.

Few men were more family-oriented than Fred Smith, and he went to great lengths to try to help kinfolk—not always with success.

In Metropolis, Illinois, across the river from Paducah, lived his favorite cousin, George "Ham" Smith, a machinist at the Illinois Central railroad shops. In 1940 Ham was laid off and went as far south as Memphis looking for work, to no avail. He showed up at cousin Fred's office but was kept waiting thirty minutes by the receptionist. Disgusted, Ham put on his hat, went down the street, and found a phone. He called Fred.

"Stay where you are," said Fred Smith. "I'll send my limousine for you." When the car pulled up, the out-of-work cousin refused to get in the backseat and sat with the driver.

Fred heard about Ham's futile job search. "Do you know anything about the restaurant business?"

"Hell, no," said Ham.

"Well, we got some restaurants called Toddle House. I'll give you a start. You wash dishes, learn something about cooking, serving people. All told I want you to practice three weeks, then I'll make you a manager, and you've got a good job!"

Cousin Ham jumped up. "Hell, no! I didn't come down here for a handout. I don't want that damn job. I'm a skilled machinist. I just came by to say howdy!"

▶ ▶ ▶

In his livestock and cotton-farming ventures, Fred Smith experimented to enhance quality and efficiency of his products. But the modern way didn't always pay off on the plantations, as he discovered with the mechanical cotton picker. Mrs. Evelyn Smith, wife of the Holly Grove plantation manager, recalled: "When we first went there it had been a hard, wet winter. The former owners of the plantation had left the cotton in the fields because they couldn't get it out. My husband had heard of a mechanical picking machine in Memphis. Mr. Smith brought it out. It was the first one we'd ever seen. It worked good, got the cotton out, saved him quite a bit of money because he was going to lose it all and have to plow it under. After that, though, they didn't use the mechanical picker. They had field hands do it—cheaper and get more cotton, wouldn't lose as much as the machine does."

On cattle, however, he set his sights high—and refused to compromise. At the annual auction of Aberdeen-Angus blooded stock at Miami, Oklahoma, in 1947, he took a fancy to the best bull of the lot, Prince Eric III of Sunbeam.

So did two other cattle breeders with deep pockets—W. G. Mennen, the talcum powder king from New Jersey, and Stephen Birch, vice-president of Anaconda Copper Company.

"We all were bidding fast and furious," Fred Smith said. "Mr. Mennen dropped out at $20,000. Then Mr. Birch bid $20,500. I really wanted that bull—and I went to $21,000. And I got him!"

A reporter asked if he intended to insure the bull. "Well, I hadn't thought about that. Come to think of it, he's such a dignitary, I may just put him up at the Peabody!"

In the same auction he bought a $5,000 heifer to add to the herd from which he was annually selling fifty to sixty bulls at $350 to $1,000 for commercial breeding stock. He was the largest Angus breeder in the mid-South.

It pained him that his prize cattle were hidden away in remote fields. He considered moving some of the Angus bulls and heifers into the Memphis suburbs. A large tract went on the market when a physician and his wife divorced, and Smith looked at it longingly.

"I'd like to buy this place," he told Sally. "But seven hundred dollars an acre is a mighty steep price just to be near enough to the road so people can drive by and see a great prize bull like Prince Eric. I guess I'll pass."

Eventually the physician's acreage was purchased as the site of Elvis Presley's home, Graceland.

To rechristen one of his plantations, Smith was inventive enough to amalgamate the names of his wife and three children. "Now I have it all worked out," he said. "The 'Sal' is for Sally, the 'ch' is for Charlotte [daughter Charlotte Fredette], the 'an' is for Laura Ann, and the 'ick' is for little Frederick. Isn't 'Salchanick' a nice name?"

It struck his fancy so much that he also used it as the name for his next yacht.

In May 1948 Fred Smith was escaping business cares at his cabin on Moon Lake, Mississippi, fifty miles south of Memphis. It was the retreat where he spent most weekends with Sally and Freddie.

Now just four months past his fifty-third birthday, he was at the zenith of a stunning business career that gave him diversified holdings worth around $17 million. His Greyhound buses rolled 1.5 million miles a month, carrying passengers across nine states. In 170 Toddle House restaurants people were eating good meals and steadily coming back. His plantations were growing cotton and producing valuable herds of black Angus cattle, while he dealt in commercial real estate and dreamed airily of transforming a World War II subchaser he had bought from the navy into a luxury yacht. He decided to call her the *Lysander,* after a Spartan general (395 B.C.) he'd become fond of in his extensive reading.

He had more entrepreneurial dreams. South America intrigued and beckoned him. As soon as he could arrange his Memphis affairs, he planned to go to Brazil or Argentina to see if he could establish in either country a bus line. He hoped vaguely that the *Lysander* would be finished at the Gulfport, Mississippi, shipyard in time to carry him south for that adventure.

After reading the Sunday papers on the breezy porch of his lake cabin, he felt some discomfort and pressure in his chest. Within thirty minutes pain developed in his left arm.

"Let's pack up and go home," he told his wife. "I'd better talk to the doctor."

In their Lincoln sedan, Sally drove him back to Memphis and summoned his physician, George Bowers, to the mansion on East Parkway South. "You've had a heart attack," said Dr. Bowers. "I'm sending you straight to Saint Joe's."

Smith arrived at St. Joseph's Hospital in critical condition and showed little improvement for two or three weeks. "Now they could do something about that, of course—then they couldn't," recalled Sally Smith. After eight weeks in the hospital, he recovered enough to go home—and right back to work.

From his bedroom, via the switchboard on his desk, he relayed orders, made decisions, and generally kept his hand in all his business affairs. He fumed impatiently about the slow pace of work on his new yacht. "He could work under pressure. He liked a challenge," said Sally Smith. "He never knew the word *stop* or *quit*. He just pushed on and on. The only time he stopped was the few weeks he was in an oxygen tent."

Through the summer and into the fall, Smith remained an invalid, confined largely to his home. Then, on the evening of Tuesday, November 16, 1948, he became suddenly quite ill. "I could hear this fluid gurgling in his chest," said Sally Smith. "His doctor was on vacation in California, so I called our next-door neighbor, Dr. Lyle Motley. He took him right to Baptist Hospital and gave him a shot that took off the fluid—ten or fifteen pounds in a day or two."

The children were taken to see him in the hospital. Fredette recalled: "He was under an oxygen tent, and I was frantic. This vivacious man. He was on top of everything. He just filled the house, and he made everybody hop. I kept saying, 'When are you coming back?' He gave some answer, but it was muffled, and I couldn't hear."

His wife remained with him day and night, sleeping on a cot in his room. About six A.M. on Friday, November 19, he woke her. Sally Smith said: "He said, 'Honey, I'm sick at my stomach.' I said, 'You want me to get the pan?' So I got up and put the little pan under his mouth for him to upchuck. He fell over dead."

6 ▶ IF I DIE FLYING . . .

Eight-year-old Freddie Smith watched as the Memphis orthopedic surgeon held the X-ray of his right hip to the light and explained to his mother the cause of his limp.

"The medical term is Calvé-Perthes disease, or osteochondrosis of the capitular epiphysis of the femur," the physician said. "Simply put, there's an interruption in the blood supply to your son's hip. The knob at the top of his right thigh bone is not developing properly. The cause usually is obscure. Perhaps he had a respiratory infection that shunted bacteria to his femur."

The doctor saw Sally's alarm. "Don't worry. This is not uncommon in children. Of course, it must be carefully treated. Fortunately, you caught it early. We can have Freddie good as new, I believe, in a year or two."

Freddie was put on crutches and required to wear a leather strap from his left shoulder through his crotch to keep weight off his right leg and allow the hip joint to heal itself.

"The doctor said it would probably take a week for him to get used to the crutches," said Sally Smith. "Well, he was running up and down the stairs the first day on those things. It was push and drive he inherited from his father. Had to be doing something all the time."

Being on crutches two and a half years did not slow him down much. From kindergarten on he had been a good student; his first report card was all A's and one B. The teacher had told his mother she didn't want to make him into "a swell-headed little braggart." In elementary school he won the A. W. Dick award for leadership. Unable to play baseball, he was made team manager. "He was all boy," said his mother.

In his first fatherless years, Freddie fell strongly under the influence of his uncle, Major General Sam T. Wallace, adjutant general of the Tennessee National Guard. In August 1952 the general's slightly pudgy eight-year-old nephew strapped on a holster and a .45-caliber pistol and skittered around on crutches as the unofficial mascot at the Tennessee National Guard encampment at Fort McClellan, Alabama. The *Memphis Press-Scimitar* published a photo of him at the camp talking to World War II hero First Lieutenant Vernon McGarity of Memphis, admiring his Congressional Medal of Honor.

"My brother was in the National Guard forty years, and Freddie's interest in the military came from our family background. That goes back a long way—Wade Hampton, the Confederate general over in South Carolina, was a relative of ours," said Sally Smith.

His mother encouraged him to read the history of the War Between the States, saw to it that he acquired a large collection of toy soldiers with which he could reenact the famous battles between the North and South, and took him several times to the Shiloh battlefield on the Tennessee River. As a boy he considered a military career via West Point.

Several summers in his boyhood were spent near Jackson on the farm of his uncle Arthur Wallace. "Both my brothers became sort of father figures for him," said Sally Smith. "They had a great influence on his life. Fred pretty much grew up unspoiled. He would go down to the farm for a week at a time, riding the pony, fishing in the pond. I have pictures of him looking like a little urchin. He worked in the hay field, all that sort of thing."

Her oldest son, Gary West, eight years older than his half brother, also served as a role model. "They grew up together in the same house, and there was a great love there. Gary is just the opposite of Fred, artistic—he taught art in school down in Florida later. His influence on Fred as a teenager was strong, like maybe

Fred wanted to do something and Gary would say 'No. You don't do that.' "

Freddie was unaware he was heir to millions until an aunt mentioned the family fortune to him. "He was about thirteen or fourteen," said Sally Smith, "when she told him something like 'You are going to be wealthy one of these days' or 'You are wealthy and going to get it when you are twenty-one' or something like that. I didn't like it at all. I wanted him to be just one of the boys, and— Of course everybody knew it. But I wanted him to think in terms of not having a lot of money."

The boy asked his mother about it. "I said, 'Yes. But you just don't think about it until you get it. It's a lifetime trust.' We never discussed it but that once. Fred was the type who never wanted to feel like he had more than someone else, and then he wanted to share it. He's very good-hearted."

Because Freddie was only four when his father died, Sally Smith tried to impress his heritage on her son. "I kept his father alive in his mind all those years. I told him how much big Fred loved him, and how much he wanted him to have the best education possible. And how he was certain his son would surpass his achievements in business."

Frederick Smith, Sr., signed his last will and testament on April 11, 1947. It was filed for probate on November 24, 1948, five days after his death. But settling the estate was a complicated, drawn-out affair. In fact, twelve years would transpire before executors finally handed over to his children personal mementos like a $50 gold pen-and-pencil set, a $150 Hamilton eight-diamond strap watch with Greyhound emblem, a $150 white gold thirty-second-degree Masonic ring, two watches worth $25 and $50, and a $50 chronometer.

The bankers and lawyers in Memphis were hard at work trying to downplay the value of Smith's holdings. They didn't want to pay heavy inheritance taxes; it was that simple. Even though later his combined Dixie Greyhound and Toddle House assets were sold for an estimated $22 million, the executors ultimately argued the Internal Revenue Service into accepting a total estate appraisal of only $717,315!

There were many financial complications. One was that the IRS was trying to collect $87,212 for Smith's 1946, 1947, and 1948 tax deficiencies. The National Bank of Commerce, which was both executor and trustee for the majority stock in the Frederick Smith Enterprise Company, lamented that Fred Smith had "let his bills pile up," had mixed his children's funds into his personal account, and owed money on his plantations, cattle, and yachts. The bank sold the farms and cattle and "recovered fair value."

It was an entirely different matter on the half-finished yacht *Lysander,* still "unusable and unsalable" in the boatyard at Gulfport, Mississippi, even though the estate had $165,000 tied up in it.

The executors searched frantically for a buyer. None was to be found until King Paul of Greece offered to buy the ship for $220,000. A high-level government flap erupted.

In Washington the State Department concluded that American taxpayers would object to such a costly transaction at a time when Greece was receiving millions of U.S. dollars to regain her economic balance. The Greek prime minister retorted that the *Lysander* would be much cheaper to operate than the destroyer currently used by King Paul to inspect the Greek islands.

Since the *Lysander* was once a navy patrol gunboat, the law required the sale to be cleared by several federal agencies. The munitions division of the State Department made an adverse recommendation, and the Greek deal was dead.

In the end J. C. Stedman, the founding partner in Toddle House, took over the project, thus stopping the heavy cash drain on the estate. Almost as much a dedicated mariner as Smith, Stedman completed the yacht handsomely and, ironically, died aboard her on a cruise to Houston in November 1950.

Fred Smith's will gave wife, Sally, $500 a month "until she shall remarry" and occupancy of the East Parkway South mansion. He specifically directed that the home be purchased as a permanent residence for his children, but the executors decided to reject that provision on grounds that "they are not there all together."

The bulk of his wealth was, of course, incorporated in the Frederick Smith Enterprise Company. He had split this stock four ways, establishing a trust that gave the National Bank of Commerce supervision of the assets as well as majority control. The shares held by the bank were to go eventually to his grandchildren and great-grandchildren. Of the remainder, he gave 25 percent to Laura Ann, 35 percent to Charlotte Fredette, and 40 percent to Freddie.

The company had been incorporated in Delaware, but executors had it converted to a Tennessee corporation, which would permit trustees to make loans to stockholders "and thus enable them to pay their taxes." The will made no bequests to Charlotte Clark Smith or Dorothy Dickman Smith, saying they had been adequately provided for, but it did allot $150 a month for life to first wife, Bessie, then living near Jacksonville, Florida.

Fred Smith was interred in the large mausoleum at Forest Hill Cemetery, with two hundred uniformed Greyhound Bus drivers marching into the small chapel and holding their caps over their hearts during the burial rites. Later his casket was moved to a private $25,000 wing with twelve crypts that his will directed to be added to the Forest Hill mausoleum for exclusive use of his and brother Earl's families.

Subsequently, when Elvis Presley died in 1977, his coffin was temporarily placed in a crypt in the same Forest Hill mausoleum, about thirty feet down the corridor from the Smith family chamber. During the four or five years the singer's body was in the mausoleum before being moved to a new and final resting place at his Graceland mansion, thousands of his fans made pilgrimages to Memphis and stormed the Forest Hill mausoleum. On the walls of Elvis's crypt they scrawled bold dark graffiti that is visible today. So hungry were the visitors for mementos or souvenirs from their idol's burial site that they savaged the exterior of the Fred Smith chamber, breaking escutcheons and other ornaments off its iron gates.

▶ ▶ ▶

For seven years after Fred Smith's death, his widow and children continued to occupy the house at 527 East Parkway South. Executors of the estate kept a close eye on expenses, but the children, as scions of wealth, had the luxury of attending private schools. Laura Ann graduated from the famous Miss Hutchison's School for Girls in Memphis. She went to Brenau College in Gainesville, Georgia, fell in love with a local youth named John T. Patterson, and married him at age nineteen. Fredette graduated from another top-flight Memphis girls' school, Lausanne. A talented artist, she attended Bennett College in Millbrook, New York. She eloped to Florida at eighteen with a bright young Memphis electronics whiz, Bryan Eagle.

Fredette's relationship with Freddie was close and intense, but Laura Ann more or less kept her distance from both of them. "I loved my little brother very much, and I was very proud of him as a young man," said Fredette Eagle. "If you met Fred then, you would have been dazzled by him. This man was charming, articulate, and just winning. You would follow him anywhere as a leader. Kind of like D'Artagnan. Sometimes Bryan reminds me of Fred. They start waving their hands around, and they conjure up these images, and your checkbook bounces into your hands, and you are ready to follow them over the next hill, and wherever. It's just wonderful. Both of them are terrific salesmen. They make fantasies come alive."

Those early years of widowhood were somewhat awkward for Sally Smith. "I knew very little about business. I had never even written a check when Fred died. The bank took care of everything, and we just went on with our lives." But friends asserted that rather than go through a third degree every time the dentist, landscaper, or grocer demanded payment, the widow let the bills accumulate and with a sheaf of them made her trips as infrequently as possible to executors at the bank.

"That's not quite true," said Sally Smith:

In Tennessee a wife is entitled to one-third of her husband's estate, and I could have gotten that. Fred was very generous in giving me things that had nothing to do with the will.

Although I love being comfortable, I have never cared all that much about a lot of money.

Many things Fred left the way he did he had planned to change, but he died before he changed them. The house was in trust for Laura Ann, which was set up when he and big Charlotte were divorced, and his plans were to buy that house from the trust himself. We were going to build on our plantation down in Mississippi and move down there with all the kids.

Of course, when things are tied up in trust with a bank, you are supposed to get permission for anything extra you do. The bank did what they were supposed to do; I never asked for anything extra that I didn't get, in other words the increase in living for the children and so on.

By 1955 the household was basically down to Freddie and his mother. "Things started changing," she said. "I felt like the place on Parkway was a real big house, too big, and I sold it, or rather the bank sold it. I could have had nearly any place I wanted, but I got a house with four bedrooms and three baths. It was at 1130 Audubon Drive. That's the street where Elvis Presley bought his first house. We lived a very simple life. Very plain."

The year 1959—when he was turning fifteen—became a watershed year in Fred Smith's life.

He enrolled in Memphis University School, the college preparatory school to which the wealthy of Memphis had sent their sons since 1893. Totally recovered from his lame hip, he played football for four years, starring as quarterback, made varsity basketball, and put in two years on the MUS baseball team. Whatever his mother had told him of his dad's ambition for his success through education seemed to take hold. He made the National Honor Society his junior and senior years and was sports editor as well as cartoonist of the school paper. In his senior year he was elected class president and voted "Best All-Around Student."

Girls from Miss Hutchison's, which was practically next door to the boys' school campus, came over in their sweaters and flannel skirts to serve as cheerleaders for the Memphis University School athletic teams.

Thus footballer Fred met brunette Linda Grisham, a Memphis socialite his own age who was one of the eight cheerleaders from the girls' school.

"They started dating when they were about fifteen," said Sally Smith.

At that age Freddie also took his first step into business entrepreneurship—joining two other fifteen-year-old MUS classmates in opening a recording studio. The idea was sparked by John Fry, Jr., son of a wealthy lime and cement manufacturer. At his family's residence on Grandview Avenue, he had converted part of the garage into a "studio," using microphones and recorders his parents had given him as birthday and Christmas presents. His goal was to become an electrical engineer specializing in design of radio stations and intercoms for ships and hospitals.

"I think we could really go into the record business," he told Fred Smith and their buddy John S. King III, son of a cotton compress executive, while they were brainstorming their futures.

"Great! Let's give it a try," agreed Smith.

With $5,000 borrowed from their parents, they bricked up and soundproofed the Fry garage and installed seven microphones, three tape recorders, three turntables, a control booth, and a sixteen-track master board. They decided to call their operation Ardent Record Company—and then scrambled to audition musical artists willing to take a chance on a kiddie outfit.

"We have undoubtedly heard the worst singers in Memphis," John Fry told the *Memphis Commercial Appeal*. "Suddenly all your friends know how to play a musical instrument or sing."

With help from disk jockeys at Memphis radio station WHHM, the youngsters signed their first recording contract with Freddie Caddell, a professional singer from Jacksonville, Florida. His initial release on the Ardent label was "Rock-House," with a flip side of "Big Satin Mama." They arranged to distribute through two Memphis companies, Music Sales Company and Sharina Music Publishers. These schoolboys certainly posed no threat to any music studio in New York, Hollywood, or Nashville. "Even so, they about broke even on the first release," said Sally Smith. "Not bad. And they had a lot of fun."

For Fred Smith it was only a hobby. In a couple of years he dropped out of Ardent. Several years later so did John King, though he became a nationally known pop critic and Memphis music historian. But Fry stuck it out, moving into a modern three-studio complex, upgrading to a forty-eight-track master board, and recording such musicians as ZZ Top, Bar-Kays, Led Zeppelin, Willis Alan Ramsey, Freddie King, and Isaac Hayes. By the 1990s his company had expanded into television production services and ranked as one of the largest such facilities in Tennessee.

And at age fifteen Fred Smith developed another new passion— airplanes and flying.

When he first broached the idea of taking flying lessons, his mother vetoed it. "You're too young. Maybe later on."

However, the subject came up again that summer when Freddie and his mother attended a National Guard conference in Nashville and talked flying with Colonel Fred Hook, a Memphis air force officer Sally Smith knew. That discussion would not only pave the way for young Fred's flying ambitions, but give him a surrogate father and bring romance back into his mother's life.

"I was at the Nashville conference as a social hostess for my brother, Adjutant General Wallace, because his wife was ill," Sally Smith said. "Fred Hook was a military friend of my brother, and I had met him at a party while I was going with Fred Smith, and I couldn't stand him. He was handsome, but I thought he acted too cocky. I didn't see him for years and years—until this National Guard convention. He was a Pentagon air force liaison with the air National Guard. Of course, he was in favor of my son taking up flying."

Back home the fifteen-year-old again badgered his mother. "Fred is one of those people who never gives up if he wants something and you say no. He just goes on and on. So finally he talked me into letting him take lessons. He said, 'Mother, you can always say if anything happens to me, I died doing what I wanted to do.' So I said okay."

She asked Colonel Hook to recommend a Memphis flight instructor. "Fred's instructor told me he took to flying like a duck to water," said Sally Smith. "I was his second passenger when he soloed. First he took up Colonel Hook, and then he said, 'Mother, how about you?' It was a little single-engine plane [Aeronca Champ], and he flew me all over Memphis that day. We landed at Memphis Arrow, the old airport, and because commercial planes had priority for taking off and landing we had to sit there for forty-five minutes. It was so hot I got a little nauseated. Later he said, 'Mother, you are just afraid, that's why you got sick.' And it could have been."

If anyone could have empathized with the boy's yearning to fly it was Colonel Hook. As a teenager he had hung around the West Memphis airport, washing private planes and running errands to pay for flying lessons. Craving excitement, he became a Memphis motorcycle policeman, then a crop duster, barnstormer, and air show acrobat. Next he was a Chicago and Southern Air Lines copilot and finally a P-51 fighter pilot in China, protecting General Claire Chennault's Flying Tigers.

As an air force officer in the Pentagon, Hook was sent to Cuba as an American military attaché, became friendly with President Batista, and got involved in the 1959 Castro revolution. For his efforts to save a Cuban officer from the firing squad, he gained Castro's hatred. Dictator Fidel reportedly ordered him assassinated, but Hook, his wife, Jewel, whom he married right out of high school, and his daughter, Linda, who was born in Havana, safely escaped.

When he retired from the air force in 1965, Fred Hook returned to Memphis, divorced, and married forty-six-year-old Sally Smith— the year before her youngest son was to graduate from college.

In August 1962 Fred Smith hiked across the peat bogs in Ireland near Lake Isle of Innisfree. His host and fellow hiker was colorful Memphis attorney Lucius E. Burch, Jr., owner of the Lodge at Dromhair, a three-story twenty-room vacation retreat built amid the ruins of a thirteenth-century Irish castle.

"Freddie came over to Ireland very cocky about walking and hunting with Mr. Burch," said Mary Lindsay Dickinson, who was there as a guest of the lawyer's daughter, Lucia, her classmate at Miss Hutchison's. "He had to quit and come back and go up and lie down. He was gone! Mr. Burch had just walked him into the ground. Freddie didn't have the hang of the bogs—every step your foot sinks down four or five inches. You can't imagine his exhaustion!

"We were all kind of waiting to see how he would handle it when he came down to dinner. Because it was a crucial thing. The Burches were kind of like the Kennedys on a challenging level. If you were going to play on their turf, you had to survive certain ordeals, so to speak. And Freddie was fantastic. He was a changed man. He was so gracious and funny about himself. It didn't take more than a couple of minutes, but it was really a neat moment."

Fred Smith, just turning eighteen, had already been hazed on arrival. "There was a landscaped bank, about twenty-five feet straight down," said Mary Lindsay Dickinson. "It was well known that Mrs. Burch, who had an incredible sense of humor, required every guest to ride the donkey down the hill. The donkey, which has no withers, lowered its head and his back turned into this impossible slippery slide, and you fell off. Freddie got dumped, and it didn't sit too well with him. Then that hiking disaster. But he was really in great physical shape, and in two or three days he was back up to speed."

The outing with the attorney to Ireland was one step in a strong friendship. Through the years they would spend many days together hunting and hiking, diving for sunken treasure, talking about life and philosophy, and flying. And later, when Fred Smith's reckless financial gambles threatened to destroy him, Burch would act as his defense lawyer, fighting to save him from prison.

The lawyer rejects the idea that he was a father figure to young Fred. "Some of my law partners are young. I've had the same relationship with them. Flying all over the country—diving— fishing—drinking whiskey. Fred was just an interesting young man, and I was glad to have him around. He was good company and vigorous and interested in things I was interested in. We talked about hunting and we argued about Salukis [Egyptian hunting dogs] and the Coriolis force [which alters direction of ocean currents and wind at the Equator]. Not many young men can talk about things of that kind. He is very bright. He is a person of fresh ideas and I'd say a liberal outlook. And one of the greatest qualities that he has, that anybody can have, is he's a vociferous reader. You could talk to Fred Smith about government or literature, a whole range of things kids his age didn't know much about or care much about."

During the visit, Lucius Burch, then fifty-eight, escorted his young guest to Scotland to hunt stag on an eighty-thousand-acre game preserve he leased. Did they kill any? "Sure we did—several. He's a fine hunter. Tough and energetic. Whatever Fred does, he likes to succeed in it."

Since Lucia Burch attended Miss Hutchison's, a romantic link between her and young Fred might be assumed. "No," recalled Lucia, now a divorcée with two children. "we had a couple of dates, but there was no magic between us."

His steady sweetheart was Linda Grisham. "Linda always had him," said Mary Lindsay Dickinson. "There never was any opportunity that you could move in on Freddie. No way. He was an all-round boy in high school, and she was popular and gregarious. And he and Linda seemed very content."

Another of Miss Hutchison girls who recalls Freddie is Jeanne Coors Arthur, daughter of Dr. George Coors, a prominent Memphis surgeon who would later become personally involved in the Federal Express saga. (Her husband, Bill, a classmate of Fred Smith's at MUS, was to become one of the first executives when the business started up in Little Rock.)

"I knew Fred when he was a young boy," said Jeanne Arthur:

It is no secret that he was overweight and had water on the knee and all that sort of stuff. As he grew older he lost all that weight, became very fit, was quite an athlete, and was very good as quarterback. He threw a touchdown that won the final game of the season. His coach, Jake Rudolph, was the winningest coach in Tennessee high school football—something like five hundred victories.

Fred was very respected by his peers. Very interested in history. He collected and painted those little lead toy soldiers, and he would study great battles. He was particularly interested in Napoleon, and General Nathan Bedford Forrest—"Get there fustest with the mostest!"

Fred's mother had an uncanny ability. She was very much the driving force behind Fred, although he didn't know it. She was wise enough to surround him with well-respected men who gave him the feeling of confidence that he later developed. I think it helped him as a leader in the marines; it helped him in business.

Sally Smith's mind control over her son is transparent in the way his choice of a college was made. Asked why he chose to go to Yale University, she said simply: "I think that was born in him. Well, his first choice was the University of Virginia. He applied to several colleges. I think he thought Yale would be more of a challenge. I had a letter from the University of Virginia, and they were sorry he had declined."

His mother recalls he was accepted at all the schools, and they discussed his options. "He did everything I wanted him to do. I wanted him to go to Yale. I believe that was his third choice. I just thought Yale was a fine school, and as his father had told me when he was real small, he wanted him to have a good education. Really, I let him decide. I told him I liked Yale. But it was his own decision. From the time he was a little boy he always pretty much made his own decisions. I thought I was making them, but after it all ended up, I realized that he had got his way."

Earlier that summer of 1962, while he was still seventeen, Fred Smith got an unusual taste of political campaigning by piloting planes in which Memphis City Commissioner Bill Farris hopped all over Tennessee in the Democratic primary for governor.

Farris, at thirty-one, was being called the "boy wonder of Memphis politics," and the young pilot could equate the experience of landing in small town after small town across the state with the kind of barnstorming he'd heard of in earlier open cockpit days.

"We borrowed any plane we could," Bill Farris recalled. "Probably six or seven different ones. I knew Fred through his mother's family, fine people. And there was a lot of flying in that campaign. I didn't get in it until April, really didn't give myself enough time.

"Fred also flew Governor [Gordon] Browning somewhere a time or two to make a speech for me. Fred told me he had a little scare on one of these trips because the plane started acting up. He didn't know Governor Browning had palsy, and somehow his shaking hands did something to the controls. But nothing bad happened."

Unfortunately Farris came across too cold and aloof to gain the approval of Tennessee voters. Frank G. Clement won the race, polling 270,939 votes to 176,863 for third-place Farris. Despite his poor showing, Bill Farris, a lawyer, would in later years persevere in politics and become known as a power broker and kingmaker in Tennessee. He also was to continue his friendship with Fred Smith, especially in raising campaign funds for candidates they both favored.

7 ▶ YALE—AND SCARS OF GUILT

The eventful chronicle of Fred Smith's four college years could begin either of two ways. Written prosaically, the chapter would depict him at Yale University in the fall of 1962, eager to go about the task of acquiring the top-notch education that his father desired for him.

A more urgent and dramatic opening would show him writhing just one year later in St. Joseph's Hospital in Memphis, battered, angry, confused, in mental agony—blaming himself for the horrifying death of his best friend. His remorse, say close friends, helped goad him into the Vietnam War, deliberately exposing himself to danger as a way of seeking expiation.

Fred Smith arrived in the Yankee precincts of New Haven, Connecticut, somewhat sensitive about being a southern boy. He took along a Confederate flag, which he proudly hung on his dormitory wall.

He went out for football. His mother worried that his smallish build would make him too fragile for the college game, but it didn't matter, for he twisted his knee in an early practice session and had to drop out of Yale athletics.

He looked around for other avenues he could follow. With his Memphis rock and roll recording experience, he applied for a disk jockey job on campus radio station WYBC—and got it.

His ebullient Confederate panache won him important student

friendships. He was tapped for a fraternity—Delta Kappa Epsilon. Flying remained a passion, and when he learned that the aviation club for Yale students organized in the 1930s by Pan-American Airways' Juan Trippe was now defunct, he searched for some way to get it going again.

He felt preordained to put in some military service; the family tradition had been drilled into him by his mother and his National Guard uncle. It would have suited him just fine to get into marine aviator training, but that didn't work out; his eyes might not have passed the test. He did join the Marine Corps reserve and was assigned to the student platoon leader training program. That would require a stint at Quantico every summer, and he looked forward to it.

At Memphis University School he had been in the top of his class. Now his Ivy League competition was stiffer. Perhaps the most illustrious Yale cachet was to become a member of the elite secret society Skull and Bones, which dated from 1832. Almost daily, in virtually the heart of the campus, Fred Smith passed the Bonesmen's drab windowless sandstone clubhouse called the Tomb. Therein reposed an assortment of skulls, one of which was alleged to be the head bone of Geronimo, the Apache chief, purportedly stolen in 1918 by Prescott Bush, whose son George was to become a Bonesman in 1948. Another story was that five wealthy Yale men in 1926 paid $25,000 for the acid-bleached skull of Mexico's celebrated *bandido* Pancho Villa. The society yearly sifted the senior class for qualified members and selected a mere fifteen. Fred Smith hoped that by his senior year he might be among them.

Meantime his freshman year sailed along. "I was a crummy student," he confessed. The reason was simple: he was into a great many sidelines, spreading himself too thin to excel in the classroom.

Being away from home caused him to become more clearly aware of the extent of his mother's beneficial role in his life. At times he thought of her just as "Mimi"—the pet name her children had concocted years earlier. Did he fully appreciate the years of dedication and devotion she had lavished on her fatherless brood, especially the youngest son?

Perhaps he could do something to show his gratitude in a material way, while she would still be able to enjoy it. When he came of age he could exercise some options that governed his inheritance. He was aware of a legal device called a Clifford trust, by which the owner of stock could retain its ownership but assign all its dividends to another party for a specified period of time.

He notified the bank that as soon as it was in his power to do so—three years hence—he planned to draw up and sign a document that would for ten years divert directly to Sally Smith all the income from perhaps 200 of his 380 shares in the Frederick Smith Enterprise Company. That would be a substantial sum—amounting to at least one million dollars or more in such a time frame.

▶ ▶ ▶

On Saturday, August 24, 1963—thirteen days after his nineteenth birthday—came the shattering episode of tragedy and death.

Home from college and his Marine Corps encampment at Quantico, Virginia, Fred Smith was going with a group of boys and girls from MUS–Miss Hutchison's for a weekend at Pickwick Lake, a boating resort 110 miles east of Memphis on the Tennessee-Mississippi border. In the party were two of his closest friends, Jeanne Coors, daughter of Dr. George Coors, the surgeon; and Mike Gadberry, also the son of a Memphis physician.

"I was supposed to ride with Fred," recalled Jeanne Coors (now Mrs. Bill Arthur). "But he had a brand-new Corvette—red, I believe. Mike was crazy about cars and wanted to ride with him. I said that would be all right. [Dr. Coors recalled also that his wife objected to Jeanne making the trip in a convertible.] I had already put my suitcase in Fred's car. So they went on and the rest of us followed, riding in a station wagon."

Dr. Eugene Gadberry, now retired after being in general practice and on the staff of the Memphis Veterans Administration Hospital, recalled his son's departure in the Corvette. And his wife explained: "I think he had some anxiety. Mike had told his father, 'I think Fred drives too fast. I tell him to slow down.' "

Mike Gadberry, eighteen, tall, slender, and dark-haired, was a 1963 graduate of East High School in Memphis. In a week or two he was to begin his freshman year at University of Tennessee at Knoxville. Not interested in pursuing his father's profession, he played guitar and hoped for a career in music.

Dr. Gadberry remembered his parting words: "You-all boys be real careful now, and don't get yourselves hurt."

By 1:45 in the afternoon, zooming along two-lane State Highway 57, the Corvette reached the outskirts of the village of Michie, within ten miles of their destination.

Milton Huggins, nineteen, an air force enlisted man home on leave, was driving from Pebble Hill with his sister, Mrs. Nettie Pearl Robertson, twenty-five, to visit their grandmother in Michie.

Just as Huggins's car came up alongside Michie High School and started to enter the Highway 57 intersection, he heard a thundering crash. Startled, he looked up and saw geysers of dust shooting up along the highway.

"That car was flipping end over end," Huggins recalled twenty-eight years later.

> It was bouncing high in the air. It would hit on one end and flip completely over and hit the ground again, and then flip again. For the car to act like that, it had to be running seventy-five, eighty, even one hundred miles an hour.
>
> The car landed upside down in the ditch. When I got there, one of the boys came running up and said, "Are you the one who turned in front of me?" I said, "No, why?" He looked like he was in shock. He said, "Somebody turned in front of me and we had to leave the road."
>
> I went to the boy lying in the ditch. The car was upside down several hundred feet on down the highway. At once I saw he was bad hurt. He was lying on his back, struggling to breathe. If he'd had immediate care, he might have made it. But he just literally choked on his own blood. That was my impression. He was gurgling and bubbling blood. Of course I got it all over me. I tried to give him mouth-to-mouth resuscitation, but it was a losing battle. He couldn't get air. When he hit the ground, it must have busted him up inside.

A crowd of passersby had gathered. Sammy Clements, young pastor of the nearby Michie Church of God of Prophecy, a friend of Huggins's, came up. "Can I help, Milton?" he asked.

"You can pray," said the airman.

In the interim, Huggins said, the driver [Fred Smith] "just continued to go from person to person to ask if they were the one who turned in front of him, just kind of rambling around, out of it. In shock, I suppose."

Tennessee State Trooper Melvin Holland arrived and summoned an ambulance. Little of the Corvette was left intact. The twisted frame and motor lay in a ditch; pieces of torn metal and broken glass were scattered a hundred feet along the road. Holland discovered a smashed bag of women's clothing and promptly crawled beneath the wreckage to see if it might conceal a girl's body.

"The trooper had a container of water and poured it over my hands so I could wash off the guy's blood," said Milton Huggins. "I was shaken and nervous. I had never seen anyone die before. So my sister and I turned around and went back home."

The station wagon with Jeanne Coors and the others in their group came along Highway 57 through Michie within an hour of the accident.

"We did not realize we were seeing a wreck," recalled Jeanne Coors Arthur, "because the road on that stretch is built up and the fields are down ten to fifteen feet. I saw some people over on the side of the road and thought maybe a hitchhiker had had a heat stroke or something. It was a hot summer day.

"We continued on to Pickwick. Fred and Mike did not arrive, and I was extremely upset about it. Maybe you would call it ESP. I did not go out that afternoon, hoping they'd get there, and they didn't. Then I got on the phone and called local hospitals and the highway patrol and didn't find out a thing.

"I called my parents, and it was sort of like I knew something was wrong because the first thing I said to my mother was, 'What happened?' And she started crying. She said, 'Are you all right?' and I said, 'Yes.' She said, 'Well, they thought you were riding with Fred.' That was because my bag was in the wreck."

Smith was taken to St. Joseph's Hospital in Memphis. Physicians treated him for concussion. But his greatest problem was guilt.

"He told me," said his mother, "that he had just a split second to decide—either to hit a car full of children that was making a big ole country left turn in front of him, or leave the road. [Exactly what caused the accident is unclear in police and eyewitness versions.] It made an old man out of him overnight!"

Smith's severe depression alarmed Sally Smith. After he had been in the hospital four or five days, she asked Dr. Coors to see him.

"So I went over," said Dr. Coors, "and we had a couple of good talks. We just talked about different things, and I tried to get his mind on at least a positive side. He was so down!

"He was not critically hurt. He had concussion; they called it shock then. It wasn't true shock where the blood pressure bottoms, but he was confused and depressed and sort of not in control of himself in general. He couldn't sleep. I think it had a great effect on him because he thought in his own mind that if he hadn't had the car, or if he hadn't had a convertible, or if Mike might not have been there, or something . . .

"I don't know all the details, but if Sally said it made an old man out of him overnight, I'm confirming that."

In Dr. Coors's opinion, the residue of guilt from the wreck marked Fred Smith's future behavior. "I still think that that experience had a great influence on Fred in his life in terms of what he did. I think he felt very badly, and I think he pushed himself to the limit in everything he did. He probably would say, no, that didn't have anything to do with it, but I always thought that it might have."

A few weeks after the accident an insurance investigator interviewed Milton Huggins at his Panama City, Florida, air base. "I just put two and two together and figured the boy [Fred Smith] was telling the truth," the airman said. "That somebody did turn in front of him. Whoever it was went on, so I can't say if there were children in the car. I took the driver to be an elderly person."

Dr. Gadberry wrote Huggins to thank him for helping his son and offered to buy him new clothes. Huggins said: "I thought about going to see him, but I was afraid he might think I wanted something."

Dr. Gadberry filed a damage suit in McNairy County, scene of the fatal wreck, and a settlement was reached without a trial. "I won't say how much I was paid," the physician said.

Even twenty-eight years later the Gadberrys felt bitter pangs. "I think that boy was going at least one hundred and ten miles an hour," said Mrs. Gadberry. "Mike's neck was broken; the driver didn't even get a scratch. Please don't try to talk to Dr. Gadberry anymore. Mike was his only son. Bringing this all up again is so painful. Last night he couldn't sleep at all."

With its big engine roaring, the Grumman Bearcat landed at New Haven airport. It was spring 1964. Fred Smith and Neil S. "Mike" Waterman, Jr., a classmate and fellow flier, watched Professor Norwood Russell Hanson climb out of the cockpit. Only thirty-nine, Hanson had 2,600 hours as a marine fighter pilot, degrees from Chicago, Columbia, Cambridge, and Oxford, undeniable guts, and the admiration of everyone at Yale who thought man deserved wings.

Getting "the Flying Professor" as an ally was critical to Smith's plan to reactivate the old Yale flying club. He and Mike Waterman already had the promised backing of Howard S. Weaver, Yale's presidential assistant. The university would take no responsibility. Fred Smith & Company must arrange for aircraft, instructors, insurance—everything.

Nobody on campus was more zealous about flying than Hanson. Noted for his skills as a stunt flier, and for his good-natured iconoclasm, he hoped with his personally owned Bearcat—last of the navy prop fighters and capable of 421 miles an hour—to break the world speed record for single-engine piston-powered aircraft, then held by a German. He was delighted at the chance to help revive the Yale flying club.

"Fred was really looking for a less expensive way to fly," recalled Mike Waterman:

> He perceived also there was a real need on campus for a way for people to learn to fly. So he put the deal together.
>
> Fred put up flyers on bulletin boards. He held an organizing meeting on campus and got enough show of interest to convince the management of New Haven Airways to get the planes and so on. Yale required a faculty sponsor—and that's where Hanson and Weaver came in. It was like financing a start-up company, and Fred was good at that, too. He convinced the Piper Aircraft people to lease us some planes. We started with a couple of small aircraft. But Fred wanted four-seaters that could fly across country and finally got a Cherokee 180, in which he made many trips to visit friends, especially in Memphis.
>
> Hanson as sponsor gave it legitimacy and would lecture and talk to the club about flying. He was sort of the glue that bound it together because of his personality and his style. Fred was a good promoter. He got it structured. They were a good team.
>
> With their leadership, Yale once again had a real flying club. It was popular. We had a lot of people in it. As near as I know, it's still going.

Waterman was already a professional pilot when he attended Yale, and he spent one summer as copilot of the *Caroline,* the Kennedy family Convair 240. After graduation he returned to Dallas and built flight simulators. Later he became executive director of the 6,500-member worldwide Young Presidents Organization.

"The flying club was Fred's baby, and I just tried to help," Waterman said. "Fred was an all-round good guy."

A year after Smith graduated from Yale, Professor Hanson took off on April 18, 1967, in his Bearcat from New Haven for Ithaca, New York. En route to give a lecture at Cornell University, he ran into a storm and was killed when his plane slammed into a small mountain.

▶ ▶ ▶

Professor Challis A. Hall, Jr., read the twelve or fifteen pages Fred Smith had typed up as his 1965 term paper in the course designated Economics 43A. For a few minutes he thought about the hub-and-spokes concept expounded, and he debated what kind of grade it deserved. Then he picked up his red pen and wrote "C."

At the time it was not important, not even to Fred Smith. But later that paper—and its grade—became a paradoxical Yale University legend, if not embarrassing, at least whimsical.

"Fred is a man with a good mind, obviously very bright," said Dennis Tippo, one of his Yale roommates. "I wouldn't say he was a diligent student, in the real sense. He would do things at the last moment, such as a paper. That probably was the style of operation for many of us in those years. We weren't as diligent as students are now. We usually pulled all-nighters before a big exam or when a paper was due. So Fred was operating in that kind of style."

Tippo, now alumni director of Phillips Academy at Andover, Massachusetts, recalled the paper. "I remember reading it. When he got it back, I think Fred joked about the grade. This idea always seemed to be in the back of his mind. You knew he was going to do something about aviation. He was going to devote his life to some aspect of it. In some of our bull sessions, all of us talking about life and things in general, several times he brought up the concept of Federal Express. I think it was germinating. It was in his mind."

"I don't remember reading Fred's paper," said Bob Frame, another roommate. "We probably discussed it. The fact that he got a C was, you know, at that point not a big deal. On occasion we all got C's on stuff. But the idea was clearly there. I wish I could tell you I remember it word by word. But I don't."

Exactly why Professor Hall had such a poor opinion of Fred Smith's paper will never be known. It could have been the context rather than the concept. But the incongruity of the C did not become a public matter until the early 1970s when newspapers, magazines, and television began probing the hows and whys of the phenomenal growth of the upstart Memphis air express company. By that time Professor Hall was already dead, victim of a heart attack on September 15, 1968, at age fifty-one.

There is no great mystery to the "hub and spoke" concept. As Smith visualized the plan, the "hub" would be located in a middle America location—he was thinking of Little Rock or Memphis—with "spokes" radiating out to Boston, Los Angeles, Seattle, Miami, and other cities—the far corners of the country.

A package from Boston destined for the West Coast, for instance, might be flown in on the Boston spoke in a few hours to the Memphis "hub," where it would be sorted and routed out on the plane that had just brought in shipments from Los Angeles, and it would be aboard when that plane flew back home, arriving before dawn. In other words, Boston to Los Angeles overnight! Or vice versa. Or Atlanta to Seattle. Everything went to the "hub" in Memphis—and then from there on to its destination.

Fred Smith thought of his system as similar to the telephone network, where all calls are connected through a "central switchboard" routing process.

Dr. Richard Corbin Porter, chairman of the Yale Economics Department when Fred Smith was a student (now at the University of Michigan), recalled nothing of the paper but offered a clue as to how the hub-and-spoke concept might have been germinated:

By the mid-sixties computers were quite capable of handling linear programming. We now teach it to our students as kind of an archaic joke. Computers will do nonlinear programming now. But linear programming was much talked about in the late 1950s and up through the mid-1960s. One problem was known as "the traveling salesman problem."

The traveling salesman problem required setting up a computer program that speedily solved the following: What is the route that takes the least number of miles for a salesman to travel to every state capital in the United States? And you can start 'em anywhere; obviously it doesn't matter where. So as to minimize, you don't go back and forth across the continent—from Washington to Maine, to California, and back to Georgia.

This set up a whole lot of transport costs, minimizing problems that could be handled linearly. This whole airline hub business would have fallen in neatly. You could show that with a hub and with people going to the hub and then out again, you could somehow minimize the total cost in terms of flights and miles and so forth.

A good student might well have picked that up and worked that out. Not something that a weak student would have done. The discovery that a hub system somehow reduced costs would have been something that you could have worked out in linear programming in the 1960s. I have no idea who first worked it out. But now with twenty-twenty hindsight, sure, put me back in the mid-1960s and I'll write you a nice paper about how hubs will be cheaper. Now it's easy. Always any discovery in economics, any uncovered theory, or whatever—everybody sees it afterward. "My God, why didn't I think of that!"

▶ ▶ ▶

In his Yale years Fred Smith was able to maintain a close relationship with his sister Fredette. Her husband, Bryan Eagle, was a graduate student at Harvard, and they had a house in the Boston suburbs.

"We bought the Dr. Paul Dudley White house in Belmont, 200 March Street, or Mass Street, as they call it," Fredette Eagle said. "The heart surgeon. Ike's doctor. He had a charming wife, Irma. Had this lovely farmhouse. Went to look at it. She said, 'You like cats?' I said, 'I don't mind cats.' They'd had several offers for it; it was a very nice house. She said, 'The one who's going to get it is the one who will take care of the cats.' I told them I'd take care of the cats."

Her brother made a number of weekend visits to the Paul Dudley White house, bringing Yale classmates. Going back to his roots, or at least keeping up family ties, apparently helped him ease and lessen his remorse for the Mike Gadberry tragedy of the summer of 1963.

So apparently did unburdening his soul—to a limited degree—to his Yale buddies. Said Bob Frame:

I know about the accident. I think it was a very significant factor to Fred. I don't know about his mother saying he got old overnight. All I can say is it was a very significant factor in Fred's life, and probably did markedly change his outlook. It was a very sobering, maturing experience. . . .

We knew about it because he mentioned it when he got back. It was not something we dwelled on. That was it. The nature of college is that it was not something you talk a lot about. But clearly it impacted him—it had a very major impact on how he ended up looking at things.

I think Fred had a charisma about him, a sort of self-confidence. And he had those entrepreneurial instincts, like getting the flying club going and being president of our fraternity. He had an aura about him that was very impressive to people. And legitimately so. I think his leadership, and his entrepreneurial instincts, and seeing what ought to be done, were there at Yale. And people recognized that.

That view must have been shared by the powers in Skull and Bones. In his senior year Fred Smith was selected as one of the elite fifteen—in a class of almost one thousand men.

8 ▶ WAR AND LOVE

Alert for snipers and booby traps, Second Lieutenant Frederick W. Smith cautiously led his marine patrol along a dim trail into the steamy Vietnam jungle. Suddenly, from a hidden nest close by, enemy machine guns opened up.

At once the marines returned fire, and bullets flew for several minutes. The first volley instantly killed the marine on one side of Smith as his men scrambled to take cover. Momemts later the soldier on Smith's other side fell, and he died in agony with a VC bullet in his throat.

Just as an enemy bullet knocked Smith's pistol out of his hand, he caught sight of a Vietcong soldier creeping up on the patrol. Smith grabbed his rifle and fired, killing the man at ten yards.

This was late summer 1967. Just turning twenty-three and only months off the Yale campus, Smith was tasting the murderous fury of his first tour in Vietnam. Amid heat that sometimes rose to 120 degrees, he learned to dodge death in the twelve-foot-high elephant grass, ancient jungles, hills, and rice paddies. Lying in wait for him and his marine comrades were snipers, sappers, bloody mortars, and hidden *punji* sticks and land mines.

He felt fear—just as any normal person would. At the same time, Fred was in a strange way fascinated by actually being in mortal combat. These contradictory emotions puzzled him. He studiously avoided giving any hint of the horrors of war to his mother; but he candidly, and in colorful detail, related this and other battlefield exploits later to several associates at Federal Express, and likewise laid bare to his soul-mate sister Fredette Eagle his innermost feelings about Vietnam.

Fully illuminating this chapter of Frederick Smith's life required considerable research into official military dispatches (formerly secret but now declassified) at U.S. Marine Corps headquarters in Washington, D.C., particularly the commanders' combat chronologies filed daily from the battlefield.

In those hundreds of single-spaced pages covering the period of his tours of duty, he is mentioned numerous times as "Lieutenant Smith" and sometimes identified only as commander of a platoon or a company. These official histories, couched in military jargon and keeping cryptic score on American and enemy casualties, confirm that he was almost continually in the thick of the fighting.

To get more personal accounts of Fred as a warrior, it was necessary to track down for interviews his battlefield superiors, in the main generals and colonels now retired and scattered across the country, plus several frontline buddies. His former companions in arms remembered him well and favorably; all agreed that Fred Smith was a dedicated and gutsy soldier.

Even while showing bravery and daring that at times bordered on reckless daredeviltry, Fred discovered that the battlefield presented a deep and puzzling personal emotional conundrum. He hated having to place himself in danger, of course, yet discovered that precisely that very peril somehow drew him, as strongly as a beguiling seductress.

Smith was human enough when exhausted, hungry, and tired of being shot at to honestly wonder "what the hell" he was doing in Vietnam. When he tried to explain it, the best he could do was recall that Oliver Wendell Holmes had once expressed the opinion that a man should share the passion and action of his time at the risk of being judged not to have lived.

Even so, after a few weeks in the war zone he began longing for a return to the luxuries of civilian life in the United States, yearning especially for a chilled drink, a soft mattress, and a woman's smile.

In the Vietnam jungles, Smith was caught in a gut-tearing,

up-and-down emotional storm—the exciting lure of adventure, his honest fear, his wonder, his rage, longing, and loneliness, and at times his disgust at what seemed the futility of the Marine Corps campaign and the high cost of American dead and wounded.

But in spite of everything, later when he was free to escape the battlefield at the end of his first tour of duty, something inside him—family tradition, conscience, Marine training, or emotions even more personal—made him volunteer to go back. . . .

▶ ▶ ▶

When Smith graduated from Yale, his commission as a second lieutenant in the U.S. Marine Corps was waiting. It was his reward for those hundreds of hours in platoon leader class on campus, plus his summers in the Quantico marine encampments. The marines needed him in Vietnam, but before being shipped out, he spent weeks in a corps school in California studying the Vietnamese language. Then he flew the Pacific to join the Third Battalion, Fifth Marine Regiment, First Marine Division. His marine forces were operating in what was known as the I Corps sector, five Vietnamese provinces extending about two hundred miles south of the DMZ, territory so deadly that by the end of 1967 marine casualties would be 5,479 killed in action and 25,994 wounded in action.

Second Lieutenant Smith was quickly shunted through marine headquarters in the port city of Da Nang, about the middle of the I Corps zone. Lieutenant Colonel W. K. Rockey, the battalion commander, welcomed his new shavetail and assigned him to lead a rifle platoon in Company I (India). The other companies that made up the Third Battalion were K, L, and M (Kilo, Lima, and Mike). Under Colonel Rockey's command were about a thousand men and thirty to forty officers.

After about a month with his rifle platoon, Lieutenant Smith was put in charge of the mortar platoon, which with ninety-four men was the largest in the battalion. From summer into the fall his battalion was in the field on search-and-destroy missions.

Portrait of Captain "Jim Buck" by the late Memphis artist-architect
Nowland Van Powell. (Courtesy Fredette Smith Eagle)

Stern-wheeler *R. Dunbar*, under command of Captain "Jim Buck" (forward on the
texas [third] deck, standing near the bell). A one-horse Jewel Tea Company wagon
on the landing is delivering supplies. The steamboat was the pride of the Ryman
Lines' Cumberland River fleet, circa 1911. (Courtesy Fredette Smith Eagle)

James Frederick
Smith at about age
two. (Courtesy
Fredette Smith Eagle)

Fred Smith at about the
time he started Smith Motor
Coach Company in Memphis.
(Courtesy Charlotte Smith)

Greyhound Bus Lines executives gather in Memphis for meeting with Fred Smith in the 1930s. (Courtesy Lindsey Smith Brady)

Earl Smith, Sr., brother of Fred Smith and partner in Dixie Greyhound Lines and Toddle Houses. (Courtesy Lindsey Smith Brady)

Charlotte Clark, at age twenty-two in 1934, when she became Fred Smith's second wife. (Courtesy Charlotte Smith)

Dorothy Dickman at the time she became the third wife of Fred Smith in 1940. (Courtesy MSU Mississippi Valley Collection)

Charlotte Smith on one of the riding horses her husband stabled for her at the Memphis Fairgrounds in the 1930s. (Courtesy Charlotte Smith)

Portrait of Fred Smith in his uniform as a navy lieutenant commander in World War II. (Courtesy Fredette Smith Eagle)

Marine lieutenant Frederick W. Smith poses in Vietnam with his silver star. (Courtesy Robert W. Sigafoos)

RIGHT: Newspaper photo of Fred's first wife, Linda Black Grisham. (From files of *Memphis Press-Scimitar*)

BELOW: The second Mrs. Frederick W. Smith, who as Diane Davis Wall was his secretary, christens the newest FedEx DC-10 with a silver bowl of champagne in Memphis on March 20, 1980, as Fred handles the mike. (Courtesy *Memphis Commercial Appeal*)

Lucius Burch, Fred Smith's attorney and pal on adventures, at a Wolf
River Society luncheon May 2, 1991, in conversation with Prince
Cambless. (Courtesy *Memphis Commercial Appeal*)

Air Force Colonel Fred G.
Hook, who married Fred
Smith's widowed mother,
Sally, and encouraged him
to take up flying and was
his partner in Arkansas
Aviation Sales in Little
Rock. (Courtesy *Memphis
Commercial Appeal*)

Fred Smith in Little Rock in 1972 with his first Federal Express Falcon jet. (Courtesy *Arkansas Gazette*)

Once, Smith later related, an enemy bullet severed the chin strap of his helmet without as much as giving him a scratch. Another time, in the jungle darkness, he started to ask the man nearest to him for the time only to discover it was a Vietcong infiltrator who had slipped across into marine lines. As Smith recounted to several FedEx colleagues, he was lucky enough to beat the Vietcong soldier to the draw.

The marine high command's Operation Swift in September 1967 threw Smith into some of the Vietnam war's most ferocious and sustained—and bloody—engagements. His battalion was badly mauled; his own unit took heavy casualties.

Pinned down, the marines could not move their dead for two and a half days. Fred's platoon had the detail of loading the bodies on the choppers. There is a dramatic photo of marines evacuating their wounded in another battle in a *Life* magazine Vietnam War special edition. The face most visible is that of an anguished young officer holding a bandaged comrade atop an armored carrier. "That's Fred," Fredette Smith Eagle told me in an interview, displaying the torn-out *Life* page. "I'm sure."

One casualty in Operation Swift was one of Fred Smith's closest battlefield comrades, a black platoon sergeant, twenty-eight-year-old Richard B. Jackson of Philadelphia. They had chatted for hours in bull sessions. "Sergeant Jack" had spent eleven years in the marines; he had a lot of military wisdom to pass on to the twenty-three-year-old as well as powerful information on another subject—life in the underclass. Of this Fred knew little, having always associated with the youth of privilege and wealth. "A lot of people in my platoon had an influence on my life," Fred Smith said later in a *Memphis Commercial Appeal* interview. "The one who made the strongest impression was Sergeant Jack. . . . He was not very well educated, but he was probably the wisest guy I ever met. He had wisdom about what people who aren't officers think and want. That has stood me in good stead since as a manager." These were lessons remembered—and used. Smith credits the philosophy expounded by "Sergeant Jack" with making him aware of the concerns of rank-and-file employees in the critical formative years of Federal Express.

▶ OVERNIGHT SUCCESS

The battalion was on a search-and-destroy mission in Quang Tin province, west of Chu Lai, on September 6, 1967, when hostile fire hit Staff Sergeant Jackson in the face, neck, and shoulder. His was one of the bodies that had to wait sixty hours before Smith and his platoon could load them to be choppered out.

▶ ▶ ▶

By November 1967, Fred had been promoted to first lieutenant and assigned to Company L (Lima). On the night of the eleventh, with a combined force of half USMC and half Vietnamese, he helped capture an ancient temple and crematorium.

Luck still rode with him; his troops suffered no casualties, but killed at least four of the enemy. The tension and the agony of the fighting were beginning to unsettle him. It bothered him a great deal that he had learned to so matter-of-factly see fellow marines die. Yet he knew it almost had to be that way or he wouldn't be able to do the job expected of an officer—even though he could never erase from his mind the fact that the next bullet from the enemy might have his name on it.

▶ ▶ ▶

Although he may have felt like an old man at twenty-three, and bullets daily interrupted his romantic reveries, Fred Smith nonetheless was strongly imbued with the juices of youth and felt passionate fire in his veins.

He looked forward later in November 1967 to his turn to take R and R because he'd wind up in Hong Kong, Hawaii, or Australia, where he could take a hot bath for a change and dine in style, enjoying a gin and tonic—and look for girls.

As it turned out, Smith spent his six-day leave in Sydney, Australia. He found the city beautiful, the residents wonderfully friendly—not the least of which were half a dozen pretty young women.

When Fred had left Memphis for Vietnam, his relationship with the sweetheart he had begun dating in high school, Linda Black Grisham, seemed uncertain. Discussing the matter later, several of their closest friends concluded that they had all detected a cooling off of the romance.

Fredette wrote that she was moving from the Boston area to McLean, Virginia, across the Potomac River from Washington, D.C., because her husband, Bryan, was going to work for the Central Intelligence Agency.

He answered, requesting her address and asserting that her new house sounded beautiful (which is accurate) and would be just the spot for him and a bottle of wine and a pretty girl when he returned stateside.

Nineteen sixty-eight began as a furious killing season. The Vietcong slipped through the jungle villages, working in cells made up of four to seven guerrillas. They were joined periodically in quick and deadly strikes by regulars with their Chinese assault rifles and mortars. In the first six months the enemy would kill 3,057 more marines and wound 18,281.

The commander of Third Battalion's Company K, Captain L. W. Farmer, was killed in a skirmish January 29, 1968. Colonel Rockey needed an officer of captain's rank to succeed him but had none available, so he gave command to First Lieutenant Smith, not yet twenty-four.

Everywhere in the I Corps area the enemy was attacking, hard and swift. Rumors were rife that a peace effort, some sort of disengagement of forces, was being explored secretly in the back channels of diplomacy. American commanders assumed the North

Vietnamese generals were trying furiously to take strategic territory to enhance their hand in event they went to the bargaining table.

One of Fred Smith's closest Yale friends, Second Lieutenant Richard W. Pershing, twenty-four, had arrived in Vietnam three or four months earlier with the army's 101st Airborne Division. Like the Third Marine Battalion, the 101st was caught up in the fury of these seesaw engagements.

In New Haven they had been fellow members of Skull and Bones, had run in the same social set, and had graduated together in the class of 1966. Dick Pershing played soccer, hockey, and all-Ivy lacrosse. Slim, handsome, good-humored, he talked of becoming an architect or joining his father's Wall Street brokerage firm. But first he had to serve a hitch in the army—he was the grandson of General of the Armies John J. (Black Jack) Pershing. His father and brother John likewise followed the army tradition.

Joking once with Smith and other classmates, Pershing said the only resemblance he could see between himself and his illustrious grandfather was a slight bowleggedness. "I tell you, everybody in my family has been bowlegged except my mother."

Looking for a missing airman, Pershing was leading a patrol the last week of February near the hamlet of Hung Nhon. Slogging through calf-deep mud, he took the exposed point position. From a hidden bunker came a rocket-propelled grenade that hit a rice dike five feet away from him. Shrapnel mangled his head and neck, killing him on the spot. (He was buried beside his grandfather in Arlington Cemetery.)

The news of Dick Pershing's death enormously saddened Fred Smith, and it angered him because of the difference in tactics in the marines and the army. When a marine fell, his buddies made every effort to retrieve him from the battlefield, whether wounded or dead. Fred knew the army philosophy was that when contact was made with the enemy, the troops would pull back and call in air strikes and artillery even though that meant abandoning their dead and wounded comrades on the field.

What upset Fred the most was discovering that Dick Pershing had gone back to try to rescue one of his own men who had been left after his unit was forced to withdraw from an engagement.

About the same time Smith himself was injured. Time in Vietnam became a jumble of days melting into weeks. He counted the weeks he had been Company K commander—ten. On Tet night Company K saw a lot of action—and he caught a small piece of shrapnel from an enemy mine. It hit him in the eye, but he said there were no lasting effects.

Nor was he badly wounded some time later when he got his second Purple Heart—a piece of shrapnel hit him in the back. The marine surgeons found it so small that they elected to not remove it.

While Fred Smith could speak candidly to others about bullets that sang of death, and of trip wires and hidden mines that tore off marine buddies' arms, legs, and heads, he censored his own letters to his mother, who was then living in Little Rock, married to Colonel Fred Hook, who had bought into an aircraft fuel and repair business there. "He never wrote me anything bad," Sally Smith Hook recalled. "He wanted to spare me."

The Third Battalion got a new commander March 28, 1968, Lieutenant Colonel Donald N. Rexroad, who at thirty-six was the marines' youngest combat battalion chief. "For a matter of only about three weeks," Colonel Rexroad remembered in 1991. "They got younger, or I got older."

When he looked over his four companies, he was surprised such a junior officer headed Company K. "Fred was very young to be a company commander in terms of time in the Marine Corps, time in grade, but his experience was tops. I think without question he had the best company in my battalion. They operated better, they accomplished their mission better, they just functioned better as an entity. A rifle company isn't a small organization—two hundred marines. It's no mean task to be a good company commander in a combat situation."

Colonel Rexroad, who retired to Tallahassee, Florida, where he is in the insurance business, recalled as one of his battalion's most hairy excursions a search-and-destroy assault on Go Noi Island, only about four miles west and south of Da Nang. Fred

Smith's Company K was accompanied by Companies India, Lima, and Mike, numbering nine hundred to a thousand men. Said Colonel Rexroad:

> We were on Ga Noi for about two and a half weeks. It was very frustrating. The elephant grass was twelve feet high. You couldn't see who was killing the person next to you. Higher command decided to pull us back so B-52s could drop bombs—they call those arc light strikes. For some reason we didn't get the order [by radio] until later. We were in contact with the enemy, and had to break off in a hurry.
>
> They made the arc light strike and we were just marching off Ga Noi Island toward a place where we could ford the river. One of Smith's patrols encountered some hostile fire and we went after it. As we advanced, the fire just kept getting heavier and heavier. It turned out that we had stumbled onto a North Vietnamese major headquarters; of course they were well defended.
>
> We had a two-and-a-half-day battle. I remember our major effort was made by Smith's company. One of his platoons was led by an acting sergeant who had only three or four years in the corps but was a fantastic guy.
>
> My command post was usually two hundred to four hundred yards back of my rifle company, and I remember Smith coming back. If I remember right, he was crying. He told me the sergeant had just been killed. He'd briefed me before about the man, and we agreed that when we got back we were going to do what we could to get him commissioned. That loss seemed to hit Fred hard, very hard. Fred did well in combat, I think, because he was a very adventuresome person. Some people do well under stressful conditions, dangerous situations. He was that kind.

Occasionally Smith tried to enlist family and friends as stateside supply sergeants. He was anxious for them to scrounge up interesting books to help his men avoid the boredom of waiting for action. Fredette sent packages of books.

Among colorful tales about the true origin of Federal Express is one that depicts young Lieutenant Smith on a hill in Vietnam watching warplanes streak across the night sky while randomly thinking about his Yale paper. As fast as a snap of his fingers, the entire concept popped into his head.

But that legend does not wash; for even while winding up his military service he let his family know he was still in a quandary about the future, and never once suggested that it included airplanes. To the kinfolk back home Smith seemed to be considering three options: to enroll in law school, find a job that would permit him to travel abroad, and take a stab at his dream of becoming a writer.

Then, too, he did not appear in a hurry to quit the battlefield. In April, 1968 he was considering extending his Vietnam tour for six months, and definitely would do so if he thought he could keep his company. By the end of his first tour he would have eleven and one-half months in the field, which he thought was probably some kind of a record.

Colonel Rexroad urged Smith to transfer from the reserve and become a career marine officer. It was no sale. But Colonel Rexroad didn't give up. He got in touch with the commander of the First Division, Major General Carl Albert Youngdale. Smith subsequently was called up to Da Nang headquarters for an interview.

The general got him seated and fired probing questions. Then he called in his senior aide, Captain Mike Sweeney, and both of them grilled Lieutenant Smith for a few minutes.

Finally General Youngdale said: "We have a slot here for a junior aide. Someone to back up Captain Sweeney. I'd like to have you come aboard."

The challenge was appealing—something new and different. Fred Smith already knew he couldn't, as he had hoped, keep Company K; he was being rotated out in conformance with combat policy. He decided to extend his tour of duty and then see what life was like as junior aide to the division commander.

But first he would take leave—and go home. So he turned over command of Company K to Captain D. W. Myers and headed across the Pacific for Memphis, Tennessee.

America was more deeply disturbed about Vietnam than Smith had thought. True, the war was not going well. The United States had lost its ten thousandth plane. The USS *Pueblo* spy ship seizure aroused disgust. Lyndon Johnson had abandoned plans to run for reelection; at the same time he slowed down the war by stopping United States air and naval bombardment north of the twentieth parallel.

The home front was torn also by the assassinations of Martin Luther King in Memphis and Senator Robert F. Kennedy in Los Angeles, and by riots by war protestors in Chicago, where the Democrats nominated Vice-President Hubert H. Humphrey to succeed LBJ.

Nonetheless Smith felt he owed an obligation to the marines and his country.

The bankers responsible for his inheritance—the Frederick Smith Enterprise Company—suggested it would be wise for him to abandon the military and take up business affairs. That would have to wait, he told them.

His return to Memphis did not seem to accelerate his interest in his high school sweetheart, Linda Black Grisham. Their mutual friends got the distinct impression that Fred Smith was no longer very much interested in her, nor in any other girls in the old crowd.

His chief interest clearly was the war in Southeast Asia. In an interview he explained to a *Memphis Commercial Appeal* reporter why he was going back for a second tour of duty: "It's not that I'm more patriotic than anyone else, but there are five hundred thousand Americans over there, and there is a job I've been asked to do. I'm not being conceited, but I have had a year's experience and I know I can do it better than any new officer they might send to replace me."

But the "war" to which First Lieutenant Smith returned in October 1968 was nothing at all like the one he had left. No longer did he march in hundred degree heat lugging forty pounds of equipment, or eat C rations and shave in cold water; in his new job he wore a starched, neatly creased uniform, and his boots were polished. He was about bowled over by the laid-back luxuriance of First Division headquarters in Da Nang and slightly startled by General Youngdale's mess. Smith saw plenty of the commanding general's mess;

he was assigned to oversee it. Consisting of a dining room and bar and recreation room, with a small kitchen, manned by a chef and stewards, it operated like a club for all generals and full colonels in the division.

The meals were excellent. Although he had been a master sergeant, machine-gunner, and former boxer, the chef could whip up superb entrees, served on china embossed with gold USMC globe and anchors. Even so, Smith undertook to brighten up the menu, writing his folks at home for sprightly menu suggestions.

Fredette Eagle immediately sent cookbooks. Smith thanked her by return mail, reporting that General Youngdale and his staff were mightily pleased with the chef's new culinary delights derived from the pages of the *New York Times*. Smith had also written his mother, asking for her "family spaghetti" recipe.

"I didn't send it," Sally Hook recalled. "It was too complicated."

She was thrilled, however, when the Little Rock newspapers reported that her son had been awarded another medal for combat action. His entire Fifth Regiment was given a Presidential Unit Citation on October 17, 1968, by President Johnson for its fighting earlier that spring in Quang Tin and Quang Nam provinces, which inflicted three thousand casualties on the enemy. In presenting the citation, the regiment's seventh such honor, at the White House Rose Garden, the president declared that the marine battalions had faced "the terrible test of courage and character" and come through "with flying colors to make every American proud."

The *Arkansas Democrat* noted that Lieutenant Smith was on his second tour and had been wounded twice and received two Purple Hearts and the Bronze Star medal.

His new assignment wore on Smith; he began looking forward to the end of his second hitch—which, he calculated as of October 4, 1968, had ten months and eleven days to run. The part of being a general's aid that he liked most was occasionally to be dispatched as a courier. In mid-October he flew to Tokyo to spend six days running official errands and managed to bump into a friend from Yale, Dr. Ben Baline, a Marine Medical Corps captain.

The division commander recalls that he had "a very good relationship" with his junior aide and described him as "a very, very fine young man." General Youngdale, who retired in 1972 and lives in Virginia Beach, Virginia, said he met Mike Sweeney after the war for lunch in San Diego, and they had a chuckle about how laid-back was the junior aide.

"The story Sweeney tells," said General Youngdale, "is that Fred was getting ready to go on leave—I think to Hong Kong—and had gotten a check for his pay. And he continually left it lying around on his desk. Sweeney kept telling him he'd better pick up his check and so forth. Finally he decided if this kid isn't going to take better care of money than that, he'd hide it.

"So he put it in his drawer. The next day Fred was getting ready to go and saying good-bye, and Mike Sweeney said to him, 'Where's your check?' 'Oh, I don't know. Around here someplace.' So Mike gave it to him and said, 'Money doesn't mean anything to you.' And Fred said, 'Well, my dad had a small bus outfit down in the South.' 'Yeah? What was that?' 'Greyhound.' We chuckled a lot about that."

Uncertainty about the future—both in the marines and later in civilian life—was again preying on Fred's mind. He considered remaining in Vietnam through June 1969 in a "very interesting" high-level G-2 (intelligence) job, which would give him a chance to see different places around the Orient. But there was also the prospect of getting an "early out" to return home by August 18.

Around the close of 1968 Smith left his assignment and switched back to the bloody combat zone. Major General Ormand R. Simpson came in as the new First Division commander, and General Youngdale was promoted to a higher headquarters, III MAF. Smith asked for an assignment in the air, as a member of the marine observation squadron at Marble Mountain Air Facility, overlooking China Beach on the Da Nang perimeter.

At Marble Mountain Fred Smith's life was no longer dull. The marine VMO-2 squadron had just received a hot new reconnaissance plane—the North American OV-10 "Bronco," which had been developed for counterinsurgency missions and artillery spotting, and Smith flew two hundred missions. Broncos occasionally took hits from ground fire. On one sortie a bullet pierced the cockpit, grazing him. If reported, the wound would have entitled him to a third Purple

Heart—but also would automatically have ejected him from the combat zone, since at that time under Marine Corps SOP it was three hits and out.

In some fashion he got a corpsman to treat the wound—which was apparently a graze—without reporting it officially.

Smith related that episode a few years later on more than one occasion to close colleagues at Federal Express. He had some other hair-raising tales that occurred while he said he was piloting both OV-10 Broncos as well as A-D-4 Skyhawks.

Roger J. Frock, who made one of the original air cargo feasibility studies for Smith and later was among the initial group of executives hired at Federal Express, said:

> Fred mentioned on one occasion he had a South Vietnamese observer sitting behind him. The guy took a hand grenade and clay and stuff like razor blades and glass, and worked it up into a ball. A homemade bomb. When they were flying, if they saw a target, the guy would throw this thing out. It would explode and spread this stuff all over.
>
> The reason I specifically remember this is because Fred said on one occasion just as the observer was throwing it out some ack-ack gun went off nearby and so close that it kicked up the airplane, and the hand grenade bomb fell into the wheel well, and it actually blew off the landing gear.
>
> I guess he had to do a belly landing back at the base. He said he jumped out and ran because he was afraid he'd be court-martialed—not for the bomb incident, but because he was out of uniform. It was so hot all he was wearing was his bathing trunks and a gun belt.
>
> That is the story he told. It may be about someone else; I don't know. My recollection is he said he was doing the flying, but he did talk about being an observer as well.

When spring 1969 arrived at the Marble Mountain Air Facility, Fred Smith again put in a request for leave. He was anxious to go back to "the world" in time for the March 22 wedding in New Haven of Dennis Tippo, his Yale roommate. He got leave and spent thirty days in the United States, stopping off in McLean, Virginia, to see his sister and her husband, Bryan Eagle, and their three children. Then he went on to Memphis for several days. There he again saw Linda Black Grisham, and their old romance was decidedly rekindled.

By early May he was back in the combat zone with his observation squadron, enduring stifling heat and recovering from a bout with tropical fever. He had been anxious to get out of the military, overjoyed that his second tour had been cut 30 days, which would put him back home no later than July 15.

Smith now rarely mentioned romance, and never marriage. But at Marble Mountain he received an urgent letter from Linda. After reading it, Fred Smith went straight to his commanding officer and requested a short emergency leave to go to Hawaii. He was asked to state the nature of the emergency.

"I want to get married," he said. "My bride will meet me in Honolulu."

Friends from Miss Hutchison's school saw off the bride-to-be at the Memphis airport. Sally Smith Hook and others in the family, including Fredette Eagle, also boarded Hawaii-bound planes. The wedding took place June 7, 1969, in a small Honolulu chapel.

There was no time for a honeymoon. Smith hurried back to duty at Marble Mountain. But six weeks later, at 3 P.M., July 21, 1969, he was discharged, with the rank of captain. (That was also a day he would never forget for an entirely different reason—Apollo 11 landed, and Astronaut Neil A. Armstrong walked on the moon.)

By any measure, the USMC sent home a genuine hero. Fred Smith had stayed on the battlefield, killing his share of NVA and VC warriors, to within three weeks of his twenty-fifth birthday. Gone were three years of his young life. What to show for it? Being alive, and grateful for that, of course—though wounded. Medals enough—the Silver Star, the Bronze Star, two Purple Hearts, the Presidential Regiment Citation, the Navy Commendation Medal, and the Vietnamese Cross of Gallantry—to reflect his courage and heroism. Newly honed leadership skills and inspirational "tricks" that would prove useful in the world of business, learned on the killing fields—where a soldier discovered that every fresh sunrise had been bought at a very steep price.

9 ▶ LITTLE ROCK BRAINSTORMS

From night-and-day action in Vietnam, Smith returned home to be confronted with the task of rescuing a run-down airplane gas and fix-it shop that was going bankrupt in Little Rock, Arkansas.

Smith was forced to accept the chore because of the bad luck or ineptness of Smith's stepfather, Colonel Fred Hook. At the center of the problem was the fixed-base operation called Arkansas Aviation Sales, Inc., at the Little Rock municipal airport, Adams Field. When Hook retired from the air force and in 1965 married Sally Smith, he was enticed by a friend to buy half interest in Arkansas Aviation, which he understood to be both sound and profitable. There was a problem—Hook didn't have $50,000 for a down payment.

But his new stepson did. When he had turned twenty-one on August 11, 1965, Fred Smith was handed by trust officers in Memphis ten thousand shares of Squibb-Beechnut preferred convertible stock, free and clear, which he promptly converted to cash. He thus had a bank savings account of at least $750,000.

The Squibb stock was just the first installment of the inheritance he was to receive from his father's estate. The bulk of assets from the Greyhound and Toddle House businesses were still tied up in trust in the Frederick Smith Enterprise Company, with the principal cautiously guarded by Memphis's National Bank of Commerce, but it was paying substantial dividends.

It wasn't that Smith was an easy touch. Hook was an engaging daredevil pilot, a military officer who knew everything about airplanes. Since his teens Smith had looked up to several surrogate fathers, such as Lucius Burch, his uncle Sam Wallace, and Dr. George Coors. As a flying pal and sometime confidant, Hook also captured Smith's trust. So Smith willingly wrote his check for the down payment to buy Arkansas Aviation—only to soon discover that the firm was in trouble.

On the day he reached his majority and was in a position to access his inheritance, Smith's first action had been to make a gift to his mother that amounted to one million dollars. From the time he was old enough to comprehend the injustice dealt his mother by his father's will, he had vowed to make amends. At the outset, under Tennessee law she could have broken the will and seized one-third of the elder Fred Smith's fortune. Instead Sally elected to make do with a bequest of five hundred dollars a month. If she remarried, under the terms of the strict will, even that modest stipend would stop. Thus she remained a widow for seventeen years and married Colonel Hook only when her son was safely in his final year of college.

So on his twenty-first birthday, son Fred examined the yield of his shares of the Frederick Smith Enterprise Company left by his father.

There was no doubt that big Fred intended the fortune he had accumulated to benefit future generations—specifically his grandchildren. Of the 2,200 total shares in the company, he placed the majority interest under control of the National Bank of Commerce trust officers as executors. On reaching majority Smith received outright ownership of 380 shares. Fredette got 250 shares and the other sister, Laura Ann, 200. Of the shares the bank held for "remaindermen," Fred received the income from an additional 486 shares, Fredette from 409.5 shares, and Laura Ann from 292.5. In the Union Planters Bank in Memphis was a similar trust holding 200 shares for Earl Smith's family.

Under the rules of the Clifford trust, Smith was permitted to divert dividends from 100 shares of his stock directly to his mother, for a period of ten years. At the end of that time the stock reverted to him. Even so, since these shares paid about $100,000 in dividends annually, his generosity represented a million-dollar present to Sally Hook.

But he feared that the financial windfall he had just made available to her would be imperiled by the continued losses of Arkansas Aviation Sales, Inc. Fred Smith sat down in the little office in the hangar at Adams Field and studied the books. His stepfather, for all his aviation laurels and charm, was not a good businessman. For his mother's sake, Smith would have to clean up the mess.

The Arkansas Aviation debacle was not totally Colonel Hook's fault.

The company had been founded in 1956 by David W. Feltus, a World War II and Korean War air force officer who quit as a Memphis corporate pilot to become Arkansas distributor for Piper Aircraft. Within two years he shot up to number one in Piper sales nationally and was financially able to build his 28,000-square-foot hangar at Adams Field. As a promotion stunt in 1959, Feltus removed one propeller from a twin-engine Piper Apache and put it on display in the lobby of a Little Rock bank. Then his pilot took off in the crippled plane and flew 1,304 miles on one engine, setting a record for such a flight—and demonstrating the Apache's safety.

It was Feltus's partner, James Woodward, who sold his 49 percent to Colonel Hook and Fred Smith. Sally Smith Hook recalled:

> My husband had just gotten out of the air force and was not, I guess, the greatest businessman in the world. They came wanting him to buy Woodward's part of the business and gave him all these figures showing it was so much in the black. Actually it was that much in the red. Well, when he found out the true situation, he went to court and sued Woodward for $63,000 damages, and lost. In Arkansas, if you are not an Arkansas native you don't win, plus the fact that the judge who heard the case knew nothing about aviation law.
>
> Then Feltus died. And my husband kept the place going out of sheer guts and determination. He was a man who didn't know what it was to say quit.

Woodward had lied, and my husband did not have anything on paper, just a handshake—so there was real bad blood between the two of them.

Their feud was still raging in 1968 when Woodward was director of the Arkansas State Aeronautics Department. Hook and others were attempting to get him ousted. On the night of May 10 at Little Rock's Aero Club, they met in the men's room and got into a fistfight. Woodward's nose was broken and Hook's spleen ruptured. As they fought, said the *Arkansas Gazette*, they traded "derogatory remarks" about each other's wives.

The fisticuffs provoked Hook to again sue Woodward, asking $101,685 for malicious assault; but a jury in circuit court (July 20, 1970) refused to award any damages.

The upshot of the crisis at Arkansas Aviation Sales, Inc., was that in the fall of 1969, only a few weeks after he had been married in Hawaii, and then been discharged by the Marine Corps, Fred Smith went to Little Rock to buy control of the failing business and run it.

He and Linda liked Little Rock, a quiet state capital and Arkansas's largest city, although its population was only 170,000 (less than one-third the size of Memphis). They bought a house in a good section of the city and quickly made friends. That winter they did not socialize much because Linda was expecting. On January 19, 1970, their first child, a girl, was born. They chose the name of Fred's paternal grandmother—Laura Windland—and called her Wendy.

At age twenty-five the former combat officer was getting his business baptism. He was young and untried in any business—except for this teenage music studio fling. Now he was getting inaugurated in the rough-and-tumble, haphazard airplane service field. Unlike his stepfather, he shrugged off having been hoodwinked in the initial purchase. But he saw little prospect of much profit or adventure selling aviation gas and offering hangar services.

Laboring over the dismal ledgers, he began to look for a fresh idea—anything—that would convert Arkansas Aviation into a money-maker.

Aviation, he realized, intrigued, soothed, and satisfied him.

The corporate jet had become popular. Executives all across the country in the late 1950s and early 1960s opted for status by having their own business airplane, a small jet that could do better than five hundred miles an hour. Hundreds of these were in the air. They were expensive; the smallest and least costly could run a million or more.

Smith observed that the corporate jet market was volatile. Some corporations unloaded their planes, finding them no more than prestigious toys. Still, others were anxious to buy one. The idea of becoming a jet airplane broker intrigued him. At the same time he detected a gap in the supply lines of parts and equipment for these jets. He moved to fill the gap. As he explained later in an interview in *Professional Pilot* magazine:

> It seemed to me that there was a need in this area for a central inventory of used turbine equipment for bizjets. I built up a stockpile of corporate jet parts and found plenty of buyers. We established our position as a fast delivery, low-priced turbine equipment component center. Total sales volume of the company shot up about 1,500 percent within a year, and profits went up astronomically. The operation remained profitable.
>
> I went on to buy and sell used bizjets, too. Still, I was looking for something more than just buying and selling jet parts and planes.

Under his leadership, Arkansas Aviation Sales prospered, doing $9 million in business in two years, earning $250,000. Smith obviously had the same natural knack of effective salesmanship that had launched his father to quick success. His timing was fortunate, too, because the used airplane market was burgeoning.

But as a long-term profession, airplane brokering was not for Fred Smith. He recalled: "I really didn't like this business. It was full of shady characters. I just didn't feel comfortable dealing with a lot of these people."

At the same time he was "infuriated" by another business problem—frequent snafus in receiving airplane repair parts. When Arkansas Aviation ordered a rush shipment by air express, it might arrive in two days, in five days, as late as one week.

"It's terrible," he told Fred Hook. "We can't count on getting any air freight shipment on a timely and reliable basis. It's just unpredictable. . . . Somebody ought to do something about it!"

Timely air freight service had never, in fact, been very good. Such service started on an organized basis at the end of World War I with barnstormers flying the mail between New York and Washington. The Railway Express Agency began flying shipments in 1925, and three or four other freight movers followed their lead.

Over the years the approach to customer satisfaction was lackadaisical at best, nonexistent at worst.

The commercial airlines woke up to their opportunity around 1960. Why not handle boxes of freight along with the passengers' baggage? American, United, Eastern, Delta, and others envisioned a new profit center. When the jumbo jets came on the scene, their underbellies seemed to offer room for small trainloads of freight. Airline executives expected the big industrial concerns to seize the advantage afforded by the 747s, the L-1011s, and the DC-10s.

But the airlines had figured wrong. Getting freight on and off the jumbo jets turned out to be awkward and inefficient. Simultaneously, the pattern of airline travel began to change. With more seats in the wide-bodied planes, airlines found they could move just as many passengers by combining flights. Routes were reduced and concentrated on the profitable major hubs, leaving scores of medium-size cities across the country with severely restricted access to air freight.

The worst blow of all came when the airlines began curtailing or eliminating nighttime and off-peak-hour flights. Freight forwarders had been accustomed to receiving outgoing shipments from their clients as late as five or six o'clock in the evening, with every assurance they could catch a flight out by ten or eleven o'clock for arrival at destination—even all the way across the country—for next day delivery. That quickly disappeared; the airlines couldn't do it profitably. In 1970 United lost almost $20 million in its air cargo division; other airlines also had big deficits. They all largely abandoned cargo and went back to doing what they were good at—flying passengers.

In 1970 Smith became intrigued by the speed and compactness of a little ten-passenger French-built Falcon fan jet owned by Little Rock financier Jackson T. Stephens. Smith strolled across Adams Field frequently to watch mechanics servicing the airplane in the big hangar of Little Rock Airmotive. Jack Stephens owned that company, too. He had hired his own mechanics to reduce the high cost of contracted jet maintenance and modification. Then he branched out, doing work for other jet owners. Soon Stephens had one of the country's most highly regarded jet modification facilities, as well as the largest bond house outside of Wall Street.

Smith was curious to learn whether the Falcon fan jet 20 could fit into his latest plan, one he shared only with his closest confidants at Arkansas Aviation.

For what he had in mind, the Falcon fan jet seemed ideal. Smith liked the fact that the jet was small, compact, and fast. Avion Marcel Dassault, the French manufacturer, intended the aircraft to carry ten or eleven passengers, at a speed of up to 550 MPH, with a range of 1,400 to 2,000 miles. From nose tip to the tail, the Falcon 20 measured fifty-six feet, three inches, with a forty-foot wingspan, not too large to land at even small airports.

Smith discovered that he could buy Falcon jets at a bargain price. As an airplane broker he knew that Pan American World Airways, North American agent for the Falcon, was selling only a few. This was a time of depression for American business. Few corporations were willing to buy executive jets. Pan Am had ambitiously created an inventory of dozens of brand-new Falcon 20s, which they stored out in New Mexico. Its executives were, with good reason, skittish about having so many Falcons on hand; they had bought and paid for the jets. The Falcons could not be sent back to the manufacturer in France.

For hours at a time Smith hashed over his plan with his controller and executive vice-president, Irby V. Tedder, a retired air force colonel and accountant who previously had been Little Rock Airmotive's first manager.

"Pan Am has to move 'em or eat 'em," Smith told Tedder. "The guys in New York are willing to let me buy 'em for a million three each. That's a real bargain! Maybe we can start by getting a couple. Have to take out the seats, convert 'em for cargo. The door's too small—have to enlarge it. I've got some ideas on that. Gotta work out something with the Civil Aeronautics Board."

Irby Tedder, having flown warplanes himself for eight thousand hours, was impressed and startled by the intensity, fire, and brilliance of this young ex-marine.

"He was a kid, but smart as a whip," Tedder recalled. "Sharpest person I've ever run into. Had a photographic memory. He could sit down and digest a ten-page document, then turn around and tell you what it all said, and know the figures."

It was clear to Tedder that Smith had come back from Vietnam with a goal—a very large ambition. "He wanted to do something constructive," said Tedder. "He wanted to do something that nobody else had done. That was his main objective. I guess he liked flying, and wanted it to be something connected with aviation."

Smith swore Tedder to secrecy. "We really were hiding behind Arkansas Aviation," Tedder said. "He didn't want anybody to know what we were doing."

As a matter of fact, Smith wasn't traveling in a straight line himself. He tried first one project and then another. All of them were built around his idea of acquiring and operating a fleet of Falcon jets.

"We tried several things," Tedder said. "It didn't start out as a package outfit."

The first idea was to pioneer a flying courier service for bond houses.

"Fred discovered that a lot of money was lost in the 'float' on issuance of bonds," Tedder recalled. "That's because of the time delay in sending them from say, New York to Little Rock. They may have to go through several banks, maybe by way of Philadelphia. Takes several days. So somebody has lost money on the float."

Fred Smith conferred with one Little Rock bond house, T. J. Raney, and found interest high, especially because air shipment might cut down on the high incidence of theft from bond shipments.

"It was a good idea," said Tedder. "We could fly bonds down here in one day. Worth the cost. But we couldn't get insurance. Fear that a plane carrying bonds might crash, or even one of our pilots going nuts and making off with a sack of bonds. So that shut that idea up right quick."

Then Fred Smith decided the U.S. mails needed overhauling. "We sent a couple of guys up to Washington," Tedder said:

They got permission to go into any phase of the postal service and, you know, check out the possibility of doing it better.

In the meantime, we asked IBM to build a computer to sort mail in the air. Their engineers didn't think much of that. They wouldn't tackle it. We were just ahead of our time; they do that now, I heard, to a small degree.

We still wanted to haul mail for the post office, but after our boys were up there for a while, they said the postal system was so bad there was no way we could integrate what we want to do in flying cargo with their system. It would be superimposing a 1970 system onto a 1905 model. It was that bad! The post office is computerized now; it wasn't then.

During 1970 Smith worked to get himself known and entrenched in Little Rock business circles. While he made major use of his own money to buy used jets, sizable financing usually was essential. So he developed ties with many Little Rock bankers, especially at the Worthen Bank, where he kept his personal and business accounts. It was clear to them that he had important financial resources; but from his action, Tedder said, the average person wouldn't know Smith had a thousand dollars in the bank. It was generally known that he came from a prominent Memphis family, was articulate and appeared well read, and was modest about his Vietnam heroism. He was energetic and innovative in handling business. "He's one of those golden boys," said one Worthen officer. "He'll go far."

Linda Smith had been prominent in the young social set in Memphis and, with her baby daughter now in hand, yearned to mingle in Little Rock society. Her husband, however, spent many more hours in his Adams Field office than he did on the dance floor. For some reason he did not join the Little Rock Country Club. Though she was eager to go out for dinner and dancing, Linda also was known as a dutiful mother and hardworking helpmeet.

"I remember seeing Linda steaming off the wallpaper in their bedroom" recalled sister-in-law Fredette Eagle. "Her face got all red and puffy, but she didn't quit until the task was finished."

At that point the close relationship still existed between Fredette Eagle and her brother. "I went to visit them in Little Rock," she recalled, "when Wendy was still in her crib, two or three months old. They had just moved in, and I brought a house present. A painting, I think."

Fred Smith took her into his confidence, discussing the failure of his initial ideas for using fast planes for air cargo—and disclosing what she thought a brilliant new idea.

For months it had been percolating in his head. The genesis was twofold: his habit of voracious reading, especially history, economics, and business affairs; plus several deep discussions with bankers about the inner machinery of the Federal Reserve System.

The length of time required for checks to clear through the Federal Reserve System frustrated bankers and depositors alike. The mechanism was old-fashioned and unwieldy, inefficient, slow. Checks received in each district Fed bank had to be sorted there and then dispatched in bundles to other individual Federal Reserve districts where the acounts drawn on were located.

"It takes two or three days, sometimes a week or ten days, to clear a check," one banker complained. "That's a heck of a time lapse between receipt of checks and crediting accounts. The whole Fed system handles close to eight billion three hundred million checks and cash letters a year. I figure that's a 'float' of about three million a day. That's just the way it works!"

But it didn't have to stay slow and cumbersome, Fred Smith reasoned. He could speed up the check clearing by applying to the process his Yale University "hub and spoke" air freight technique.

He proposed to go into business with a small fleet of jets that would nightly pick up in each Federal Reserve district that day's checks and fly them to a central sorting hub. There they would be processed at once by Federal Reserve employees and sorted into bundles for transfer to the appropriate Fed bank. His pilots would take off before dawn to return to each Fed district its package. That would eliminate the time lag; checks would be cleared overnight— all across the United States.

On fire with his newest brainchild, Fred Smith struggled to get an audience with officials of the Federal Reserve System.

"Boy, I'll tell you!" said Irby Tedder. "Did you ever try to get into a Federal Reserve Bank? Pretty hard. It's practically impossible. Guys standing around with these guns, looking you over. . . . But Fred finally found a friend somewhere who said he could get him into the Kansas City Federal Reserve Bank. Oh, boy, when?

"There was another phone call, and Fred told me, 'We go in the morning!' We got in a plane about five-thirty A.M. and flew up there. We got a complete briefing on the Federal Reserve System. Then Fred worked up a complete deal and took it up there before the top Fed board that meets only about twice a year."

The initial response of the Federal Reserve Board appeared favorable. Smith felt at last he had found a means for going into the air express business. The Fed did not give an immediate answer; he knew the idea would crawl through a lot of bureaucratic red tape. But he was confident they would buy his scheme, because it would certainly save time and money.

In a rush to get ready, he began in May 1971 to build the nucleus of his airplane network. He tentatively placed an order with Pan American Airways jet salesmen for two of their Falcon 20s. This new venture would require considerable start-up financing. Of course, he would invest his own money; but more than he could muster would be required. He felt that his air express plan could be a beneficial investment opportunity for the family trust, the Frederick Smith Enterprise Company, Inc.

Discord had already broken out about the handling of the fortune his father had left. The trust was estimated to be worth between $13 million and $15 million. Smith agreed with Plato that wealth is the parent of luxury and indolence, and poverty of meanness and viciousness, and both of discontent. His sisters were unhappy with the trust officers at the National Bank of Commerce. These bank executives, as members of the board of directors of the Frederick Smith Enterprise Company, Inc., were all powerful and had largely decided since the trust started in the 1940s how its resources were used. The bank's policy was to safeguard the funds, rather than try to invest them aggressively.

As she grew up, Fredette Eagle felt these bankers treated the heirs with disdain; she called Grattan Brown, the head of the National Bank of Commerce trust department, an "ogre" and felt the inner maneuvers of the company were purposefully kept mysterious and confusing to the heirs. Her disenchantment probably began, Smith once said, when the bank turned down her request as a teenager to draw cash from her inheritance to buy a convertible.

She and her half sister, Laura Ann Patterson, had caused their husbands, Bryan and John, to become directors of the company to represent their interests. Both men thought the bank was too passive, unwilling to take any venture capital risks, content merely to accept stock dividends and pass them on to the heirs. Instead of being an operating concern, the Frederick Smith Enterprise Company, Inc., was actually a holding company, set up primarily as an umbrella for tax purposes. The original Greyhound and Toddle House interests had been disposed of through two mergers that left the umbrella company owning 164,800 shares of Squibb-Beechnut stock worth better than $13 million.

In the late 1960s Bryan Eagle and John Patterson would fly to Memphis for quarterly board meetings of the Frederick Smith Enterprise Company with questions and challenges. They finally persuaded the bank's chief trust officers, Brown and William Richmond, to employ outside analysts to consider more effective use of the assets. Eagle proposed liquidating the trust, even though that would require payment of several millions in capital gains tax. While each heir would get immediate money, the amount would be sharply reduced by the big tax bite. He was anxious for Fredette's share to be invested in some growing business. He was an electronics specialist and knew there were fortunes to be made by investors in that field.

Patterson suggested the trust resources could be leveraged, permitting his wife to pledge her share of the Squibb-Beechnut stock as

110

collateral for a large loan. She would then invest the cash elsewhere for a higher yield. Both husbands argued also that the Frederick Smith Enterprise Company, dangerously, had not diversified; if Squibb-Beechnut stock fell, the heirs' income would plummet, too.

The bank officers adopted a neutral position, but not Smith. Since his return from Vietnam, he had become active in the company and was elected president. He strongly opposed liquidating the stock holdings, arguing that such action would be contrary to his father's desire—on two counts.

"Specifically I had been instructed by my father to insure that the family remained together and that we pursued business interests together—that was in his own hand, which was given to me [by a trust officer in a sealed envelope] on my twenty-first birthday, and to the girls," he stated.

"The letter . . . said that he wanted to make sure that the money he had left us would not be idly spent, that we would not live the life of a fop, if you will, that we would try to be productive with our lives, and that we would always keep the family together through the vehicle of Enterprise Company with me as leader of it, or words to that effect."

The liquidation proposal had come to a head in a board meeting August 31, 1970. It was rejected.

Apart from investment income considerations, the squabbling over the holding company took on soap opera overtones. Bryan Eagle had been hired by the Central Intelligence Agency as an electronics expert. His marriage to Fredette was breaking up. Laura Ann Patterson was likewise at odds with her husband, became basically a recluse, and was largely out of direct touch with her financial affairs, although John Patterson still sat on the board.

Faced with the possibility of divorce, Fredette Eagle had a number of talks with her brother. At one point Fred Smith dispatched lawyer Lucius Burch to Washington, D.C., to make certain that his sister had competent legal counsel. Burch reported she did. Fred Smith felt that with a divorce coming up, Bryan Eagle, who incidentally was a close friend and had Fred's power of attorney during the time he was in Vietnam, should resign from the board of Enterprise Company and be succeeded by Fredette. That change occurred in February 1971 at around the time the Federal Reserve airplane check plan first surfaced.

When challenged as to why he voted to seat Fredette as a board member, Fred Smith stated: "Because of the letter that my father had written me, because she owned shares in the Enterprise Company, because she was scared to death of the bank, and because she is a very bright girl."

▶ ▶ ▶

Smith had informally sketched the outline of his Federal Reserve flights not only to Fredette, but also to William Richmond, vice-president of the Memphis bank's trust office. He felt he had their support.

Now with all plans in place, he went at it in a rush.

On May 28, 1971, he convened the Frederick Smith Enterprise Company board in Memphis, presented his Federal Reserve proposal, with the help of Colonel Tedder, announced he was investing $250,000 of his own, and asked the board for a matching $250,000 to make the company his partner. The proposal was adopted unanimously.

On June 18 he incorporated in Delaware a company he called Federal Express Corporation, feeling certain "Federal" would be apt when he got his contract from the Federal Reserve System. Eleven days later he again convened the Enterprise Company board and presented an additional request. This time he wanted the directors to guarantee a $3.6 million loan from the National Bank of Commerce of Memphis (the trustee) so he could buy his first two Falcon jets, for Pan American Airways wouldn't deliver the planes without a credit guarantee. The directors promptly voted Fred Smith's way. Two weeks later he had his loan, backed by collateral of fifty thousand shares of Squibb-Beechnut stock worth $4 million.

Fred Smith had his new jets flown to Little Rock and began awaiting the decision by the Federal Reserve System. He had everything figured out. As soon as the Fed said "yes"—which he was certain it would—he felt he could negotiate a profitable five-year contract. This in turn would serve as a guarantee to finance the acquisition of the needed additional Falcons, which Pan Am had optioned to him at bargain prices.

And once the Federal Reserve flights were running smoothly, he would merely build on top of that a larger air cargo express system that would serve the whole country for delivery of small packages—the gap he had identified as a real profit-making opportunity, if he could get there first.

He liked the idea that the government in effect would be financing the creation of the Federal Express air cargo system.

The Federal Reserve said no. Fred Smith had not realized that each district bank in the Fed system was jealous of its own turf. They were too competitive to create the co-op scheme he proposed. Each would arrange for its own sort and distribution, as before. The proposed Federal Express Corporation was essentially dead.

Irby Tedder recalled why the bank check scheme was shot down. "The way it turned out, it depended on the Fed at Kansas City working with the Fed at St. Louis. Changing their work schedules around so we would have certain times to pick up and drop off, and so forth. And do you know, they were so politically oriented that the people were not willing to change their work schedules to do it. And the Fed would not make them do it. So that killed that one."

Several years later the Federal Reserve System would, on its own, adopt Smith's scheme, authorized by federal legislation establishing an "interterritory system" known as ITS. Today a fleet of forty-seven airplanes—jets, turbos, and propjets—nightly move 13.2 million checks through five hubs, located in Cleveland, Chicago, New York, Atlanta, and Dallas. Including ground couriers, the annual cost is $33 million, paid basically by fees from national banks. "This system," explained Tom McFarland, who directs the operation from the Federal Reserve Bank in Boston, "cuts the float close to one to two days, instead of ten days before."

In the late summer of 1971 Fred watched his entrepreneurial plan collapse, reeling from the disappointment. He had invested a lot of late night study, many trips to New York and Washington, hundreds of hours of explaining, negotiating, and haggling to lay the groundwork. In his hangar were two Falcon jets, idle, on which he owed $3.6 million to the National Bank of Commerce in Memphis. That wasn't a big worry. He was sure he could sell them and make a profit on the transaction.

But he had no intention of parting with his Falcons. They were still essential to his future plans.

10▶ *THAT DAMNED PURPLE AIRPLANE*

The dark-haired young man in a crew-neck sweater sat in the back corner of the Little Rock Airmotive conference room. Arthur C. Bass noticed him as he began his pitch for Aerospatiale's new Corvette jet, but he couldn't place him. Most of the others were connected with Jack Stephens.

Tall, blunt, and hard-driving, Bass, a thirty-nine-year-old aviation marketing consultant from New York, was on tour trying to line up Corvette distributors. He gave a forty-five-minute talk.

The man in the crew neck came up to him after the lecture. "That was the most unusual presentation I have ever heard," he said. "I'm Fred Smith. Would you do a study for me on an idea that I have?"

"What is it?"

In a few sentences Fred Smith sketched his air express concept.

"I don't think much of it," Bass responded. "It sounds like a dumb idea. But I'll take a look at it, and at the end of the day you'll probably owe me a lunch. Okay?"

Bass remembers that first meeting—in November 1971, when Fred Smith was struggling to recover from the unexpected rebuff by the Federal Reserve. "My feeling at that time was just like a lot of other people's feelings," Bass recalled. "The cost of running a Falcon would be prohibitive for that kind of a business venture. That's number one. And number two is the length of time it would take to create a network, and then get market acceptance. You

115

couldn't just fly between two places and assume people were going to cull out a trade for you."

Fred Smith was learning not be be disheartened or dismayed by negative reactions. He saw other high hurdles ahead. Even so, he had definitely found the right airplane, he thought, having rejected as unsuitable another corporate jet, the Gulfstream G-1, as well as the roomy but slow and ancient DC-3.

Starting up would take a lot of money. Another uncertainty was how to convince shippers to use his air express line. That was the matter he wanted Art Bass to look into.

In reality, at this point Smith was just an untested entrepreneur with a clear-cut idea but not enough personal business training and financial experience to make everything go.

In fact, he was stymied even before he started.

His plan was to fly under Civil Aeronautics Board (CAB) air taxi regulations. That would permit Federal Express to fly anywhere, anytime, not restricted to certificated routes. However, he ran afoul of the reg known as Part 298, which limited air taxis to a maximum takeoff weight of 12,500 pounds. The Falcon could not possibly operate under that limit! Even equipped and empty, the aircraft weighed 15,200 pounds. With fuel tanks full, and loaded with packages, the plane would gross at least 26,000 pounds.

Part 298 had been written thirty years previously, when air taxis were planes like the twin-engine Otter that weighed around 4,000 pounds and carried perhaps twenty passengers with baggage that might add another 4,000—before the day of the heavier, pressurized jet aircraft.

Others might have given up, but Fred Smith just slogged ahead, hoping luck would be with him. He believed he could get the CAB to rewrite and modernize Part 298 to permit greater takeoff weight, unless he stumbled and stirred up objections from present or would-be competitors. He also needed the CAB to permit the Falcon to carry a payload of 6,500 pounds, otherwise the cost of flying the plane would absorb any profit.

At this juncture, and for the next three or four years, many strangers would be coming into Smith's life—and their reaction to his personality and their perception of the soundness of his dream would determine whether they were willing to become part of his entrepreneurial team. His keen knowledge of aviation, plus his undeniable charisma, won over most recruits.

Art Bass, for instance, recalled: "I didn't know what Fred's business experience was, but I knew that he had done very well in an industry [airplane brokering] that had been managed very badly for a long time. I thought he and I hit it off rather well. I liked him from the start."

Earlier, an Arkansas native named Harmon L. "Buck" Remmell had entered Smith's circle of colleagues. Remmell was a vice-president of the Wall Street banking investment firm of White, Weld & Company, with offices in New York and Chicago.

Smith was introduced to him by a banker in Little Rock. Getting a southerner like Remmell on his side would be a good move, Smith thought. Sam Walton, the Arkansas small-town discounter who then was trying to launch his Wal-Mart chain, was working with Remmell and White, Weld to raise the financing on which Walton hoped to become America's biggest retailer [a goal he achieved in 1991]. A native of Newport, Arkansas, Remmell "talked our language" and understood the Dixie mind-set, which Smith believed would make it easier to deal with Wall Street men. Smith asked him about getting investors to put $15 million to $30 million in Federal Express.

"You won't get to first base," Buck Remmell said, "until you have the cold, solid facts on the domestic air freight industry. Get some independent research done. By qualified experts. Verify this gap you see—and find out just how much potential business is out there."

"Makes sense. I will."

"We can show that data to potential investors. If it looks good, we ought to be able to raise money."

In December, a month after he had talked to Art Bass in Little Rock, Smith flew to New York to arrange for market research. He had tentatively committed to Bass, who with two partners operated as Aero Advanced Planning Group, or AAPG. An ex–marine pilot with ten thousand hours in jets and helicopters, Bass had been an aviation magazine writer before turning consultant. His free-spirited,

117

unorthodox partners were ex–New York advertising executive J. Vincent Fagan, and S. (Sidney) Tucker Taylor, a 1967 Yale University graduate, a former aviation writer, and sales rep for Pan American Falcons.

They agreed to make the market analysis for $75,000.

When he reported his progress to Remmell, the White, Weld official was both skeptical and critical.

"Shouldn't you have hired an outfit that is high-powered and has national standing? People with money to put into something this new and untried are going to be skittish. They probably have never heard of AAPG!"

"Art Bass is first-class, impressive, a straight shooter," said Smith. "He created all the strategies for introducing the Dassault Falcon in North America. Pan Am thinks he did a hell of a job. Also, he created basic marketing strategies for Cessna and Piper Aircraft that are still in use. And his partners have good experience. Vince Fagan sold twenty million dollars' worth of Falcons in one year. Tucker Taylor was coeditor of *Who's Who in Aviation* and *Inside Private Aviation*."

"Well," said Buck Remmell, "in my opinion you need some outfit that's better known. A name Wall Street will recognize, won't quibble about."

Smith made inquiries and settled on A. T. Kearney & Company, a national consulting firm that since the 1920s had specialized in transportation economics. The project manager assigned to him was Roger J. Frock, thirty-five, who had an industrial design degree and an MBA from the University of Michigan. He was particularly suited to direct the Federal Express study because much of his twelve years at Kearney involved high-profile research and design on distribution logistics and cargo handling operations for airlines, motor carriers, railroads, and steamship lines.

Frock listened to Smith describe the feasibility analysis he wanted. The consultant felt considerable skepticism.

"Our study," Frock recalled, "was to address the operational feasibility of the concept. Was there a market for it? Would customers use it? And the third thing—was it financially viable to do it?

And in the course of doing that, we were to establish the kind of organizational structure it should have."

They agreed on a fee of $75,000—exactly what he was paying AAPG.

"Fred Smith was a young guy with an idea, and it was kind of interesting," Frock said. "But I had been through a number of these things. I told the guys that we ultimately assigned to this study to give it our best shot, but I imagined the best thing we were going to do was allow him to not throw a lot of money down the drain for something that wasn't going to come to fruition.

"As I'm sure you are well aware, ninety percent of people who have those kinds of ideas just wind up tossing good money after bad."

The visitor from Arkansas wanted immediate action. But instead of plunging into the job, Frock decided it would be prudent first to check out his new client. "It was not every day," he recalled, "that we signed a large contract with an unknown." A Dun & Bradstreet check showed that Fred Smith was a millionaire and could easily afford the work.

It was only then that A. T. Kearney & Company got serious.

Smith did not tell either research company that he had hired the other. And they never found out until the entire project was finished.

The three AAPG partners, as well as Roger Frock, were destined to later join Fred Smith's circle of "partners" in the ever-quickening FedEx adventure. All were mavericks, true nonconformists, courageous and "crazy."

For four or five years in the early 1970s their lives—and Fred Smith's even more so—would be always hectic and too often harrowing.

Flying in from Los Angeles, Rick Runyon landed his Cessna 310 at Adams Field, parked outside Fred Smith's hangar, and entered the cramped little office from which Federal Express was run.

"God, it was so smoky in there, I nearly died," Runyon recalled. "Fellow at Pan Am—the guy in charge of back-hauling strawberries to Europe—knew about my design work and sent me to see Fred. He spent a couple hours explaining what he wanted."

Three weeks later Runyon was back with a sheaf of sketches. He put them up on the conference room wall, about two dozen twelve-by-sixteen-inch renderings. Each showed the Falcon painted in different color combinations.

Then the designer led Smith to the door. "I want you to walk in, just glance at these, and point to the one you like—real quick," he said. "Don't stand there and think about it."

Smith went in and swept the wall with a quick gaze.

"What the hell!" he said, pointing. "What's this goddamned purple airplane?"

Irby Tedder was sent in the same way—with the same result. Runyon next sent in Fred Smith's secretary. She came out and said, "I'll bet the men would all pick that purple one. But I like this other one."

Irby Tedder recalled: "It was funny—her knowing the men would pick the purple job. We sent in the rest of the staff, and that purple airplane was the one that stood out."

"Purple!" Smith snorted.

"I wanted to use plum color," the designer explained. "But it's fugitive. I've researched the paint. After a year plum has a two percent fade factor."

Smith kept scowling at the drawing, which emblazoned FEDERAL EXPRESS across the top side of the Falcon jet in a combination of purple, orange, and white.

"What about the logo?" he asked.

"I've done Getty Oil and a lot of other big companies," Runyon replied. "People just don't have time to figure out what the hell a logo means anymore. With your small budget, we can just make the name and the lettering, the logo." He had designed a distinctive alphabet, with ligatures, so the lettering could not be stolen.

Smith was not convinced. He wanted to incorporate a big dollar sign in the logo. (Fredette Eagle later whimsically suggested using the name "Rapid Air Transport Service" so the lettering on the tail would be RATS.)

Before a final decision, the purple-orange-white design was shown to one other "expert"—Fred Smith's mother.

"Finally," Runyon recalled, "Fred said, 'God damn it, Runyon—okay!' He picked up the phone, got the guy at Pan Am, and told him, 'Rick is working for me now, okay?' And I helped strip the first Falcon we painted."

The adventure appealed to Rick Runyon, who had learned to fly at fifteen and made his way through art school working as an aircraft mechanic. He entered the design competition for the Carlsberg beer bottle and sold his car to finance his entry to Copenhagen. He won.

Through the early 1970s Runyon would remain on call for Federal Express, designing stationery, brochures, trucks, and buildings. "I even ferried Fred back and forth to Memphis in my Cessna. We spent a lot of evenings together, out to dinner, and so on. For quite a while he was short of money, but I finally got paid. We have remained friends."

To spray the FedEx plane with purple paint was simple, but gutting the plush Falcon interior and converting it into a "minifreighter" was complicated. At Adams Field were experts who could handle the work. Smith had been using Little Rock Airmotive whenever modification was needed on jets he brokered. So he conferred with Lucien Talliac, CEO of LRA, and Roland Corriveau, head of engineering and electronics.

In passenger configuration, the door was 31 ½ inches wide and 59 inches high. "It must be larger," Fred Smith told them. "We'll be loading pallets with a forklift, things as big as a mainframe computer. The door should be sixty inches wide and seventy-four inches high."

"Fred loved the Falcon and had made an in-depth study of it," Talliac recalled. "He decided the Falcon offered the best combination of weight, speed, and economy. We had to certify many, many changes to convert it to cargo.

"For example, the Falcon had emergency rudders that were activated from the rear. If the airplane is full of cargo, you can't get to these. Provisions were made to bring those controls forward to the cockpit. Of course, cutting a large hole in the fuselage [to install the bigger door] was not very simple, either, and took months of engineering and testing."

Smith knew the Falcon was sturdy; the French had used it for paratroop jumps. He told Rick Runyon that being able to open the door in flight proved the fuselage was strong. He flew to Paris and conferred with Marcel Dassault, the Falcon manufacturer, and his engineers. Upon his return to Little Rock he brought a head full of technical information and laid out the changes he wanted Talliac and his men to make. LRA contracted to modify each Falcon for $300,000 and tore into the project.

The strain of long hours, worry, and financial pressure began to take a toll. Smith fought off irritation—most of the time. Occasionally he would kick over a wastebasket or let fly a few choice epithets. But usually he was the calm person of the group, patiently cooling off other hotheads.

Lucian Talliac, a World War II B-17 pilot who spent ten years in marketing at Delta Air Lines before coming to Little Rock, recalled: "He was very bright, very brilliant, and very supportive. And the type of man who proves—well, you could go into his office ready to tell him to go . . . you know, where Polly put the nuts, and five minutes later go out of there beaming."

Smith had in hand a couple of purple Federal Express jets and a minisize corporate staff; but he didn't have the start-up capital he needed, nor yet the market data that might lure investors. Worst of all, he still needed government approval to fly as an air taxi!

His immediate worry was that the national recession would ease and the market for corporate jets would pick up. In that case the Pan American business jet division, at the moment desperately in need of cash to avoid bankruptcy, might suddenly see prospects and raise the $1.3 million price they'd set for each new Falcon 20 he needed.

To lock up enough planes for his fleet, Fred Smith flew to New York and signed a contract to buy twenty-three Falcons from Pan Am for a total of $29.1 million. He agreed to take delivery of one plane a week beginning September 28, 1972.

It was an "if, and, or but" deal. The Pan Am executives were well aware FedEx couldn't use the planes unless the air taxi takeoff weight limit was raised; they agreed to refund Fred Smith's payments if the CAB didn't make that change. Even so they wanted option money up front—$1.15 million.

Smith was short of ready cash. So once again he decided to try to get backing from the millions his father had left in the family trust. He summoned Frederick Smith Enterprise Company directors to meet in Memphis on December 17, 1971. Privately he had been boosting up the scheme with Laura Ann by telephone and on visits with Fredette Eagle.

If he could nightly fill his proposed fleet of twenty-five Federal Express jets, he crowed to them, the annual revenue would be almost $67 million, leaving a gross profit before taxes of almost $43 million. A bright picture indeed! His enthusiasm made it appear almost certain.

Fredette admired his aggressive vision. "I was always interested in what he was doing, and excited about it," she recalled. "I wanted to help him as much as I could. But I had financial concerns of my own at that time. I had separated from Bryan in 1969 and was going through a bad and expensive divorce."

Again Fred got help. His sisters and the National Bank of Commerce trust officers were willing to back him up. They voted to put up another block of the Enterprise Company's Squibb stock to guarantee another bank loan for the Pan American option.

Even with two of the Dassault jet planes on hand and twenty-three under option, Fred Smith still wanted more Falcons. He went out on the open market and found eight used ones. Still short of ready cash to buy them, he turned to friendly bankers in Memphis and Little Rock. Trust me, he told them, all I need is short-term loans, demand notes. I know how to sell used planes at a profit. Even if the Federal Express scheme goes sour, I can easily sell all these Falcons—especially, he said, fitted with the cargo door he had invented. His new door was, he said, such a highly regarded design that if others used his pattern, he would charge them a $25,000 royalty for each plane modified.

Worthen Bank in Little Rock was so proud of lending $500,000 to finance six of the used Falcons that it ran television commercials in early 1972, showing the purple Federal Express prototype taking off into the Little Rock sunset with the slogan "Worthen helps a good idea fly."

To give directors of the Frederick Smith Enterprise Company an on-site view of his embryonic Federal Express, Fred Smith flew one of his used Falcons to Memphis and brought them to Adams Field.

"It was a Falcon that had belonged to Frank Sinatra," Fredette Eagle recalled. "It was beautifully furnished. The interior was done in a sort of oatmeal-colored raw silk, and burl wood, and teak—all beige. It was very elegant.

"I told Fred, 'I hope you will keep this for the company plane.' And he said, 'No. No. We are about to gut it."

On the flight from Memphis, she sat in the cockpit as her brother tried to explain the functions of the various instruments. She had flown with him a number of times. "I remember once he took me up in a little plane in Memphis. We were just flying around. Rashly I said, 'Show me what you can do.' And he laughed and did a loop the loop!"

To push his marketing researchers, Smith frequently flew into New York with chief financial man Tedder and a battery of attorneys. He had two Little Rock lawyers working for him, Frank L. Watson, Jr., and William N. Carter. His personal attorney was Robert L. Cox of Memphis, who also served as secretary of the Frederick Smith Enterprise Company.

They barged through the A. T. Kearney offices so fast, Roger Frock recalled, Smith didn't take time to introduce his companions. "There was a mystery to it all," Frock said. "There was an urgency to it all."

There also was developing the reckless spirit that permeated the close-knit "band of brothers" pioneering the Federal Express scheme. Recalling some of their sallies into New York, William Carter said: "I remember we all got drunk one night and got thrown out of the Regency Hotel."

But the standard mien of Fred Smith was serious and intense. "Fred never played," Irby Tedder said. "He was always serious-minded. We'd go somewhere to do business, maybe three or four of us, and we'd hit the hotel and have a martini. He'd have maybe one, and that would be it. He hardly ever relaxed, rarely went off for a weekend to have fun. Once in a while, when he was really under stress, but didn't have anything big to do, we'd slip more martini in his glass, and get him drunk."

Relief from Part 298—which barred his use of the Falcons—was high on Fred Smith's agenda. The CAB began hearings on the regulation in January 1972. Owing to bureaucracy's slow pace, the decision was not expected until the end of the year. But the ever-optimistic entrepreneur was confident the weight limit would be raised.

It was imperative Smith be made to understand the complexity of successfully achieving adjustments in United States government regulations. "You need an old Washington hand, somebody who knows the territory, and the people—especially those in Congress," he was told. "Try to get Ramsey D. Pott's law firm."

That firm assigned Nathaniel P. Breed, Jr., to represent Federal Express; he found the outlook unpromising. Even if the CAB granted relief, rival air cargo haulers most likely would not take that lying down. "I would expect some of them to appeal," Breed told Fred Smith.

If Federal Express managed to start large-scale operations, there would be such a howl from other airlines that Smith eventually would have to apply for CAB certification status. "That would be a real snakepit," Breed warned.

"We've got to get the limit lifted, or we can't do a damn thing," Smith said. "Take the risks! Charge on!"

Not all was gloomy. Favorable reports began to trickle in from both New York market researchers, neither yet aware the other was working on the same project. Art Bass and Roger Frock, separately, had lost their early skepticism and were telling Smith the same thing.

There was a high degree of dissatisfaction all across the country with existing air freight. The industry was dominated by Emery Air Freight and Flying Tiger, both launched at the end of World War II. Each was generating annual revenues of $100 million. But their deliveries were erratic and frequently late. Both shippers and consignees felt air freighters were generally unreliable, timewise. The researchers were confirming the "gap" that Smith had been alert enough to discern on his own. The aftermath of World War II had markedly changed the industrial map of the United States and thus the attendant pattern of traffic in essential material and supplies. Getting large shipments from a factory in one major industrial city to another metropolitan business center had suddenly taken a backseat to the developing need for overnight delivery of small packages.

Smith's own travails at Arkansas Aviation Sales, Inc., had clearly demonstrated this. An electronic switch, or a bearing sleeve for a jet engine, or even an installation diagram—a shipment weighting between possibly half a pound and fifty pounds—might be needed urgently. But when it did not arrive by air overnight from a factory or warehouse in Connecticut, or Seattle, or Atlanta, or San Diego, a million-dollar airplane would sit idle and unproductive on the ground, awaiting repair until the needed parcel arrived.

In the electronic age, WordPerfect Corporation in Utah might well dispatch of set of disks to a schoolteacher in Albany, Georgia. Johns Hopkins Medical Center in Baltimore could be anxious to get X-rays to a physician in Oklahoma City. Construction engineers waited in Kansas City for blueprints from New York. Dallas lawyers were trying to rush a document to Pittsburgh to seal a merger. These were the types of high-priority, time-sensitive parcels Federal Express intended to handle.

Not surprisingly, when Roger Frock and Art Bass finished their independent studies—in May and June 1972—they came to the same conclusion: there did exist the eager and untapped market for fast, on-time air express. Moreover, it could be lucrative: the potential revenue for the air freight industry was as much as $1 billion a year.

A. T. Kearney and AAPG estimated it would require between $6.5 million and $15.9 million in capital to establish the network Smith had in mind. His scheme called for about thirty Falcons to pick up packages in as many or more cities around the United States and arrive around midnight at a hub at Little Rock's Adams Field. There an army of night workers would sort, assemble, and load the packages for departure around three in the morning to the appropriate destination cities by dawn.

Another of Smith's notions was confirmed—the majority of air express users wanted their parcels not only to travel overnight by air, but to be delivered promptly by ground courier. They indicated they were willing to pay a premium for door-to-door service.

"Based on our calculations," Frock told Smith, "it will only take six months or a year to generate earnings. And to break even, Federal Express need only carry 1.6 million packages a year, plus haul ten thousand tons of charter freight. And you can do that by grabbing just one percent of the domestic air freight market that exists today."

Art Bass said substantially the same thing. Hearing it, Smith smiled, already thinking past running merely a successful air express service. His fleet of Falcon minifreighters would be in use only at night, making their runs to Little Rock and back to their home airports. That meant they would be available for other duty during daylight hours. Two things came to mind—charter flights for heavy shipments, and some sort of passenger service, probably short commuter schedules.

The nation's airways were "asleep" at night, the research showed, which left the skies uncluttered. Thus his Falcons could take off and land at practically any airport without being hampered by congestion that might disrupt their tight schedules. In fact, 90 percent of the nation's 2,200 airliners were on the ground between ten at night and eight in the morning.

The gap, Art Bass pointed out, was bigger than Fred Smith had estimated. Sixty percent of all air freight moved between the country's twenty-five largest markets; yet 80 percent of small, urgent shipments originated or terminated outside them. Which meant shippers and receivers at these smaller places could get only second-class, untimely service. Further, at least one hundred major cities were not currently receiving any overnight air freight at all.

"There's plenty of business to go after," Bass assured Smith.

▶ ▶ ▶

In the darkness at Adams Field, Smith paced beside one of his Falcons, glaring at it. He wanted to take off for Miami. The pilot compartment side window wouldn't close, and nobody could fix it. Finally an emergency call went over to Little Rock Airmotive for a mechanic.

Rousted from home, Alvin J. Jeffrey appeared. He took a look and went to his toolbox. He came back with a screwdriver and neatly flipped the window catch over the stop and closed it.

Smith stared at him and then beamed. "How would you like to work for me?"

"When?"

"In the morning—at eight."

"Okay. I'll be here."

Certainly not all of the original Federal Express staff was recruited in such a haphazard manner. Jeffrey proved a good hire, competent enough to later become supervisor of FedEx hub ground maintenance. Smith took a personal liking to him, occasionally dropping by for breakfast with Jeffrey and his wife, Johnnie, and inviting them to his home as dinner guests. But the boss and mechanic quarreled and parted years later when Smith thought Jeffrey was trying to overcharge him on a race car FedEx sponsored.

In early 1972, when the nucleus staff was assembled, Federal Express had no such thing as a personnel department. Everything was casual.

J. Tucker Morse, a young lawyer clerking for federal judge J. Smith Henley in Little Rock, got his job because his father, a former mayor of Little Rock, lived next door to the Federal Express entrepreneur. One evening they began talking over coffee at the Morse's dinner table.

"Fred said he needed an in-house lawyer to do a lot of the day-to-day work," Morse recalled. "He was an engaging fellow, and he would pay me as much as I made clerking [$700 a month]. I shared a little bitty office with two or three people. I reported to Irby Tedder. He was the elder statesman of our group. He was a sobering influence on us young farts. We were all full of mustard and ready to go, and knew no fear."

To an experienced manager like Irby Tedder, the people around Smith, and the boss himself, didn't know how to manage anything. "They all came in," Tedder told one business historian, "with a lot of wild ideas on how to put Federal Express together, and only a few of them made any sense. They were an impetuous bunch."

Fred Smith was single-handedly trying to run the operation, in a totally imperious mode. He was described as a "nitpicker—he had his hand in everything. He worried about little bitty problems other people could handle." And that created confusion and delay. The accounting department was a mess, with no internal controls. Reports were rarely on time. Smith's tinkering, for instance, fouled up the cash flow because of a lag in billings.

"With Fred it was always business," Irby Tedder recalled. "I'll tell you the truth, we worked for three or four years, and the only time I had off for over six hours was Christmas Eve and Christmas Day. We worked around the clock trying to get everything done, checking and double-checking, and all that. That was back when computers were just coming out. Much of our work was on calculators—you know, the old style."

Tedder recalled many late night meetings to set policy or solve problems that turned into "knock down, drag out" affairs. Tempers flared, especially Smith's.

"Fred would get real tense," Tedder stated. "Once in a while he would throw something against the wall. So we would try to get him drunk at some bar, hoping it would relax him and perhaps keep him away from the office next day."

But the boss, not yet thirty and healthy, had an iron constitution.

"Early next morning," Tedder said, "he'd come bouncing back ready to take on the world again."

Ten thousand passengers a month were landing at Little Rock's municipal airport—and many of them went away talking about seeing purple airplanes!

Smith had started converting his Falcons into cargo planes. At times, ten Federal Express jets were lined up in a row at Adams Field. That was the full extent of Smith's fleet in early 1972—the two new Falcons and eight used ones. And it was just as well he hadn't been able to take delivery on any more from Pan Am. He couldn't do much with his minifreighters as long as the CAB's air taxi rules kept them from hauling cargo.

Getting this fat nucleus of the fleet on site so promptly was a major accomplishment. But disturbing glitches were dogging Fred Smith's plan. The main problem was money—the terrible scarcity of it. He was actually dancing on the edge of an abyss. The financial crisis worsened by the day, almost by the minute. So much was going out and so little coming in that Federal Express verged on dropping over the precipice without having a chance to try its wings.

The villain in this melodrama was Smith's own business naiveté. He just didn't understand how difficult would be the task of getting hard-bitten investors to back his dreams with their dollars.

Buck Remmell and White, Weld & Company wanted to be able to show prospective investors market data that confirmed a legitimate and viable need in America for on-time overnight air express. By spending $150,000, Fred Smith got it. White, Weld was enthusiastic enough to send a senior executive, Homer Reese, to Little Rock to check the situation personally. He went back to New York seemingly impressed, but still there was not a lot of action on the investment capital front.

In his lack of financial sophistication, the Federal Express entrepreneur misunderstood White, Weld's role. They clearly agreed to *try* to raise $20 million in capital; somehow Fred Smith had it in his mind that this was a guarantee—in other words that they were committed to coming up with that amount.

By the time he understood their true role, Federal Express was in such a desperate hole that it seemed only a miracle could save it.

But all through 1972 Smith plunged bravely and blindly ahead.

Thinking of his charter freight sideline as an adjunct to his yet unborn overnight parcel express, Smith sent out his Arkansas Aviation salesmen to drum up business with industrial clients.

Ford Motor Company wanted to send a load of auto parts from

Ypsilanti to Kansas City. Smith was legally stymied. Without relief from the CAB's takeoff limit, using the Falcon would be illegal. Hoping to get Ford business later, Smith piloted the plane personally and then dodged any infraction by not charging for the flight. "Just showing you what we can do," he told the somewhat confused Detroit executives.

To ease his money pinch, he considered—with considerable repugnance—bidding for U.S. Postal Service contracts. Six routes were open in the Midwest for five nightly flights a week.

"Bidding for the mail contracts was Fred's idea, and I didn't like it," Tedder recalled. "I thought it was going to spread us too thin and would interfere with starting Federal Express. But he had the other approach, and he was one hundred percent correct and I was wrong.

"Fred said if we got the mail contracts, we could go before investors and say, Look, we've got mail contracts, which is a guaranteed deal, and all we have to do is perform. It turned out that it was a real good selling point. So he beat me out on that."

Several small operators were bidding on the contracts, so Federal Express lowballed them. "Fred bid way too low. We left money on the table. But he wanted to be sure we got the bid. He had an overall plan, and it worked. Once we got the first bid, and had the planes to perform, we could have gotten anything we wanted, with a lot higher income."

But he could not have flown the mail except for a lucky break. The CAB suddenly lifted the air taxi weight limit! On July 18, 1972, Part 298 was modified to permit planes to carry thirty passengers, with a 7,500-pound payload. That was all Federal Express needed (Two air carriers and the Air Line Pilots Association challenged the action in the U. S. Court of Appeals, District of Columbia Circuit. That cloud was eventually lifted when the court ruled on December 5, 1973, that the CAB acted properly in liberalizing Part 298.)

Being freed from the old weight restrictions also meant that Federal Express could proceed with the purchase of additional Falcons under terms of its option with the Pan American business jets division.

But again Smith faced his old bugaboo—not enough money.

Baltimore was the home of Commercial Credit Equipment

Corporation (CCEC), a large finance company Smith had dealt with as an airplane broker. He applied there for a loan of $13.8 million with which to purchase ten of the optioned Pan Am Falcons, repayable in ten years. He offered a mortgage on the airplanes and cited the Kearney and AAPG market studies to convince CCEC executives of the bright prospects for his proposed air express service.

CCEC was agreeable to the mortgage, backed by Fred Smith's personal guarantee, but demanded more—a pledge of $2 million collateral from the Frederick Smith Enterprise Company.

Smith, buoyant over the outlook, saw no difficulty in this request. He had used backing from the family trust before.

But this time it was different. He was going to the familiar well just once too often—and planting the seeds of tragedy.

Calling a meeting of the Enterprise Company in Memphis, he again got the directors to give him even more than the $2 million loan guarantee. On his recommendation, the company voted also to invest $2 million in Federal Express.

Fredette Eagle was agreeable to this action, but she was asked to pledge all her shares to CCEC to indemnify the loan. She refused. Of her 250 shares, 5 had already been pledged to cover the mortgage on her beautiful Potomac River estate in McLean, Virginia.

"I'm willing to help you as much as I can," she told her brother. "I'll strap myself to do it. But I have to save out some shares for myself for income. My divorce is expensive. I have lawyers to pay. And mortgage payments. I must have some income."

She agreed to pledge 145 of her shares and keep the remaining 100 for dividend income. Fred Smith said that was fine. But later Bobby Cox, who wore three legal hats—Federal Express corporate counsel, Fred's personal lawyer, and secretary of Enterprise Company—pleaded with her by phone. To finalize the CCEC loan, she must sign over all her stock. Again she offered 145 shares—no more.

Two or three weeks later, on an afternoon when she was giving a garden party at her McLean home for two hundred guests, a taxi arrived about three-thirty bearing her brother and Bobby Cox.

"The party was at four," Fredette Eagle recalled:

The caterer had just come in. The bartender was asking where to set up. You can imagine just how hectic it was.

They handed me a sheaf of papers and said, "Here is what we talked about." I said, "Did you save me the one hundred shares I told you to?" Fred said, "Yes. We have done it exactly like you told us to. Sign here."

I said, "I can't sign right now. I'm extremely busy. I'll sign it, and get it to you." Fred said, "No. No. We have to make a plane. Can't stay. You've got to sign it right now."

I said, "I haven't read it." He said, "It's exactly what we talked about. Trust me. Sign it!" And I'm sorry to say I did. He said he would send me a copy. I never got it. I called him two weeks later, and said, "Where's my copy?" He sent it to me, and, of course, I had signed away all my shares.

I was betrayed. He had just cut the legs out from under me. That's the whole story.

But it was by no means the whole story.

Fred Smith had taken a foolish and reckless step. It was a mistake to destroy this close and intimate relationship of over a quarter century. His obsession to get the purple Falcons flying was warping his usually keen and balanced judgment.

There was trouble ahead, serious trouble, and a price to pay. Fredette as a loving sister was one thing. An angry divorcée with bills to pay and no income was an entirely different matter.

Fred Smith should have known that.

11 ▶ *PUT IN ALL THE FRUIT SALAD*

"Hi, Charlotte, how you doing?"

Coming into his Adams Field office, Smith threw the question casually at his secretary. Impishly Charlotte Curtis blurted: "Oh, I nearly cut my toe off this morning."

Smith, head bent, reading a report as he walked, didn't miss a stride. "Oh, that's fine," he said. "That's wonderful."

Charlotte Curtis, recalling her days with him between 1972 and 1976, said: "So preoccupied. In such deep thought all the time. Constantly thinking. Such late hours. Sheer determination. There was no doubt in that man's mind where he and the company were going."

J. Tucker Morse was also "always intrigued" by Fred Smith's "enormous powers" of concentration. "You could walk in and he'd be thinking about something and literally wouldn't know you were in the room. That is one sign of a great mind—the ability to concentrate."

In that period two critical items dogged his mental agenda—recruiting staff and finding investors. The former was fairly easy, the latter almost impossible.

Charlotte Curtis, in her twenties, came to FedEx after having been appointment secretary to former governor Winthrop Rockefeller of Arkansas. Hired about the same time was George P. Eremea, who had spent eight years as Rockefeller's personal pilot.

An ex–air force test pilot, Eremea was assigned to take up the modified Falcons and check their new weight balance and so on.

The most outstanding early hires were the two New York consultants who had made the Federal Express feasibility studies. Roger Frock joined the company in May 1972 as general manager, and five months later Art Bass became senior vice-president of planning.

Legends abound about Smith's sincere and passionate "killer charm" turned loose on recruits. But Frock, whose A. T. Kearney research gave him rare insight on FedEx prospects, must have been an easy sell. He took a $1,000 pay cut, signing for $36,000 a year. (Smith's salary was $35,000.)

Despite later published reports, neither Frock nor Bass was promised they'd be millionaires in four years. Smith did offer stock if FedEx succeeded, but not in writing. "I was thirty-five," Frock recalled. "I wanted to take the plunge in a risk venture."

When a recruit balked, Smith "would really go to work on them," said Bass. "Fred's face would light up, and he'd paint a glowing portrait of how we were going to be a Fortune five hundred corporation and that they ought to come along for the adventure of it all."

There were minor Machiavellian overtones to the hiring of Roger Frock. The idea was not strictly Smith's. White, Weld, on the hunt for investors, strongly suggested more window dressing at FedEx—a "high-powered man" as executive vice-president. Buck Remmell suggested that Frock's professional background qualified him.

That displaced Irby Tedder, who moved over to senior vice-president of administration. "It didn't bother me at all," Tedder said. "We worked together. Very close. No problem. Did the same thing I did before. Had my feet in all areas."

Frock immediately undertook to inject more discipline and order into the catch-as-catch-can atmosphere in the Little Rock office. Along with the MBA he received in 1959 from the University of Michigan, he had acquired a liking for the theory and practice of MBO—management by objective.

Gathering his small staff, Frock assigned each a list of projects. "Roger just didn't know how to get along with people," one staffer recalled. "He was not liked at all. He put demands on us that just tied our hands. Now most of our staff meeting time was spent determining how you had progressed. Were you meeting your schedule? If not, why not?"

Tedder was also critical. "We were stomping out fires at that point and trying to get this thing off the ground and going," he said. "Other guys will tell you the same thing." He mentioned Norman F. Timper, who joined FedEx as operations vice-president after thirty-four years of flight crew training and operations, mostly with United Airlines.

"Norm would say in staff meetings, 'This is the most childish stuff I've ever seen.' He said that many times. So did I. But Fred let Roger run it," Tedder said. "Fred's attitude was, well, he was trying to keep the show on the road and keep it attractive to investors. Fred and all of us got along perfectly."

Tedder said the staff tried to free Smith of day-to-day details. "He had enough to do to get the big things wiped out. He was tops at that. The company went on by the skin of its teeth for a long time. But Fred would go down and talk to the little guy on the line and come in and raise Cain with us because they didn't have a particular tool to work with. Little petty things."

On that point, Charlotte Curtis recalled: "He is the type of person who would walk into a hangar and see a grease spot and instead of ordering someone to clean up the spot, he would say 'Pitch me a rag,' and he would do it himself."

She said Fred Smith could see a problem, analyze it, "and nip it in the bud. He does not vacillate when a problem needs to be solved. He acts. He is a boss who makes each employee feel an important part of the company."

Roger Frock remembered plunging feet first into the middle of one critical objective on arrival at Adams Field. Because of the installation of the cargo door and new cockpit controls and the like, the Federal Aviation Administration (FAA) required a new manual to be written before the modified Falcons could be flown. George Eremea had been working on it. Frock commented:

> After a week or two of not getting very good answers
> from George, I walked into the meeting with the FAA guys. I

said that I would sit in and see if I could help. They were kind of going round and round. I wasn't used to working with the FAA. I said, "Stop! I want to make a list of everything we have to do to get this manual done and get our certification. And no one leaves this room until I get that list!"

And the FAA guys looked at me, and looked at one another, and finally said, "Okay." So they made the list and we went over it. I think we had only about eight people in the company. I parceled out the work and we agreed we could get it done in about nine days.

I told the FAA we'd meet in ten days and give them the manual. "And I'm going to get my certificate, Right?" "Yeah."

But ten days later when we met they said, "Well, yeah, you got to do this . . . and do that. . . ." I said, "Stop! You made a commitment. I didn't write this list, you guys wrote it!" They said, "Well, we were optimistic. Tell you what, we'll make another list."

I said, "Okay, we'd do it one more time . . . just once more!" And twelve days later we finally got our certificate. . . . Years later one of the FAA officials told me we'd set some kind of a record by getting the certificate in under five months; it usually took at least nineteen months.

That kind of hustle overburdened the little staff. There were constant late nights in the office at Adams Field. "It wasn't anything to stay till two in the morning," said Charlotte Curtis. "Lots of long hours. One night Fred told me to be back at seven in the morning. Next morning when I stepped into the shower, I could only see spots. I couldn't go in, but I did manage to call two girls and send them in. The doctor found I had five inflamed vertebrae. That was before word processors. We had been typing draft after draft, with hundreds of corrections. Just too much pressure work. I was an outpatient and wore a neck brace for weeks."

Federal Express had been incorporated almost one year by the time Roger Frock arrived as general manager. But there was still much to be done before Fred Smith could start flying air express. His reaching out for mail contracts was a major effort to help stanch the red ink on his books. That helped some.

An unexpected glitch developed over the Falcon's fan jet engines, manufactured by General Electric. GE required that on corporate jets these engines be brought in every fifty hours for inspection and maintenance, at a cost of $20,000. When GE gave that edict to FedEx, Tedder exploded.

"We're not flying corporate," he stormed. "We will be on airline maintenance and overhaul schedule. We'll do our own work.

When GE stuck to its position, Smith and Tedder threatened to pull off the GE engines and get replacements from another manufacturer. The battle went on almost a year before General Electric, aware of how many engines they might lose, finally acquiesced.

At the end of 1972 the Federal Express Corporation's books showed income of $2.8 million—half of which came from hauling mail. Expenses were just over $3.7 million, leaving an actual operating loss for the year of $927,845. In addition, Federal Express, Fred Smith personally, and the family trust were in debt for $21.7 million!

FedEx's need for both operation revenue and a cadre of Falcon-qualified pilots turned out to be a company advantage. Smith had a bias against commercial pilots, whom he termed "steely, blue-eyed executives with pilots' caps." The first pilots he hired for FedEx were former military aviators and a few corporate jet fliers. In the beginning the FedEx pilots were sent to New York for training.

"It became obvious we could not continue doing that," Tedder said. "We had to run our pilots through our own school. There were just too many of them, and we didn't want to spare them for that period of time. Also, we needed to keep up a steady refresher program."

The Federal Express Training School was started in Little Rock in October 1972 to train pilots for the Falcon. Fred Smith got it approved by the Veterans Administration because all of the prospective pilots had had military service, and the government paid most of the tuition. That ran almost $9,000 for two weeks of intensive schooling.

By the end of a year about 273 pilots went through the FedEx school. Fred Smith thought he'd have to abandon the program because that was about the limit of job opportunities in his cockpits.

But he tried to salvage his flight school by making a pitch to Japan Airlines for their business. To qualify pilots for the new DC-9s, JAL was sending pilots to a school on the West Coast.

"We had a better deal for them," said Tedder, "because the Falcon was more similar to the DC-9 than what they were using to train in on the West Coast. The pilots had to go back to Japan and train on their planes, while they could almost transition out of the Falcon into the DC-9.

"Fred worked on that deal for eight or nine months. We thought we were going to get the contract. But we didn't."

Frock remembered the first revenue charter vividly. "That was done for IBM. They were presenting a new line of computers in New York at a press briefing. There they would be photographed and demonstrated. The stuff came out of Lexington, Kentucky, and it took three or four airplanes because of the bulkiness of it.

"It was so important I made sure I was up in New York to see the planes come in. That charter was worth something like twenty-four thousand dollars. I kept that document as a souvenir for several years and then had it framed and gave it to Fred."

Federal Express did get considerable charter business from the Ford Motor Company, as well as from General Motors. But this gradually dried up because FedEx was not as cost-effective for automotive supplies, Frock explained, as such air carriers as the Zantop Company of Ypsilanti, Michigan. "Zantop had less expensive aircraft—mostly Electras—that could haul a bigger payload. They were better for the automotive people."

Perhaps the greatest irony of Smith's search for start-up capital was that the very people who could have either supplied it or helped obtain it were all the while in hometown hollering distance of Federal Express.

Stephens, Inc., the large and successful Little Rock bond house, knew from the start—and to the smallest detail—exactly what kind of a venture Fred Smith had created and what he needed most to make it go. The company also knew what kinds of hurdles he was being forced to jump.

In fact, Jack Stephen's Little Rock Airmotive was involved in overseeing the conversion of Falcons into what Fred Smith would eventually call "550-mile-an-hour delivery trucks." With that role, Stephens, Inc., was virtually looking through a picture window that revealed the nuts and bolts of the first days of FedEx.

The reason Stephens, Inc., did not take a gamble on Federal Express was cold business calculation.

"I did not think it would succeed," recalled Jon Jacoby, Stephen's chief financial officer:

> We kind of do things here on a red hot basis. We try not to formalize how they are done. I had the specific responsibility for what we call special investments.
>
> I got involved in Little Rock Airmotive in 1966 or 1967. The year we started we had a pilot. So we built a garage, and said as long as we have a garage why don't we sell gas. Then we started selling radios and airplanes—that became Little Rock Airmotive. The original pilot thought he ought to get a raise, and Jack didn't think so. So he quit. But we just went along.
>
> Federal Express appeared, and we got the first contract to modify the Falcon jet with the cargo door. When Fred was trying to raise money, we turned him down.
>
> The reason we did that was that what I look for, my ideal kind of investment, is one that you spend one dollar to prove that absolutely it pays to spend ten million dollars. With Federal Express, you had to spend ten million dollars before you could open the door. In other words, nobody is going to call you and say "Take my package" if the only place you serve is Little Rock and Memphis.

In Jon Jacoby's view, to open an air express company would imply that packages could be delivered anywhere—at least in the United States. There would be few customers if half the time Federal Express didn't serve the city the customer wanted to reach.

"So they had to put in place a system covering the whole United

States, just to carry one package," Jacoby said. "Which meant you started off with all fixed costs and no variable costs. And the ideal business is you can get the first order, and make money from day one and expand on that.

"Like you open a Wal-Mart store, and if that formula succeeds and you do well, you open a thousand of them. But you don't open a thousand of them to take the first order. And so Federal Express— I called it extremely risky in that you have to put in place a business, as I recall, that had to grow at thirty-two percent a month in order to stay within the twenty to twenty-two million dollars he was raising.

"And I just thought it was impossible for any business to grow thirty-two percent a month."

Jon Jacoby, bright and friendly, sat in his downtown office in 1991 and looked back twenty years—philosophically.

"The thing of it was, it grew at sixteen percent a month. And it took fifty million dollars rather than twenty-two to get to break even. Those are rough numbers. As a matter of fact, we did look at it another time. Fred was redoing his financing, so we had a chance to invest. We did make an offer, but at that time, unfortunately, he didn't take it. We might have been a little conservative."

But Stephens, Inc., was not at all on the conservative side when it came to selling Little Rock Airmotive to Fred Smith.

The pace of LRA's work on modifying the Falcons with a larger cargo door and new cockpit instrumentation was a disappointment to him. Nearly every day he stopped in at Stephens, Inc., to chat with Vernon Giss, now in partial retirement but then the top financial officer and a power on the board that operated Little Rock's municipal airport.

"LRA is going too slow to suit us," Smith told Giss. What he didn't say was that the FedEx people felt the LRA mechanics were accustomed merely to prettying up interiors of corporate jets with new upholstery or a bar or new lavatory and had no notion of how to set up a production line that would expeditiously convert the Falcons to minifreighter workhorses.

What Giss kept worrying about secretly was a stack of bills from the likes of Douglas and Boeing and other aircraft supply companies for the cargo doors, new struts, and avionics required to modify the Federal Express planes.

FedEx was slow to pay.

Giss was afraid that Smith might bankrupt himself and never be able to pay for the LRA work. So he actually started holding up parts orders. And that further slowed down the conversion of the Falcons.

"We had to commit to Douglas Aircraft for the new cargo doors," said Jacoby. "That was five million dollars. And what were we going to do with all those doors if Fred couldn't raise the money?

"So he came to me and said, 'If I get the money to buy LRA, what will you sell it for?' He talked to Jack Stephens, and we said we would sell. And his bank was willing to loan the money to buy LRA, but not the money to buy the cargo doors. Sounds silly to me, but that's Worthen Bank down the street."

Stephens and Jacoby went over their figures. LRA had a book value of about $625,000. The only current business of any consequence was the Falcon conversion. "What was that worth, if Fred didn't have the money to pay?" Jacoby asked. By going "way out," Jacoby told Stephens, "maybe you can dream up a value of two million dollars."

Jacoby recalled: "So Jack said fine, and he priced LRA at two and a half million dollars. Fred was able to borrow the money. And Jack negotiated the deal. They reached agreement on Saturday, and Jack said, 'And I want the money today!' 'Well, the bank's closed!' 'Just go get me a cashier's check, or there's no deal!'

"So Fred went and got a cashier's check on Saturday from one of the Worthen officers."

Jacoby now sees Smith as a truly remarkable person. "He did so much that looked crazy to me. He overpaid for LRA. . . . But he was just so focused on overcoming whatever obstacles sprang up in his path. He certainly put Federal Express ahead of everything. He was almost a crazy about it."

Even though Smith paid an excessive price for LRA, he took charge, put in new management, and got his Falcons outfitted with new doors with exceptional speed. Further, a few years later when it was no longer essential to FedEx, he sold the company to British Airways and made a million-dollar profit.

► ► ►

By the end of 1972 Fred Smith and his crew had come to the conclusion that as a center for their forthcoming air express hub, Little Rock would not do.

But to move from Arkansas would be perilous because it well might incur the wrath of powerful Arkansas congressman Wilbur Mills. Mills, who had enormous clout in Washington as chairman of the House Ways and Means Committee, had done favors for FedEx because the company was headquartered in his native state, because he had admiration for Smith, and because he had confidence in the success of the scheme.

Born in 1909 to a storekeeper in the village of Kensett, Arkansas, Mills graduated from law school at Harvard and went to Congress in 1939 after serving as a judge in White County. His forty-two-year congressional career was to be devastated after his Tidal Basin involvement with stripper Fanne Fox made headlines and he had to admit his alcoholism.

But Mills was one of the Capitol Hill powers in the early 1970s when Smith needed his help—and he gave it freely. Trying to reciprocate, Fred kept one of his Falcon jets as a passenger plane, just in case Mills needed to make a trip in a hurry. The Falcon carried Mills on a number of personal flights, but he did not call on the courtesy to excess.

Roger Frock recalled him as a stand-up straight shooter and by no means a patsy. "If something was right," Frock said, "Mills would help do it. If it wasn't, he would not touch it."

As the national hub for an air express system, Adams Field had several deficiencies. Fred Smith appealed to the airport commission for help in correcting them, but he got nowhere. The commissioners pleaded poverty and tax shortfall.

The biggest drawback was that Little Rock's municipal airport had only one runway. "It was equipped for instrument landings in both directions," said Irby Tedder, "but it was not too big. If you had a strong crosswind, you couldn't land; you'd have to go someplace else. It just plain didn't suit. The other factor was that the Little Rock airport didn't have any facility that could be used for sorting packages."

On the other hand, Memphis, Fred Smith's old hometown, was willing to go all out to get the FedEx hub. Everett (Ned) Cook, chairman of the Memphis airport board, not only had vision, but knew the Smith family from early Greyhound–Toddle House days.

Cook quickly made available a group of sturdy hangars and acres of ramp parking and induced the commercial airlines serving Memphis to endorse a $2.9 million bond issue to build a modern sorting hub with first-class conveyers.

"Memphis was so much better for us," Tedder explained. "That field had parallel runways north and south and east and west. With an instrument landing system. That meant you have eight different directions to land from.

"Having parallel runways is very important. Sometimes a little private plane will come in with the gear up and crash on the runway. Happens quite a bit. In Little Rock that meant the runway would be shut down to all traffic two or three hours. In Memphis you just land on the parallel runway."

Fred Smith finally telephoned Mills and told him of the decision to pull up stakes and move to Memphis.

"He got very upset," Tedder said. "Fred talked to him a while, trying to explain. Mills was still pretty mad, so Fred invited him to come down for a briefing. There's a major factor you might not think of. About sixty or seventy percent of our flights would be going east and returning from the east, and Memphis, of course, is east of Little Rock. There would be about thirty minutes extra flying for those planes to come to Little Rock. That's a lot of fuel. We worked that out in dollars and cents, and it was a fabulous figure.

"That was one of the things Fred pointed out to the congressman. It was just a business decision. Mills finally saw that and got over his anger.

► ► ►

On Friday, February 2, 1973, the American Airlines flight from New York brought an explosive priority letter to Smith in Little Rock. As he tore open the envelope, he was already on edge, under extreme pressure. The message from White, Weld was one more staggering blow, and a surprise.

It did something to Fred Smith, something to his normally impecable judgment and sense of business ethics. The White, Weld demand—for money, of course—goaded him into reckless and tragic action that would threaten him with prison.

The letter from White, Weld was a bitter pill for Smith, already unhappy with the lazy pace of the Wall Street firm's search for the financing he needed. Now, in this document, they sent a last minute demand that he come up with an additional $1.5 million in cash to put into Federal Express, on top of the $3.25 million already invested by himself and the Frederick Smith Enterprise Company.

White, Weld's ultimatum was that paid-in capital of $4.75 million by Smith and the family trust was essential to trigger their efforts to place $16 million in equity securities and $4 million in 8.5 percent second mortgage notes due in 1980.

That very day two of Smith's lawyers were in New York, fighting deadlines, trying to keep Federal Express alive. Bobby Cox was actually in the White, Weld offices going over the final drafts of the investment house's program for a private offering to garner the urgently needed venture capital. Smith had believed the funds would be in hand in a couple of months.

At the Pan American business jet division, Frank Watson, Jr., was negotiating desperately to keep Pan American from canceling Smith's option on twenty-three Falcons. Without ready cash Federal Express had been unable to meet its promise to take delivery on one plane a week. Pan Am was running out of patience.

"I spent twenty-three days in New York trying to keep Pan Am from selling the Falcons out from under us," Watson recalled. "One of their guys, a senior officer, was a mean SOB. We had to play hardball . . . and FedEx almost died in those bitter meetings."

Smith knew that if the planes "were sold out from under us," their replacement "would have been impossible from a time point of view."

145

When the letter arrived, Federal Express was essentially "broke." Fred Smith knew he was finished unless he could promptly get his hands on $1.5 million.

His best hope was to borrow from a bank. However, he felt his credit had already been stretched thin at his primary bank, Worthen, which was carrying the paper on his purchases of used Falcons—and bragging about it in television ads.

Earlier, Smith had received friendly overtures from the recently reorganized Union National Bank. When he showed a film about FedEx to a Little Rock business group, including U.S. Senator John McClellan; one of the Union officers present was Walter T. Maloan, senior vice-president in charge of commercial loans. "I know we will not be your primary bank," Maloan told Fred Smith, "but we'd like to do business with you."

Now, in a bind for money, Fred Smith went directly to Maloan and asked to borrow $2 million, explaining the crisis and tendering a financial statement that projected his net worth at $7.2 million.

Not unexpectedly, the banker wanted some collateral other than Smith's personal solvency and the prospective corporate treasure chest White, Weld expected to open for FedEx.

Details of this dramatic episode are contained in sworn testimony given later by both parties. Smith and Maloan do not agree precisely on everything that then transpired, but both told substantially the same story.

They faced each other across Maloan's desk on the second floor of the Union National Bank building. Pending the move to Memphis, Smith still had his executive offices in the same building, on the eighth floor.

Summing up their impasse over collateral, Maloan used a common Arkansas quail hunter's expression: "Your dog won't hunt."

Fred Smith understood him. He volunteered that he had stock in the Frederick Smith Enterprise Company, which he would be willing to put up as collateral, backed by an agreement from the family trust to repurchase it for at least $2 million.

That seemed to satisfy Maloan.

"All right. Fine," Fred Smith told the banker. "I'll get you a resolution or a buy-back agreement of the stock."

What happened next is melodrama. Smith went downstairs and found a secretary—"I think her name was Mary Beebe." He asked her to take some dictation. What he gave her were the "minutes" of a meeting of the board of the Frederick Smith Enterprise Company, supposedly held on January 27, 1973, in Memphis.

"And I told her to dictate the fact that the Enterprise Company holds some shares and that they would buy them back from Frederick W. Smith, if called upon doing it," Smith later testified.

Then he handed her the Enterprise Company minutes book so she could see the style in which to write the document and told her: "Just put all the other fruit salad in it just the same and date it."

The secretary wrote up two documents: the supposed minutes of a board meeting and the "buy-back" resolution. Despite the fact that they were totally fictitious because no such board meeting was held, Fred Smith took them to his office and signed them as president of the company.

In the blank for the signature of the secretary of the Enterprise Company, Fred Smith picked up a pen, he admitted, and wrote in the name "Robert L. Cox," who was of course not only secretary of the trust, but his longtime friend and corporate and personal attorney.

Thus the documents were not only fictitious, they were forgeries.

Yet Smith felt he had acted in honest good faith. He considered that he personally *was* Federal Express, and that likewise he was the chieftain and leader, and aggressive planner, of the family Enterprise Company, and that the other directors would ratify any action he took on his own.

He took the fake papers to Maloan, who wanted to call Bobby Cox in Memphis and discuss the loan. Fred Smith gave him the number. Maloan phoned Cox's office; he was out of town. The banker then dictated two letters, dated February 5, 1973, which set out the circumstances surrounding the loan and the stock buy-back, one addressed to Fred Smith in Little Rock and the other to Robert Cox in Memphis, and handed them to Smith. When they came back to Maloan, one bore the signature of Frederick W. Smith. On the other letter, which acknowledged by the secretary of the Enterprise Company notice of the assignment of Fred Smith's stock to the bank, was the signature of Robert L. Cox.

147

Maloan handed over a draft for $2 million. Fred Smith promptly put $1.5 million into the sagging Federal Express by buying 450,000 shares of its stock. The other $500,000 was used to meet his past due obligations on Worthen Bank loans.

Despite good intentions, Smith had created documents that violated federal banking laws. (A full year was to pass before Maloan and his bank would discover that their collateral was false—when the note came due in the spring of 1974.)

Even that $2 million loan did not take the pressure off Federal Express and Smith. Weeks went by and investment capital still was not forthcoming from White, Weld. FedEx still a-borning, continued to teeter on the brink of collapse.

Smith was desperate. On that period he would later testify: "What I'm saying . . . is that with the trauma of that year, the pressure was so great on me, and there were so many events that went on, and so much travel and so many meetings with investment bankers . . . and a hundred different people that came down there . . . . I just don't recall specifics of virtually anything during that period of time. . . ."

To keep Federal Express afloat in this crisis, Smith went in June 1973 to the First National Bank in Memphis and requested a loan of $1 million.

For collateral he duplicated a page from the scenario he had used successfully at the Union National Bank, offering First National a "resolution" presumably authorized by the Frederick Smith Enterprise Company to buy back Smith's shares—even though they had already been pledged to the Little Rock bank.

The document given the Memphis bank was signed by Smith as president of Enterprise and also was attested by the secretary, "Robert L. Cox." The First National Bank handed over $1 million, which Smith promised to repay as soon as White, Weld came through with funds.

Within a few weeks word of the million-dollar loan got back to other officers of the Enterprise Company. At an explosive board meeting on July 31, 1973, Smith was accused by directors of "trickery" and "conflict of interest" in issuing the "resolution" to benefit his own airline.

Cox did not sign the document, Smith later testified, asserting that he "probably" wrote in Cox's name. One upshot of the board meeting was that Bobby Cox resigned as secretary of the Frederick Smith Enterprise Company, although he continued as legal counsel for Federal Express and as Smith's personal attorney.

Even though the deceit in the First National loan was starting to unravel in Memphis, nobody at that time alerted Union National in Little Rock that it had been similarly victimized.

While he borrowed $3 million, Smith was under pressure from Pan American in New York on FedEx's delinquent option to buy the twenty-three Falcons that were urgently needed to establish the nationwide air express service.

Pan Am executives finally relented and agreed to give FedEx until May 15, 1973, to exercise the options and pay for all the jet planes. But there were strings attached. For every plane not taken on schedule after March 31, 1973, the price went up $1,500 a day!

The people at Pan Am must have thought something good eventually would come of Fred Smith's plan because they demanded, and got, warrants to purchase FedEx stock at a later date but at a bargain price.

Jon Jacoby of Stephens, Inc., was right: Smith had to have a nationwide system in place, a willingness and ability to deliver almost anywhere overnight, before he could expect to lure shippers.

Working diligently that spring on that system, and using "headhunters," FedEx lured several experienced men from United Parcel Service, including Michael J. Fitzgerald, then thirty-seven, who set up the first hub in Memphis and hired the first couriers who drove vans leased from Hertz.

"Simply because the package was of high value to the shipper and the consignee, it was logical for us to attempt to provide the service where it never left our hands, a kind of womb to tomb comfort level," Fitzgerald said.

"So our door-to-door decision was based on solving the problem for a shipper or a receiver of how to get his package to or from an airport. It was just inconceivable that we could put together a network of independent carriers who would provide a cartage service for the company with a high degree of reliability. We had to run our own delivery trucks. It was obvious going into that kind of business that reliability is uppermost, the high service that Federal was dedicated to and still is.

"Having our own couriers was Fred's decision. He was very open and receptive to the ideas that we brought to him—provided, of course, we had thought it out. Remember, Fred had gathered around him some people with extensive background in this business. Hell, I had thirteen years in United Parcel, and let me tell you, UPS is the best boot camp in the world."

There was no letup for the man at the top. Smith was summoned by White, Weld to a dozen different meetings in the East to explain his air express concept to potential investors.

Wall Street was on the verge of a major sag. As a result investors were wary and the sales pitch by the man from Arkansas did not open any pocketbooks. According to Irby Tedder, the presentations were excellent, if somewhat chaotic:

> About four-thirty one afternoon he called me and said we had to be in New York at nine in the morning to brief a potential investor. I said, "Oh, gosh, okay. I've got to get some money." I didn't have any money to travel with.
>
> We took off that night and had to lay over in Memphis a couple of hours. He went to sleep on a bench. We went to Atlanta and then on to New York. He hadn't prepared any-thing—no speech.
>
> We do not arrive on time in New York and are thirty minutes late getting to Wall Street. He goes in and gives the most beautiful briefing you ever heard. He dozed most of the flight up, but he must have formulated that speech in his sleep; he was sharp as a tack.
>
> He was a great front man. I would give him a carload of figures when we started on a trip. He would stick them in his pocket. But, by golly, when we got there he had them exact. Get up and talk without notes ninety percent of the time.

Although by January 1973 Smith had about one hundred fifty employees and an executive nucleus in Memphis, he faced an obstacle to starting service. He had only nine Falcon jets, and all were tied up in carrying the mail under the U.S. Postal Service contracts he had obtained to keep some revenue coming in.

Roger Frock and Art Bass concluded they would have to free up at least six Falcons to launch Federal Express. Smith agreed and began canceling his mail contracts. He hoped to inaugurate air express by the middle of March.

The Memphis staff devised a network of a few start-up cities, opened offices in each, hired couriers, provided delivery vans, arranged flying schedules, and tried to get the word out that Federal Express could deliver packages overnight.

The effort was all pathetically puny. (Looking back a few years later, Smith confessed to a Harvard Business School interviewer: "The biggest asset we had going for us was our naiveté. God takes care of fools, you know.")

The cities to be served were mainly all within a mere five hundred miles of Memphis—St. Louis, Dallas, Kansas City, Atlanta, Nashville, Cincinnati, and Little Rock. Hastily assembled, inexperienced "blitz teams" of four or five salesmen invaded the targeted cities, working two or three weeks in each to presell the company's service. The agents were identifying potential big shippers and estimating their potential use of the new airline. Advertising was confined to an opening announcement in local newspapers and direct mail.

In Memphis, where all flights were supposed to bring their cargo for sorting and distribution to the outgoing flights that would depart before sunrise, Mike Fitzgerald created a temporary "hub" with one gravity-feed beltway in one of Memphis International Airport's old World War II wooden hangars.

Finally six Falcons were relieved of their mail delivery runs, and the Federal Express inauguration was announced for Monday, March 12.

On that morning salesmen and agents began calling in from along the network with optimistic predictions. They expected the planes to be pretty well loaded up. William T. Arthur, a former classmate of Smith's at Memphis University School, and son-in-law of Dr. Coors, was FedEx marketing director. He had a feeling that the salesmen were being overly optimistic. But he joined a throng at the Federal Express hangars at Memphis airport for the debut.

Standing on the ramp watching the midnight sky for the lights of incoming Falcons were Fred and Linda Smith, her Hutchison classmate Jeanne Coors Arthur, most of the corporate officers of FedEx, and all the mechanics and ramp swampers.

Also in the crowd was Henry W. (Brick) Meers, vice-president from the Chicago office of White, Weld. He recalled later: "I saw the anguish in their faces as they waited. Most were worried about their future. It was a critical moment for all of them."

Right after midnight the Falcons swooped in. Their cargo doors were flung open—on emptiness.

"It was a bust," Mike Fitzgerald remembers. "We could see what was wrong. We didn't have enough cities. And people hadn't heard of us."

In all, the Falcons brought six packages. One was a birthday present from Fred Smith to Irby Tedder, and one was a bundle of dirty laundry sent home by the FedEx salesman in Kansas City.

THE WOOING OF COLONEL CROWN

Charles L. Lea, Jr., craved action for his $100 million portfolio. Federal Express wanted him to invest. He said no. But now, barely a month later, on Thursday, April 19, 1973, he left his Wall Street office to fly to Memphis and have an important closer look.

People said Lea (pronounced "Lay"), forty-five, looked a lot like Jimmy Carter. He got his red hair from his Irish grandfather and his degree—in Chinese history—in 1952 from Cornell University. That somehow propelled him into investment banking, where he rose to executive vice-president of New Court Securities Corporation.

The international banking dynasty of Baron Rothschild of Paris was behind New Court. Lea's firm, an offshoot of Amsterdam Overseas Corporation, had been formed in 1967 principally to handle the Rothschild family's American investments. With the baron's approval, Lea was looking to risk part of the $100 million he managed in a promising venture.

Aware of that, White, Weld's Brick Meers suggested Lea take a look at the forty- to fifty-page private placement package they had written for "this airplane thing by an attractive young guy down in Tennessee." Lea read it and wasn't immediately impressed, but Brick Meers would not give up.

So Lea agreed to be at the FedEx hub this midnight—because after the March 12 inauguration, Art Bass and Roger Frock had torn apart the initial air express network and rearranged it completely. Tonight they were making a fresh start.

With Smith, all his executives, and their families, Lea stood on the ramp in the dark outside the sorting hangar and watched the Falcons swoop in. This time was better: there were 183 packages. The old start was too embarrassing; Smith just erased it, calling it an operations "test," and made April 19, 1973, the new FedEx birthday.

Ten Falcons were now flying, and the number of cities making up the April network was much larger—twenty-two. Among them were Cleveland; Columbus; Detroit; Greensboro, North Carolina; Indianapolis; Jacksonville, Florida; Chicago; Miami; New Orleans; Oklahoma City; Pittsburgh; and Rochester, New York. By summer, service would be extended to Los Angeles and San Francisco as well as to Houston, New York, and Miami.

But the small yield of April's second start-up disappointed Lea. This was small-time stuff—nothing for a $100 million portfolio to fool with. The FedEx people must be promising more than they could deliver. "We're not interested," he again told Brick Meers, and took the next flight back to New York.

Despite the better showing, Federal Express remained in desperate trouble. Expenses were soaring. Income was too thin to pay the bills.

The deficit at the end of April was $4.4 million. Every dollar Smith and the family trust had pumped into the enterprise was virtually gone. In fact, the equity of all the stockholders had dwindled to just under $290,000.

Smith was hurt and frustrated—and furious at what he considered betrayal by White, Weld, particularly Buck Remmell.

Charles Lea recalled: "In the beginning Fred said he was given to understand by Buck Remmell that when White, Weld said they'd do this deal it was an underwritten fait accompli. He did not understand, I don't believe he truly understood, that it was strictly a best efforts deal, and the money wasn't in the bank, and he had a long row to hoe.

"He jumped up and down, and said he was totally misled by White, Weld. His feelings, his strong feelings about that, were a problem later on. Because of being misled, he had made commitments and taken risks that he never would have taken."

Even so, Smith showed no animosity toward Meers. "Fred has a way of seething under a very cool exterior," said Lea. "And I could often detect anger in his subcutaneous response, if you will. But he was always very polite, even to the people he was absolutely entitled to take off on."

The group around Smith, who was twenty-eight, also were "extremely young and with limited business experience," recalled his early Little Rock lawyer, J. Tucker Morse. "In terms of starting a company of this size, we were first-grade novices. And I think that really played to our advantage because we were not fully aware of the obstacles we faced or the difficulty in overcoming them. I look back on it now and think, Oh, my God, why in the world would anybody try to do something like this!

"The essence of Federal Express is that you had a brilliant guy conceptually who was willing to risk his own money, and who also most importantly was able to run a company. He had the business skills necessary that most entrepreneurial types don't. Then he surrounded himself with some good people who frankly were able to work without creating a lot of bureaucracy early on. And we all worked well together. Everyone carried their weight. We got along incredibly well. There was very little back biting or politics until the 1980s.

"That was the beauty of FedEx to me. It was literally like a championship football or basketball team where everybody was working together. Enormous esprit de corps, enormous sacrifice. Thank God I was not married for most of that period because I would have been divorced. Worked on Saturdays and Sundays and at night. We were just consumed by this idea. That was the real secret of that company."

By any measure Smith was the dominant personality in FedEx. "I always said I thought one of the most brilliant parts of Fred Smith was his ability to deal with each person individually," Tuck Morse said. "That is a real talent that I haven't seen much of in my business career. And it was quite effective. It worked well with me. Certain things will motivate me, where other things won't.

"Some people Fred would yell at, and other people he would never raise his voice to. Some he would argue with, some he wouldn't. It was real brilliant strategy he would use, particularly with the officers. Quite effective. Looking back—his determination, his concentration, his drive, all those. Just his ability to understand people and what makes them work, and what they will be motivated by, and respond to. I was really in awe of that ability. And to have that at such a young age. I could see a guy who was forty-five to sixty years old having that history of experience being able to do it. But some fellow twenty-seven to thirty years old—that's exceptional!"

Along with their grinding work, the FedEx troops managed to enjoy themselves. "Yeah, we were hard livers," said Tuck Morse. "We had a good time. There were guys who were incredible in their ability to work all day and most of the night and stay out and drink and get up and keep going. It was wild. There is no question about it. Fred was not one of the best at doing that—but he was pretty good. He was working harder than anybody else, no question about that."

What Smith learned in Vietnam about leading troops with personal courage and confidence helped him now. Nothing seemed to faze him. Mike Fitzgerald recalled: "He rarely let you see him get down. I'm sure bad things happened to him; he kept them private. And he would constantly look for the bright side of trouble, and laugh. That was pretty infectious, so we all kind of followed suit. And some of the more devastating things—after a while they seemed to lose their thud . . . their impact. You didn't get terribly upset. We had enough of them. You kind of became ready to handle them.

"The feeling was that if you couldn't find some humor or relief, you were destined to become a crazy person. One thing that struck me in those days was the lack of finger pointing when things would go wrong. It was very, very comforting. It allowed people, I think, to operate on a far better plane, a higher plane, than they would have. . . . You didn't have the sense of having to worry about something going wrong and what it would mean to you personally. I think that was commonly shared."

The nightly "lift" grew almost imperceptibly through the rest of the April midnights. The package count wasn't rising a great deal, chiefly because few knew that Federal Express existed and could regularly make on-time next day delivery.

Operationally the air express company was running smoothly. But any expansion to serve more cities would not be feasible until more cargo planes could be added to the fleet.

The explosive element was the fact that on May 15 Fred Smith & Company's troubled and patched-up option to purchase eighteen more Falcons from Pan American was due to expire. The Pan Am people had turned unyielding on any further extension.

Only days after Charles Lea's second rejection of Federal Express, into the drama stepped a new potential savior—the powerful billionaire industrialist Colonel Henry Crown of Chicago.

Smith got a surprise call from Chicago, where Brick Meers maintained headquarters as White, Weld's resident partner and vice-chairman. A well-connected civic leader, Meers, sixty-five, sat on several corporate boards and knew everybody who counted in Windy City financial circles, Colonel Crown included. Meers and Crown were fellow trustees of the University of Chicago.

"Colonel Crown will see us Friday, May fourth," Meers said. "Can you make it?"

Notwithstanding Smith's disenchantment and feeling of betrayal, the White, Weld organization obviously was working hard to solicit the $20 million or so needed to keep Federal Express growing.

Knowing of Colonel Crown's astounding rags-to-riches rise, Meers had a hunch that the fire and zeal of his Memphis client would capture the seventy-seven-year-old financier's fancy—and confidence.

By "astounding" youthful business acumen, Crown had parlayed a small Chicago sand-and-gravel firm founded in 1919 with his two brothers into one of the world's largest distributors of construction supplies. Merging that firm into General Dynamics Corporation in 1959, Crown took control of the giant contractor. But a long corporate struggle ensued, and Crown was given $100 million and ousted.

His lifelong shrewdness in wheeling and dealing was best demonstrated when he paid $3 million in 1952 for control of New York's Empire State Building, gradually acquired all stock in the 102-story skyscraper, and sold it nine years later for $65 million.

On the day he welcomed Fred Smith and Brick Meers to his office at 300 West Washington Street in Chicago, Crown was again in control at General Dynamics. On the heels of a profit tailspin, he had quietly bought back his 18 percent holdings for only $50 million.

Not surprisingly, Crown listened with interest to Smith's recitation. He knew firsthand just how frustrating it was to a business, large or small, to be unable readily to transport time-sensitive packages. The visitors did not have to prove to him existence of the air express gap Federal Express was beginning slowly to fill.

"Colonel Crown," said Smith, "we have under option twenty-three Falcon aircraft at $250,000 each, and those aircraft today—the replacement cost is $1.5 million, and the market has become substantially more firm since the date of that option.

"Will you loan the money, or guarantee the note, for us to exercise this option, which is an integral part of fitting Federal Express together? The worst thing that can happen to us is that if you decide you don't like the program, you can sell the aircraft at a profit. Secondarily, will you give us some working capital in the interim, say, a million dollars?"

Crown was sympathetic. "Real satisfaction," he had once said, "comes from creating, building, or taking a business that hasn't been doing too well and making it better." But he couldn't rush to the rescue. For one thing his financial vice-president was hospitalized, recovering from a hernia operation. He wanted to delay any decision until that man was back on the job. Besides, Crown's style was to study a new venture cautiously.

Brick Meers earlier had warned Smith: "When the Colonel gets into your deal, he knows the size of your underwear." Likewise, Crown was concerned about the FedEx chairman's youth and lack of seasoning in commanding a large corporation.

"I would say Federal Express perhaps needs a CEO who is older and has more experience," Crown said candidly. His remark was directed to Brick Meers, and it didn't faze the blunt billionaire that Smith was in the room.

To Meer's credit, he wasn't to be stalled. He took the unorthodox course of invading the finance man's hospital room and spending the afternoon laying out their proposition. With Smith doing most of the talking, they convinced the sick man.

Their brash move seemed to impress Crown, who knew firsthand about enterprise and aggressive struggle. In sharp contrast with Fred Smith's background of wealth, Crown had been born to poor Lithuanian immigrants. He'd dropped out of school at sixteen for a $4-a-week office boy job. Fired for a shipping mix-up, he'd quickly learned to hustle. Even when young he had remarkable imagination for creative financiering. Now he rode around Chicago in his Rolls-Royce, and the *Tribune* credited him with donating $100 million to charities.

A series of meetings in Colonel Crown's office began on Tuesday, May 8. Brought into the negotiations were General Dynamic's chairman, David S. Lewis, and its executive vice-president for finance, Gorden E. MacDonald, as well as a battery of lawyers.

The upshot was that General Dynamics agreed to guarantee a short-term bank loan to FedEx of $23.7 million, but at a huge price.

Signed on May 12, 1973, the agreement provided that Federal Express would have to repay the loan—from Chase Manhattan Bank in New York—in just four months, on September 17, and deliver an option for Crown's group to acquire 80.1 percent of Federal Express stock for a total of $16 million.

Crown wanted his experts to go to Memphis and study the air express operation before deciding to exercise his option. If he chose not to take over FedEx, General Dynamics was to receive outright 6 percent of the stock for backing the Chase Manhattan loan.

Crown's lawyers found one cause for worry. Under federal

government regulations, any person or company owning control of an airline was subject to CAB approval (delineated in Section 408 of the CAB rules). As a manufacturer of aircraft, General Dynamics might find that undesirable. Crown scoffed at the lawyers. He pointed out that Section 408 would not even apply unless General Dynamics exercised the option to buy FedEx.

Fred Smith was surprised by the billionaire's outlook on legalities. "Colonel Crown's belief was that the laws of the United States are made for everyone else," Fred stated later. "So the Section 408 provision against his taking control of an air carrier was the least of his concerns. He felt that he could accomplish anything he damn well pleased in Washington, and so stated to me."

Under the loan agreement, Federal Express was restricted from modifying the new Falcons obtained from Pan American until permanent financing—not just this four-month stopgap—was arranged. This actually applied only to fourteen Falcons, since four had already been delivered and were being modified in Little Rock.

It was difficult for Smith to risk giving up control of his company to General Dynamics, but he felt he had no alternative. "There was nothing else I could do. We were in the soup." However, Smith believed he was only cleverly buying time; he did not believe Crown would exercise the option he had demanded granting rights to buy the majority of Federal Express's stock. Despite the billionaire's boast of having Washington clout, Section 408 would complicate his other holdings if he also controlled an air cargo business.

Fifteen aviation technicians from General Dynamics flew into Memphis on May 21 and spent a month analyzing all aspects of the Federal Express operation, especially the design of the bigger cargo door and what had been done to strengthen the Falcon landing gear to handle heavier payloads.

In the main, their findings were favorable. The 110-page report, completed July 12, asserted that FedEx operators took quick advantage of opportunities, moved alertly to fix problems, and had the prospect of showing a profit within a year.

David Lewis convened the General Dynamics board on July 19 and, with Smith present, recommended acquiring the 80.1 percent stake for $16 million. Several directors objected vigorously, describing FedEx as an unwholesome and risky enterprise. The bugaboo of Section 408 was also raised.

The board voted to let the option expire.

Brick Meers accepted the verdict philosophically, conceding that General Dynamics was already under financial restraints owing to a profit downturn and the expense of reopening its Quincy Shipyard in Massachusetts. Other negatives had surfaced. Crown had some holding in Trans World Airlines, and his son Lester was a TWA director as well as on the board of Continental Bank, a major aerospace financier; that might be a conflict of interest.

Smith came away from the boardroom discouraged, not that General Dynamics did not buy control of FedEx, but that the directors were not willing to support him adequately through his financial crisis. He was so rattled that his next immediate moves gave rise to one of the most celebrated legends about his struggles to succeed with Federal Express—the story of winning $27,000 in Las Vegas and using the money to meet the FedEx payroll.

"I was in Chicago when I was turned down for the umpteenth time from a source I was sure would come through," he recalled in an NBC interview. "I went to the airport to go back to Memphis, and saw on the TWA schedule a flight to Las Vegas. I won $27,000 starting with just a couple of hundred and sent it back to Memphis. The $27,000 wasn't decisive, but it was an omen that things would get better."

That's about as detailed as Fred Smith ever got about the episode. His colleagues generally confirm the tale, with slight variations.

J. Tucker Morse said: "We were sitting in the office on Friday afternoon and he called in and said, 'Well, I didn't get my deal worked out with Colonel Crown and General Dynamics. I'll see you all Monday, and maybe we will be in business or maybe we won't.'

"Apparently he left and went to Las Vegas. He did come back with the money and we did make the payroll. He said he won it playing blackjack. We didn't have many employees at the time. Most of our payroll was for pilots. I think $27,000 would have come close to it. The officers weren't paid much. I was making maybe a thousand a month."

Roger Frock's version: "The Las Vegas thing really happened. Yes indeed. At the close of business on Friday we were practically out of money. We had to pay for our fuel a week in advance. I think that ran about $28,000. I don't know if you realize how small we were at that time. Anyhow, Fred brought back the money and we got our fuel!"

The good omen that Fred Smith thought he detected at the Las Vegas blackjack table developed chiefly from the exhaustive General Dynamics study in Memphis. Meers could see that the survey report was powerful ammunition, added to the A. T. Kearney and AAPG feasibility studies, to shoot at prospective investors.

It was so persuasive, in fact, that Crown decided to extend General Dynamics's guarantee of the Chase Manhattan loan for a longer period to facilitate the search for venture capital. He was a great help, too, in getting Worthen Bank to ease its demands. Fred Smith had fallen badly behind, and the Little Rock bank was threatening to call his loan.

General Dynamics came up with $1.55 million, to apply to the note by buying one Falcon and then leasing it back to Federal Express. That gave Fred Smith a little breathing room on his Worthen debts.

Further, Crown realized that a $5 million investment would not subject him to Section 408, since that would not represent control, and he began talking favorably about chipping in that much on the still simmering White, Weld private offering.

Prudential Insurance, not known for plunging on risk ventures, talked about investing $5 million. Congressman Wilbur Mills is on record as interceding for Smith at Prudential and also with his longtime friend Colonel Crown.

These developments persuaded Meers to go back to Charles Lea with a new entreaty to get interested in FedEx.

And Charles Lea changed his mind.

"A lot of things happened," Lea recalled. "For the period April through July, we had some operational data to look at. Also the fact that General Dynamics had spent a lot of time and we had their material. That gave us a better feel for what the risks were, so we began to feel that this thing could really happen.

"We agreed to co-manage the private placement. White, Weld was an investment banking firm and had no interest other than being an agent and creating the transaction. Our interests were different. We were acting both as an agent, and more particularly from my point, we were looking for a good investment opportunity. We agreed that we would use our best efforts as an agent along with our capital interest to assemble this particular transaction."

From his New Court Securities portfolio, Lea considered investing a couple of million. His estimate was that the venture capital package would have to be in the neighborhood of $51 million.

Looking back from a vantage of twenty years, Roger Frock conceded that Fred Smith's own zeal and immaturity to a large degree trapped him in the financial morass:

> We really would have had no problem meeting our business plan, but we got screwed around by the people trying to raise the money. We didn't really know how difficult it was going to be. We had confidence in the product we had and the organization and the structure and the way we put it together. First of all it was so unique, there was such a demand for it, and we were so well structured to hit the marketplace that we could have just rolled on from day one without any problem.
>
> We thought the way the plan was laid out was to get the money before we started operations. But when we didn't, Fred made the decision that the only way we were going to get the money raised was to demonstrate to the financial market that this was in fact real, there was a need for it, there was a market for it, that we could provide it.
>
> When that decision was made, a lot of people who were going to put money in, who might have put it in on the front end in a straight venture, started sitting back, and saying, "Well, Smith is putting all his money in. Let's see how he does." And that really hurt us.

And that was probably a dumb thing in terms of the financial crunch it caused. Yet it may have been the only way it could have been done. I'm not sure of that, and in that case it may have been the problem that was due to the immaturity of Smith.

On that there wasn't a whole lot of discussion. Basically, it was Fred's money. At that time we were all in there because it was an action place and we were entrepreneurial people. We had at risk primarily our time and our careers, but certainly we were not laid out on the line the way Fred Smith was in terms of the dollars and everything.

So when he said we're going to go, that was the decision. And it was just done. His reason for doing it was because he became convinced that the only way we could get the money was if we could prove that it would happen. As a result, I think Fred really got taken to the cleaners by these venture capitalists.

In the late summer of 1973 the volume of packages traveling among cities in the bellies of the purple planes continued skimpy. A typical one-day count in August was 9 picked up in Denver and 115 in New York. The couriers got 91 in Chicago, 52 in Philadelphia, 19 in St. Louis, and 13 in Detroit.

Still, for the first time the FedEx people in Memphis saw signs of eventual victory when New Court Securities decided to team up with White, Weld.

Once converted, Lea became the longed-for saviour to FedEx.

"The first one I really believed," recalled Roger Frock, "and who put a realistic date on getting it done was Charley Lea. Fred and I flew to New York and had dinner with him at the New York Yacht Club. He seemed to be rational and to make sense.

"Charley made a very realistic assessment. At the end of our meeting, he said, 'It's going to take a long time. It's going to be very frustrating. But I'm going to tell you, it will get done!' And I think he's the one who ultimately made it happen."

In astounding contrast with today's sophisticated, computerized, sleek, and slick Federal Express operations, ground couriers in the beginning months were haphazard. As Mike Fitzgerald, the former UPS veteran, recalls: "The first office we had in Milwaukee was the doorway of a freight forwarder—it was a doorway! We would go there at three in the morning with two Hertz rental cars from a nearby Holiday Inn, meet the airplane, and get the inbound packages.

"In New York, we sorted in the street—Thirty-seventh Street. It was a storefront which we shared with a local carrier and another kind of forward broker character for the garment district.

"When it rained, we moved half a block down and sorted under a bridge. That was New York City—Thirty-seventh and around Second Avenue."

Fred Smith's leadership fired up the troops in the field. He sincerely believed his company would be America's next Xerox success. "The level of loyalty and participation was terrific," said Fitzgerald. "It was exhilarating to go around and talk to these people, and be there with them. Most of them had no patience with people who were dragging their can. They turned on them quicker than we ever would have.

"There was a great sense of David and Goliath kind of stuff. We were taking on the likes of Emery Air Freight, and being publicly laughed at by a lot of people. A fly-by-night outfit—that kind of thing. The more that happened, the firmer the resolve was."

One thing Federal Express needed was a tough, talented bookkeeper. Collections from the customers the cargo line had were running a couple of months behind—simply because the bills were not sent out promptly. In consequence creditors were threatening to sue; in fact, some did. Even the state of Arkansas wanted back taxes, and Adams Field was demanding rent on the LRA hangar.

Charles Lea and Brick Meers were touting the FedEx investment opportunity coast to coast, trying to raise new capital. At the same time, those with money sunk into the company—mainly banks—were furiously demanding theirs back.

Fred Smith & Company was in default, or right on the edge of it, on practically everything they had borrowed—even the $1 million working capital from General Dynamics. Worthen Bank in Little Rock was on the hook for more than $8 million. They got tough. Irby Tedder was fearful the bank would try to seize the mortgaged planes. Worthen had a young officer, Pete Maris, keeping track of the situation. "Every time he showed up at the airport," Tedder said, "we would radio the Falcons not to land. It was all very touchy."

In Detroit the airport parked a fire truck in front of the Federal Express Falcon so it couldn't take off without paying an overdue bill for fuel and landing fees. "We went on by the skin of our teeth for a long time," Tedder recalled. "I tried to keep all these creditors happy—especially fuel companies. We were burning fuel and not paying for it. I had it set up so that when they just had to have some money, they'd let me know, and I'd usually manage."

Former executives from those dark days assert even now that Federal Express never missed a payroll. If they didn't, they came within an eyelash. On September 14, 1973, employees got a memo from Fred Smith and Roger Frock asking them not to cash their paychecks before September 17 at the earliest. Some officers recall they just dropped their paychecks in a desk drawer and left them there for weeks.

Mike Fitzgerald recalled a dramatic—and dangerous—episode when a frustrated courier in Kansas City, who was owed $300 for expenses, pulled a gun and took the station manager hostage. Then he telephoned Fitzgerald and said: "If I don't get my money right now, I'm going to blow this sucker's head off, and shit in the hole!" Fitzgerald got the money there fast.

A large crisis occurred in October 1973 just at the time Lea and Meers had assembled a consortium of twenty-three investors, among them Allstate Insurance, the First National Bank of Chicago, and Chase Manhattan, making up a pool of $23 million.

No sooner had it formed than it threatened to fall apart. Chase Manhattan got nervous. It wanted to back out of the $23.7 million loan it had made on the eighteen Falcons unless General Dynamics continued to guarantee it. Chairman David Lewis of General Dynamics was leery and undecided.

Meers and Lea were continually on the phone among New York, Chicago, Memphis, and General Dynamics headquarters in St. Louis. They were stunned on October 19 when the Arab nations declared an oil embargo to force an American policy change on selling arms to Israel, knowing the negative effect that it would have on Wall Street, on investors in general, and on their consortium in particular.

Thus in the last week of October the Federal Express bailout came to a dead halt.

Fred Smith was frantic—and furious. In the FedEx headquarters everybody felt the investors were a greedy lot—"jackals of Wall Street" was the most used term. These "jackals" all wanted to grab a piece of Fred Smith's skin and then disappear. All the struggle, all the fighting, was left up to him.

Even General Dynamics must share blame for the events that had boxed him in, Smith said in a letter he dispatched October 26 to David Lewis in St. Louis. Yet he begged for help. On Lewis's decision about granting the Chase Manhattan guarantee rested the continued existence of Federal Express. If the General Dynamics chairman declined, Federal Express would not be able to open the doors Monday morning.

The air of disaster was so heavy that some of the "band of brothers" in Memphis organized an impromptu farewell party at the hub. Said Mike Fitzgerald: "We had a hell of a party. We thought it was over—we weren't going to open on Monday. The management guys all pitched in our money, what little we had left. On the inbound flights we brought lobster and clams from New England. We had some Coors beer flown in from Denver. We brought in sourdough bread. We had shrimp. . . . Oh, we put together a party that was pretty much good-bye."

But it was premature. Brick Meers, by no means Smith's favorite companion, made a last-ditch call to A. Robert Abboud, vice-chairman of the First National Bank in Chicago, who already knew the "horrible" plight of Federal Express.

"How much do you want?" asked Abboud.

"Ten million."

Abboud groaned.

Meers responded that he believed Chase Manhattan would be willing to match the $10 million and thus rescue the collapsing investor deal. Reluctantly Abboud said yes.

But Chase Manhattan demanded more money from Fred Smith or his family trust—another four million.

Already Fred Smith had $2.5 million invested personally, and the Enterprise Company had committed assets of $5.4 million. How much more could he ask of the family trust?

His sister Fredette Eagle was already upset and felt in the dark about the financiering, which admittedly was hard to understand for a layman. Would she still go along? What if she balked? If it ever came out that Smith had created fictitious minutes of an Enterprise Company board meeting to get the $2 million loan at Union National Bank in Little Rock, there would be hell to pay. He knew that.

But he had to call another meeting of the company board to work out a deal for the family trust to invest another $4 million in Federal Express.

He faced Fredette Eagle and the other directors on November 6 and made his plea in an atmosphere that was already tense because the circumstances had been revealed of his $1 million loan from Memphis's First National Bank (though not yet those of the Little Rock loan).

"We had a tiger by the tail," recalled William Richmond, the National Bank of Commerce trust officer and an Enterprise Company director. "We could not let go."

The board of directors went along, investing $1.5 million more outright and lending $2.5 million secured by a second mortgage on the ten Falcons already obligated to back the loan from CCEC.

Smith was wilted but relieved. Now he could go to New York and return to Memphis with long-term financing that would relieve the pressure and give his company time to develop.

Executing the credit agreement documents in New York on Tuesday, November 13, was an intricate process that took six hours.

In Memphis there was a period of euphoria, and then everybody started hustling again. Smith got up a long list of names and wrote bonus checks for all employees, ranging from $15 to $100—just in time for Christmas.

▶ ▶ ▶

Federal Express business just dragged along. The nightly "lift" was not keeping pace with projections for growth. The red ink was flowing again. Income still wasn't adequate to cover expenses. The purple airplanes had racked up revenue of $10 million, but the operating loss was at least $5 million.

In Memphis Fred Smith & Company was again shifting the blame to the investor group. Funds from the credit agreement were parceled out to FedEx "about like Mama giving a kid his Sunday school offering," grumbled one executive.

Sharp-eyed money men in the investor group had positioned themselves on the Federal Express board. They had influence. Action was demanded.

The venture capitalists and bank officers descended on Memphis on February 12, 1974, burrowed into the files, and emerged with another ultimatum. Unless investors could be found to put in another $6.4 million and banks were willing to lend $5.1 million more, the purple airplanes were doomed.

The early rapport between Federal Express and General Dynamics had essentially evaporated. Gorden MacDonald, executive vice-president of finance for Colonel Crown's company, was disturbed by some of Fred Smith's "wild, off-the-wall ideas" and worried about the air cargo line's future.

Chiefly for that reason, General Dynamics decided to forgo any further participation. This was a stunning setback in view of the fact that the rapidly approaching second round of financing was to take place on March 19.

But a greater surprise, and a personal catastrophe for Fred Smith, exploded on March 6 when Little Rock's Union National Bank called on Memphis's National Bank of Commerce for the three hundred Enterprise Company shares he had pledged for his $2 million loan a year ago, now in default.

For the first time, the Memphis bankers learned of the loan. And both banks discovered, to the dismay of all, that it was predicated on forged documents.

13 ▶ *WHEN SOUL-MATES SPLIT*

On March 12, 1974, two dozen grim men in business suits flew to Chicago and gathered in the Icarus Room of the O'Hare Hilton. They represented Federal Express Corporation's worried and unhappy investors and lenders.

It was one day after Fred Smith had gone before his own Enterprise Company board in Memphis and admitted his Little Rock bank forgery. But, curiously, that deed was not the episode that triggered the Icarus Room session; in fact, these money men seemed largely to shrug off that embarrassment.

Their concern was not morals, but dollars. They were displeased with having to come up a week hence with a second injection of money—$11.5 million—into the lame and struggling air cargo line. They feared that all they had poured into FedEx was "going south very rapidly, and the reason for that was management inexperience."

Smith, still six months shy of thirty, and beleagured on all sides, must be stripped of control and replaced, they felt. They wanted an older, experienced executive, one who had actually run an airline. Additionally, FedEx urgently needed a tough finance officer to straighten out the slapdash counting room in Memphis.

Charles Lea of New Court Securities, the leader of the dominant investors, did not exclusively fault Fred Smith and his managers. "There were a lot of external problems, too," Lea recalled. "The fuel situation [Arab oil embargo] was dreadful. There was also the fact that we had a lot of these new Falcons sitting over in Arkansas as what we called green machines—that is to say, they hadn't been outfitted as delivery wagons—and the reason for that was the banks slowed down their delivery of funds under their commitment.

"The whole thing was grinding to a general halt, and Fred had himself pretty well ground into the woodwork. We needed a front man, somebody who would be a barrier for these guys to operate behind rather than trying to do it all themselves.

"Raising capital is extremely time-consuming for the management of any company. You have to see countless people and go through those dog and pony shows, as we call 'em, just to get your message across. You have to answer every inane question known to man before people will really come down to consideration of whether they will invest in the company or not."

Lea does not remember knowing then of the bank forgery, but if he did, "I didn't pay a heck of a lot of attention to it. For what they might haul you away in a police wagon in New York, well, in Little Rock I have a feeling that country cousins are a lot more loosey goosey in terms of signatures and so on. Fred may not have crossed all the T's and dotted the I's, but he wasn't stealing."

While investors may have winked at the Union National Bank mischief, it was an embarrassment that depressed Smith and had become an unaccustomed personal albatross that drove him to the brash visit to Herbert Hall McAdams on May 15, not quite two months after his Icarus Room showdown.

Although Fred Smith told McAdams that he contemplated suicide, he obviously did nothing of the sort. In fact, the next day he wrote the Union National chairman a nice letter thanking him for trying to lift his spirits and specifically for suggesting he read the Bible verse Mark 9:23.

While no other person has gone on record to confirm that Fred Smith talked of ending his life at any time for any reason, five or six of his closest associates said in interviews for this book that in this period he was at the lowest point they ever saw him.

Fred Smith himself said, "No man on earth will ever know what I went through [in 1973–1974]."

The Union National incident fell into "the background noise" for

Lea. "We had so many problems to deal with. It was just one of them. They seemed to come at us like a waterfall."

With his sidekick Brick Meers of White, Weld, Lea recruited thirty-seven-year-old Peter S. Willmott, a highly regarded MBA from Harvard, who had been a corporate finance officer for fourteen years, most recently at Continental Baking Company.

Sent to Memphis as executive vice-president of finance and administration, Willmott, according to Fred Smith's pals, "thought he had fallen in among happy-go-lucky Martians" but quickly sorted out and made sense of the money end of Federal Express.

How helpful was the sober-minded Willmott? "Very," said Charles Lea. "He was the smartest thing I ever did at Federal Express. He got down there and didn't believe any of the figures these operating guys gave him. He recast the finances so that month-to-month operating statements began to make sense and we could see where we were and what we had to do."

To raise prices was his first recommendation. Fred Smith and his colleagues had been afraid doing so would scare off customers. Willmott argued successfully that air express was a premium service worth higher rates. Willmott was then able to predict with certainty just how many months it would take for Federal Express to become "cash positive"—in other words, profitable.

By the Icarus Room meeting, Smith had lost his position as chairman and CEO of his company, but he was left in office as president under a two-year contract. With the help of corporate "headhunters," Lea and Meers came up with the new FedEx boss, retired air force general Howell M. Estes, Jr., fifty-nine, president of a commercial charter airline called World Airways based in Oakland, California. His annual salary was $75,000, Smith's $40,000.

The career of General "Howling" Estes was meteoric in the military—he had been the air force's youngest four-star general—but his command of the lively and somewhat wayward FedEx troops in Memphis was to be highly contentious.

Two weeks after Estes's arrival in Memphis, the June 15 issue of *Business Week* skewered his new charge with a full-page article headlined: FEDERAL EXPRESS TAKES A NOSEDIVE. The subhead read

"Costs have outpaced revenues, and the company is fighting for survival." An unnamed investor was quoted on why Smith had to be replaced: "They had a group of marketing people who assembled and sold a good marketing concept, but there is not one in Memphis who really knows anything about running an airline." The article continued:

> Officials at Federal Express concede as much. Arthur Bass, senior vice-president, says: "Smith just could not play the investor game and run the airline at the same time. It was something we began to recognize and finally had to move on."

One venture capitalist was quoted in *Business Week* as saying that Federal Express really needed "some nuts-and-bolts guy to run the show."

FedEx didn't get that kind of boss. The executives in Memphis were startled, and gradually more and more amused, to discover that they now reported not to a first-name early and late hard driver, but to a "clean desk" military type as interested in personal perks as in performance of the company.

General Estes was furious over the "nosedive" article and excoriated the magazine—to no avail. Smith, exhausted and depressed, went on vacation to South America to get his second wind.

How Memphis headquarters responded to the general's arrival is recalled by J. Tucker Morse:

> When Estes was brought in, Fred was fairly mature about it. He understood. We weren't making money, and we had a lot of people's money in it, and they were concerned, particularly about all of us being so young. They just didn't think we had the maturity to run a corporation.
>
> Fred accepted the general, but just kept doing exactly what he was always doing, and that was running the company. And we all knew who the boss was, notwithstanding the title that Estes had, so we just kept doing what Fred wanted us to do. The program was not changed very much at all.

And frankly, Estes was used to being pampered. He had not lived in the real world. He had been in the upper echelons of the air force, and everybody was kissing his ass all the time. We weren't about to do that.

One of the things I had to do for General Estes was get his car license tags transferred from California to Tennessee. That was a very important deal for him.

Here we were going broke, and I had a number of very important projects to accomplish, and he was always trying to get me to do some ridiculous deal like that. Despite that kind of stuff, we had a good time with it.

Roger Frock recalled that Estes was hired while Fred Smith was away for the weekend. "They said it was with Fred's approval," Frock said. "But Fred was really rip-shit about it. Fred said, 'I knew we needed one, but I hadn't given my approval yet.' So that didn't start out too well. Fred said it was like General Eisenhower trying to run Ho Chi Minh's guerrillas. We were Ho Chi Minhs's guerrillas. We were an undisciplined lot. We knew what we were doing, and we related very well to one another. But there was so much to be done that to anyone from the outside it looked like utter confusion, utter chaos.

"I will never forget the first official act I saw out of the general. He grabbed Smith's secretary at a time when every minute counted, and had her spend a day and a half trying to get a refund on the license plate that he had brought from California because he had only used it about seven months."

Then Estes told Frock to put up signs giving the CEO and other officers private parking places.

"General, we are just not accustomed to doing that around here," Frock said.

"Well, we're going to do it."

"If you want a parking place," Frock responded, "we'll put up a sign for you. You gotta understand something—Fred Smith doesn't want a private parking place. And I don't. And the rest of the people in the company work for me, and they're not going to have signs."

Estes's reaction? "He got his sign and went on to something else. I don't believe he understood the business. There's a difference between having a position [president of World Airways] and running something. He had one of our accountants do a profit and loss on the cities that were at the end of Federal Express at that time. He made a big presentation to us and said we're not profitable because we're serving these cities—San Francisco, Los Angeles, Dallas, Atlanta, Chicago, New York, and Boston. He said, 'I want that service stopped.'

"You do that, quit flying there, and eventually you have a phone system that is connected to one other person, and it's not very profitable. We knew that, so we ignored him. We didn't do it."

Another proposal Estes presented in a staff meeting was to emphasize service to small cities. Present was Vince Fagan, another of the AAPG partners who had made the initial FedEx market study. Through his incessant cigar smoke, Fagan had habitually bantered in heavy give-and-take with Smith.

"For example," Estes said, "we should not be trying to serve New York City. There is too much competition."

Fagan, spewing smoke, grunted wryly: "I'll bet your relatives were the ones digging for gold in New York State in 1849—because there was no competition there."

The man who hired Estes, New Court Securities's Lea, had mixed feelings about the general's performance as FedEx boss:

> Fred Smith was a good soldier for quite a period of time. He put up with the general, who was a store-front dummy, in my opinion. We used him successfully. He got us through at least a very important financing. But after a while he got to be terribly out of the culture.
>
> The general insisted on his perks, and his limo, and his expensive hotel rooms, and so on and so forth, while all the rest of us were living in eighteen-dollar-a-day hotel rooms. So it really began to be an issue, not only with Fred, but with everybody else.
>
> Oh, Estes did a lot for us, when we had to do another financing. We'd take the general, who looked like Daddy

Warbucks, and he was credible. Here was Fred. He'd gotten a little run-down, and his ability to forecast the future was very sullied at that time. I couldn't have taken Fred back to these investors and had 'em put up a nickel.

You know, an investment is an act of faith, and you can do all the homework you want to, but in the last analysis it comes down to whether you believe the guy who's going to execute the plan. And Fred was not very believable in those days. So we needed somebody who was, like the general, and he served a very useful purpose.

Estes, however, was not useful in the FedEx courtship of Colonel Crown. When the general and Peter Willmott went to see him in mid-July 1974, Crown was pleasant but adamant that he no longer would carry a big debt for the cargo airline. He gave them a token $300,000.

The general also went out as a salesman to drum up business, calling on big corporations—Lockheed, Rockwell, Raytheon, McDonnell Douglas, and others. "The tour was fine," recalled Mike Fitzgerald, "but we didn't get any business, not measurably. I think it was an ill-planned strategy because some order coming down to the shipping department from the CEO to give the business to FedEx tends to get people a little aggravated . . . telling them what to do.

"So it was not the best plan. And the same result would occur today. That was no fault of Howell's or anybody else. Just wrong strategy. The kind that ignores that fact that the guy in the trenches hears what is going on."

The general also attempted to defuse a unionism threat. Mike Fitzgerald went with Estes to California to talk to the airline division of the Teamsters Union. "Our mission was to explain to them the futility of trying to organize FedEx at that point in their growth," Fitzgerald said. "That wasn't anything the company was prepared to cope with. We had all hands busy trying to hold our hat and ass together.

"Further, we were not going to just lay back and let the company be organized, and we felt . . . we did not need anybody else to help us run this company . . . because there was too much invested in sweat and belief and caring for the employees and the future of the company to do it any other way.

"Again, this group that Fred had around him believed in this very, very much. It wasn't like Fred said 'Okay, now listen, you guys. This is the philosophy of the company. You will believe this, and go forth!' Those guys were just too tough for that kind of stuff to be pulled on them.

"When you talk about a Vince Fagan—he was not a guy you sat down on a chair and told him what was his belief and his philosophy and his way of life. I certainly wasn't going to do it. Not at that stage of my life. But we did believe there was a way for that company to do something with people that had been talked about or alluded to, and had never been done before, and the belief then, too, was we had a hell of a row to hoe and a hell of a battle to fight, and we could do it with the people, those in the trenches with us. This sounds all trite and cliché ridden, but it was true."

Fitzgerald was constantly in the midst of pilots, couriers, and pickup and delivery men and women. "There were some intelligent guys in the streets driving the trucks and sorting the packages," Fitzgerald said. "The level of loyalty and participation was terrific. Guys were signing their time cards hours before they really finished work. Guys were driving routes with their wives on the weekend to teach them. And pilots were loading and unloading planes with the cargo handlers. That kind of stuff was unbelievable.

"I've thought about this a number of times. The group that Fred had around him in the beginning, I would defy any skilled management recruiters or headhunters to go out and duplicate. It was a unique group in the sense that each had a very strong personality, and there wasn't a quiet one among us unless it would be Roger Frock, and Roger was as determined as any in the crowd.

"There was a great deal of shouting and yelling at meetings and so forth, but the heat dissipated right away. We all remained extremely good friends, to this day. And Fred used the skills of the people there in a good way. He was a great guy to work for."

J. Tucker Morse recalled that "the fun people" and their humor were "one of the best things about Federal Express" and played a role in the success of the venture:

The level of humor was wonderful. We were laughing and having a good time, and I think it really helped to break the emotional stress and keep people going.

The funniest? Oh, Tucker Taylor was just a world-class character. Mike Fitzgerald was hilarious, Art Bass was funny. Even Pete Willmott got with the program. He came in like a stuffy Booz Hamilton type, and by the end he was just loads of fun.

We'd go out and go drinking and tell jokes and have a good time and come in to a meeting. It really shocked some of the suppliers coming in. Somebody would make a comment and we'd all start laughing. I think it helped us in negotiating—making the atmosphere a little bit looser. I remember the French being fairly stuffy.

Tucker Taylor hasn't changed a bit. He's irreverent as hell. Just wonderful. He's got a great background; his father was bishop of Baltimore, and his stepmother was president of Sweet Briar College.

Vince Fagan was a really fine advertising and marketing guy. He would really talk to Smith. They would argue endlessly. We would just sit there spellbound, wondering how this was going to come out. I think Fred had great respect for Vince's strategies and programs and intelligence. It was fun. There was a lot of discussion on any number of subjects. Fred would bring things up and have thought it through and have his own ideas before he threw it out on the table.

Did he want a rubber stamp? No, he wanted a real discussion. There were people there who would speak their minds. You may have heard the Mike Fitzgerald comment. Smith was in there telling one of the senior officers how something was going to be done and there was an incredible challenge to the guy to get it done. It was a very serious and very tense meeting.

Fitzgerald leaned over to the guy and said, "Listen, if Fred Smith tells you that a chicken can pull a freight train, buddy, your job is to hook it up!" That really captures the comments that were made in our meetings.

▶ ▶ ▶

In the late summer of 1974 Federal Express was again suffering financially. Peter Willmott, now guardian of the Memphis counting room, had come up with some dire, but interesting figures.

If an additional $9 million could be raised, it would get FedEx over the hump—and on a paying basis.

To Charles Lea, this third round of financing was a tough sell. If the original investors were unable to meet the call for more money, their shares of the business would be savagely diluted, in favor of those who could ante up again.

Fred Smith would take a battering. He and his family at the outset owned the controlling stock. But the effect of a third round would be to cut his holdings to just 8.5 percent and the family trust, the Enterprise Company, to a miserable 0.4 percent.

With Charles Lea masterminding the maneuvers, his New Court Securities stood to end up with 16 percent of FedEx. Prudential Insurance would own 10.7 percent. But in September success was not certain.

"It was just excruciatingly hard," Lea said. "This was the end of the road. I had begun discussions with people about bankruptcy, because that was going to be our next step if we couldn't get this thing tacked together.

"Stock for ninety percent of the business was available for just a relatively modest amount of capital. Fred was being wiped out. He was taking his medicine, but he wasn't happy. He had put his personal worth in this thing, and the Enterprise Company in, too. His claim was that they had nine million bucks going down the drain. But there wasn't a hell of a lot we could do about it."

In the crisis, Art Bass went to France and made an appeal directly to Baron Rothschild, who had decided to pass after twice putting funds into the company. Lea knew the Rothschilds felt it would just be throwing good money after bad. But Bass, a lifelong flying enthusiast, was going to the Paris Air Show. Lea told him to try to change the baron's mind.

In a scene reminiscent of Hollywood, Bass lunched with the gray-haired baron, his articulate, curly-haired son, and a nephew "who looked like Louis Jourdan" and spent an hour with them in their elegant Paris offices.

"I went through why it was going to succeed," Bass said. "When it was going to happen. Why it was going to happen. I literally educated them. We knew it was not simply adding and hoping. We had created an air express buying power index. Like shoving an ice pick into a high-pressure hose, because we weren't just getting the destination. We were getting N times N minus one. All the different numbers became multiples.

"We knew that given enough time, given a system in place, it would produce a hell of a lot of business because again there was a latent market that was never understood. It was very difficult to explain at the time. But at the end of the day the baron said to his son and nephew, 'The only way the bank will put in money is if you guys put your personal money in it.' Which they did."

Finally the impending collapse of the purple airplane cargo line was averted. Explained Lea: "The way we got the nine million dollars, I guess we ended up with three million in equity, and made the banks defer interest and principal payments for the balance. And then we got there. I'll tell you the margin was small!"

Watching all this from the inside, J. Tucker Morse started out in awe of the investors and soon grew to look on them as "just lemmings." "I don't want to be too mean about this," Morse said, "but this was the birth of the venture capital business. 'I don't want Joe to have the deal if I'm not in the deal.' It was talk like that back and forth. 'If you do it, I'll do it, and I don't want you to do it unless I do it, because you might do better than I did.' It was really hilarious toward the end, because we had three quick financings. New Court stayed with it and ended up making a bunch of money out of it."

The close relationship between Fredette and Fred went through months of disappointment and distrust, recrimination and denunciation, and finally reached the battling lawyers stage.

In November 1974 the love between them shattered abruptly and totally. Fredette sued him. To Fred, that was treacherous and unpardonable.

By "illegal and irresponsible" investments in Federal Express, Fredette Eagle charged in a suit in Memphis Chancery Court, the $17 million family trust had been reduced to about $2.5 million. She had recruited sister Laura Ann Patterson as an ally and also sued in behalf of their children. The National Bank of Commerce and the trust officers were included with Smith as defendants.

The lawsuit hit the newspapers at a very damaging time for FedEx, which was still fighting for its life and not in need of headlines tagging its creator with fraud.

But Fredette was desperate. Earlier she had hired an aggressive lawyer in Virginia and begun taking him with her to sit on meetings of the Enterprise Company board. Ironically, on these trips to Memphis she usually stayed in her brother's guest house behind his big Tudor residence on Morningside Park.

"Our board meetings were getting totally out of hand," Fredette recalled. "I could see . . . I felt I was going under.

"My attorney was telling Fred my situation and what he had done to me. Fred made a remark that was just so funny; he said, 'I may have been a little cavalier with her.' It was one of those boyishly extravagant remarks that was so totally out of place. He just cut the legs out from under me."

No longer receiving dividends from the dwindling assets of the Enterprise Company, Fredette Eagle, accustomed to an income of $110,00 a year, was in a pinch.

"It was pretty terrible," she said. "I got a job, and sold a lot of stuff, some cars, and a lot of furniture, some paintings. I fired my maid, put my kids in public school, started selling real estate, and took in a boarder. And after two years it began to get a little better.

"I'm sorry I ruined whatever ties Fred and I had, and I will always regret that. But I don't think I had any choice. I think the bankers would have been totally in control of everything I owned. I think I would never have gotten it back. I was having to beg them for income. They wouldn't return my calls or tell me what income they were going to pay or when they would pay it. It was 'Don't worry, little lady' and 'Don't bother us, little lady.' They were very patronizing and sometimes rude. They knew they were in on a lot of hanky-panky and could very well get exposed."

The Enterprise Company stock, Fredette felt, was being used to collateralize loans that gave a disproportionate share of Federal Express stock to Fred Smith personally. "As naive as I was, I could see hanky-panky going on. It turned out that his personal lawyer and the FedEx lawyer was the same lawyer who represented Enterprise Company. It became patent after a while that this was working only to Fred's benefit.

"I'd be a fool if I didn't bring my lawyer to keep track of what was happening. The very thought that I insisted on my own lawyer was considered very disloyal. If I had let them go on with what they were doing . . . they would control my affairs. I couldn't get through to them on the phone. Their secretaries wouldn't talk to me. I was just dismissed as a childish gadfly with no rights whatsoever.

"Laura Ann agreed to pay half my lawyer's salary. She was not tracking too much on this. But she had good sense, when she was tracking."

By the end of 1974 the sisters' lawyer was trying to get the United States district attorney in Little Rock, W. H. "Sonny" Dillahunty, to indict Fred Smith for bank fraud. Union National Bank likewise was eager for criminal action in the case, Dillahunty recalled.

Dillahunty said in a 1991 interview: "The bank first presented this matter to one of my assistants, and my assistant took the position that it was something that was purely civil in nature. . . . The bank's attorney, Griffin Smith, called and asked me would I listen to them, realizing, of course, that my normal position was not to overrule one of my assistants.

"And I said only if my assistant sat in, and we listened to them. When they got through, I looked over at my assistant and said, 'Bob, it's a clear case of fraud.' And we went to the grand jury with it."

▶ ▶ ▶

When the FBI began investigating, J. Tucker Morse interceded with the U.S. Attorney. "I knew Sonny well, having worked with him when I was in federal court," Morse recalled. "I went to see Sonny, and I said, 'Look, when you get into this thing . . .' I was working for Fred at the time, and there was no question where my loyalties were. I said, 'I think it is ridiculous for you to present this to the grand jury and prosecute the case. I think you are going to lose because while the facts might appear intriguing to you, the intent to commit fraud wasn't there. And other members of the family have done exactly the same thing.' He was somewhat of a zealot. He said, 'Here's a great white-collar criminal, and I can make hay prosecuting.' Sonny was a pretty eager beaver at the time, and I just don't think he used good judgment in jumping on this."

Dillahunty, no longer United States attorney, recalled: "Tucker came to me and said, 'Please, don't indict Fred!' He had tears in his eyes."

Among several witnesses called to testify before the grand jury was Smith's secretary, Charlotte Curtis.

"The people in the grand jury room must have thought I was wacky," she recalled. "I had never before been called by a grand jury. It very strange. I couldn't tell how this was going to go, or what to do.

"This would sound funny to men, maybe, but females remember these things. District Attorney Dillahunty said, 'Take your oath.' There I was, standing with my little purse in my left hand. He gave me a look and said: 'Miss, you can put your bag down.'

"I took the oath. Then he showed me some documents—two, as I recall. And he said, 'Can you tell me the difference in these two signatures?' So I said—and this seemed to strike him as funny, 'Well, one looks darker than the other one.'

"And he said, 'Can that not be attributed to the copy machine?' But did I type the document; I can't remember. I think that's where Sonny was going. I've looked back over it in my mind, and I think they were trying to figure out if I forged the signature. And I don't think I did. That was a long, long time ago."

The final rupture between brother and sister took place in the anteroom outside the Little Rock grand jury chamber.

"They were interrogating the witnesses about what Fred had done," Fredette recalled. "Fred was there and he came over to where I was seated. He was furious. He said, 'I want to talk to you! You know what you have done?' And I said, 'You gave me no choice. You betrayed me! I have no place to turn. This is all I can do!'

"And he seemed to think he would have gotten away with it if I hadn't . . . if my attorneys hadn't exposed him. And he might have. His feeling was that everything would have been papered over, and everybody would have gone off happy, if I had just not done this.

"That was the last time I saw Fred," she said in 1992. "And he never spoke to me again."

(In the late 1980s Fredette appealed to Lucius Burch to arrange for her to lunch with her brother, in hopes of a reconciliation. "Lucius got back to me after talking to Fred," she recalled, "and said, 'Now is not the right time.' ")

On January 21, 1975, Smith advised the FedEx board that he was being investigated by the federal grand jury in Little Rock.

Ten days later the indictment was returned, and the U.S. marshal began drawing up a warrant to arrest him. If convicted of using a forged document to obtain the $2 million bank loan, he could be sent to prison.

Another blow came shortly before midnight on January 31—the same day he was indicted—while Fred Smith was driving home north on Airways Boulevard from his office at the airport in his leased 1972 blue Ford LTD.

Near the intersection of Airways and Park Street, George Clifton Sturghill, a fifty-four-year-old black handyman, emerged from a nearby bar and began walking across the boulevard against the traffic light toward the east side.

By coincidence E. L. Milner, a veteran Memphis policeman on his way to work, was driving his personal car directly behind Smith's auto. What happened is recorded in his arrest report:

On Friday 1/31/75 at approximately 2335 hours officer Milner observed the defendant northbound on Airways at Park Avenue. The defendant had the green light, but a pedestrian was crossing against the light and the defendant struck the pedestrian with the right front of the above described vehicle, knocking the victim to the pavement.

After striking the man, the defendant slowed down, as if to stop, then sped off northbound on Airways. Officer Milner gave chase in his personal vehicle and was able to get the defendant pulled over at Airways and Spottswood, where the defendant was arrested for leaving the scene and returned to the scene.

The victim was transported to JGH and listed in critical condition at approximately 0045 hours on Feb. 1, 1975. Car 714 handled the accident investigation and advised to place a hold on the defendant for the Hit and Run Bureau in addition to the charges [driving with an expired Arkansas drivers license] placed by the arresting officer.

Defendant was then transported to Headquarters and allowed to use the telephone. His vehicle was driven to the city lot by Mark 20 on the 4 to 12 shift.

Sturghill died in the emergency room. Neither his demise nor Fred Smith's arrest for leaving the scene of an accident caused much of a stir in Memphis; it was not reported in the newspapers until four days later, and then as two paragraphs tacked like a casual afterthought on the end of the story of the bank fraud indictment. Even Sturghill's family in Olive Branch, Mississippi, where he was buried, accepted his fate philosophically. His stepmother and two other relatives interviewed in 1991 for this book did not know that he was killed by an automobile or that Fred Smith was the driver.

Ironically, the Friday night hit-run did not become known at Federal Express until around noon on Saturday. Top executives came in that morning for the customary weekly give-and-take session with the boss. "Fred was notorious for showing up late," recalled Roger Frock. "We would always take bets on when he would show up for the eight o'clock meeting. And that particular morning we were all frosted about it because Bobby Cox bet that he wouldn't show until twelve-thirty.

"We all laughed and said, 'He's not going to be that late.' But Bobby Cox knew that he was in jail and wouldn't get out until noon. So he won the bet!

"Fred told us what happened. He said that he was passing a rowdy Negro bar where there was a lot of noise. He thought somebody had come out of the bar and slapped his hand against his car. He didn't see anything and went on, not realizing he had knocked a man down. And a police officer who was on his way to work saw him and stopped him down the street. And that was very fortunate in one way that the officer saw exactly what happened. Otherwise maybe his story would not have been believed.

"That was probably the lowest point at which I ever saw Fred."

Smith was released from jail on $250 bond, and his case was set for trial on February 3 in division 5, city court, before Judge S. A. Wilburn. Defense attorneys are loath to rush to trial on such "hot potato" cases, however, and the hit-run charge was postponed six times and would not reach a conclusion for more than a year.

Meanwhile Fred Smith, battling to preserve his image against the bank fraud indictment, issued a statement to the press:

The original money to fund Federal Express came from myself and my family's holding company. To do this I scraped up and borrowed every nickel I could. In February 1973 while attempting to raise the money from our current institutional investors and our banks, Federal Express needed additional money to survive.

Accordingly I borrowed a large sum of money from a Little Rock bank using a buy-back agreement of my stock in the family company.

Since making Federal Express into a large and profitable company was initially hindered by high interest rates, the oil crisis, and the country's worst financial downturn in decades, my two half sisters, who strongly supported Federal Express in the beginning, instigated a very complicated lawsuit.

Largely as a result of this suit, and efforts of my sisters and their eastern attorneys to influence this pending civil litigation involving the family holding company, the U.S. grand jury in Little Rock today returned an indictment alleging that I improperly prepared the documents involving the family company to secure the loan from the Little Rock bank.

It is my opinion that the actions of my sisters were designed to discredit both myself and Federal Express in hopes of influencing the civil action.

Although it would be improper for me to further comment on the merits of this case while it is before the court, I know my intentions were absolutely correct and am confident that this complicated matter will be decided favorably.

14 ▶ WE, THE JURY, FIND . . .

Smith took the self-service elevator to the third floor of the old Tennessee Club, overlooking Court Square in Memphis. It was once the elite Memphis men's hangout where in the late thirties his own father and uncle had been members; now the building housed the law firm of Lucius E. Burch, Jr.

Smith had come to retain the lawyer who, though as southern as cornbread, took on—for no money—the defense of Martin Luther King in the Memphis sanitation workers' strike in 1968 and lifted an injunction barring his march a few hours before the civil rights leader was assassinated.

"I never cared about a harp or a halo—I haven't got any more religion than a polecat—but I would miss being a participant in what's going to happen," Burch told the *Memphis Commercial Appeal,* which added:

> Like the famous novelist Ernest Hemingway, whom he knew, first meeting him in Spain in 1928, Burch has spent a good part of his life boxing, fishing, shooting, hunting, globe-trotting, backpacking, horse-packing, mountain-climbing, and narrowly escaping from plights that would have done in lesser men. A highly physical outdoorsman, he can still walk all day, ride 30 or 40 miles in the saddle, fly a plane, and train a bird dog.
>
> "I am one of the last mastodons in the sense that I am the

only person I know who doesn't have a television. When I started the practice of law [1936], the older men were all extremely literary. Recently I talked to three young lawyers who all went to top law schools, and not one of them knew who Jefferson Davis was."

In a 1991 interview for this book, Burch, who has a slightly pixieish countenance wreathed in a neat gray beard, in a soft genial voice that at times takes on a biting edge, recalled this visit from Smith.

"I was not the family lawyer," he said. "But this was not unusual. The people who come to me with those problems are not customarily the people whose wills I've drawn or divorces I've handled. They are people who have got some problem. They've got the ox in the ditch and need somebody to get it out.

"The bank and the DA in Little Rock went after Fred hard. I always had the impression they thought they were going to convict him.

"I used to think that I lived by my brain and my sense of rationality, but as I got older I found I could rely on my guts a whole lot better. I never had a feeling they were going to convict Fred."

On Tuesday, February 12, Burch took his client into federal court and entered a plea of not guilty and then began preparing for the courtroom fight that would rescue or ruin thirty-year-old Fred Smith's career. Much—everything—was at stake. If convicted, he could be fined $5,000 or sentenced to up to two years in prison.

Smith was worried that being taken into court on disgraceful charges might undermine the loyalty of his FedEx troops. He distributed a company memo, which read in part:

I do not want to burden you with my personal problems and want to stress this matter of indictment has absolutely no bearing on Federal Express's operations, but I ask your continuing support in confronting the publicity that may result from this action.

An indictment is certainly no proof of guilt or innocence.

The criminal charges, however, startled, alarmed, and angered a number of Federal Express directors. They all flew to Memphis on February 26, just three weeks after Smith's indictment, to hold a board meeting the following day.

As disturbed as any was Charles Lea. He came in early and cornered Smith in his office for a closed-door session that lasted most of Wednesday afternoon. Then he went in and conferred at length with General Estes.

At day's end, Roger Frock and Mike Fitzgerald stuck their heads in Smith's office to say good night. They got a wan smile and a friendly wave but no comment from their chief.

Later in the evening Smith telephoned Frock at home.

"If ever there was a dark day, that was it," Frock recalled:

Fred said, "I just wanted you to know I'm going to resign tomorrow at the board meeting."

I said, "Aw, bullshit! You can't do that!"

He said, "No, I'm going to do it."

I said, "Smith, you are over the hard part."

He said, "No, there's just too much pressure, and I can't take it anymore. I'm going to resign."

I said, "Where are you? Fitz and I will come down and talk to you."

They found him in his office on the second floor of one of the FedEx hangars. "Smith had a six-pack of beer up there. I will always remember this—to me it was a marine dealing with a difficult situation. It was a six-pack of beer for the three of us, and the cans were warm."

Smith said, "I know how to handle that." He jerked a fire extinguisher off the wall and sprayed the cans with foam. That chills them. I thought it was brilliant.

So we drank our beer, and we talked to him, and we talked to him, and we talked to him. He was serious. He had written by hand a letter to give the board.

Our arguments with him were basically that the hard part was just about over. From then on, it was going to be all downhill. It was very obvious at that point he had done nothing that he should basically be ashamed of. He had done nothing that was at all detrimental to the company.

The management group, we knew, believed two things. No matter who would take over the leadership, if Fred Smith weren't there, the thing would not ultimately be successful. That is how much we believed in Fred Smith and his ability to know and understand the business, and in his charisma and his leadership capabilities. That was very sincere; we felt that way!

And the other thing was that even if that hadn't been true, we sure as hell weren't going to sit around and take orders from General Estes, because he didn't know what he was doing.

In the hangar office, the men drank their beer and talked—until five-thirty in the morning.

"We ultimately convinced him to stay," Frock said. "Then Mike Fitz and I went over to Charley Lea's room at the Hilton Hotel about six A.M. and got him out of bed. This is probably my one and only bad time with Charley. The poor guy was half-asleep.

"We said, 'Smith is not resigning at the board meeting today. That's not the way it's going to be. And we're not going to work for Howling Estes. He doesn't know what he is doing. Smith is important to this thing, and if you don't believe it, we are going to tell you that every single senior management officer in this company is walking out if Smith leaves! Because we believe the only way this company can be successful is for Smith to be here running it. If he's not here, we don't want any part of it!'

" 'Calm down! Calm down!' Lea said. 'We'll talk it out! We'll talk it out! It really looks like Smith has to go.'

" 'If that's the way it is,' Fitz and I said, 'we just want you to know that the rest of us are going!' "

The senior officers gathered at headquarters and drafted a "To Whom It May Concern" letter to the board that stated: "The following senior management people do hereby tender their resignations effective immediately upon the resignation or termination of Frederick W. Smith."

Frock said, "It was signed by every senior management officer except Pete Willmott. The board was going to make Pete president and keep Estes as chairman. So Pete kind of got caught in the middle. He was new and didn't quite know exactly what was going on, but it looked like a good opportunity for him. But all the rest of the senior guys said they were going."

The FedEx directors were not intimidated by the threatened mutiny. Behind their closed doors, they debated strategy and plotted countermoves.

Frock said:

The board meeting went on for hours—all day. We all went into the office just next door and sat on the floor and talked to one another and tried to figure out what we would be doing next week.

At one point the board called in Art Bass, primarily because he didn't pose a threat to anyone in the company. I think they thought they had a patsy in Art, who would be a good strong leader and keep the company together.

Because he was a mild-mannered, don't-rock-the-boat kind of guy who was usually trying to solve arguments and keep people cooperative, they had some respect for his leadership.

Basically, they offered Art the presidency but said under that scenario Smith would still have to leave. They told Art he would never have another opportunity like this.

And Art told them to go stuff it—he wasn't interested!

The board meeting went on, and on, and on. Finally, much to our surprise, they came out and announced that the general was leaving, that Art would be president, and that Smith would move up to board chairman. I did not expect that.

Estes left immediately. I never saw him after the board meeting. It was an unfortunate thing on his part, I think. He just didn't fit in. I think he would have made great window dressing for us, and to some degree that would have been all right. By and large he did stay out of the way, but he was such a pain in the ass. Just little trite personal things.

(In a telephone interview in May 1991 from his home in Bethesda, Maryland, General Estes characterized his stay at Federal Express as "quite successful." He got along "fine" with Fred Smith, whom he described as "very capable, a smart young guy . . . good brains . . . did well in Vietnam.")

Federal Express was expanding its network to new cities in late spring 1975. But it was still struggling financially. For the fiscal year ending May 31, 1975, the company lost $11.5 million, which meant that the total deficit for only a little over two years of operation came to $29.3 million. Then, too, there were outstanding loans of $49 million.

Could FedEx survive? That question, posed by the business weekly *Barron's,* caused some nervousness at Memphis headquarters because the magazine's writers, while applauding Fred Smith & Company for being "spunky," had doubts.

Charles Lea, particularly, was concerned. The ouster of Estes and the restoration of Smith to chairman and CEO had been in effect a smoke screen. The New Court financier had stripped Smith of policy control and established an executive committee of the board with Lea as chairman. Thus he and his committee, and not the founder, really made the decisions.

Then, for the first month ever, Federal Express chalked up a profit—$55,000 for July 1975! (Not very big, but it proved to be the turning point. From then on the operation made money, and when the 1976 fiscal year ended, net income came to $3.6 million.)

Even so, and as shackled and neutered as he was by the executive committee, Fred Smith was still chief of the airline.

In December 1975, only a matter of days before Smith was scheduled for trial in Little Rock for bank fraud, the board of directors suddenly started a search for a CEO to replace him. Two impressive candidates were interviewed—G. Michael Hostage, a vice-president of the Marriott Corporation, and Fred Olsen, chairman of the Hertz Corporation.

"I talked to Mike Hostage," Lea recalled. "I liked the guy; he went to my school, Cornell. But I'm not sure he thought he could handle FedEx. I felt Fred Olsen was the only one who was tough enough and smart enough to actually run the business."

The directors who conducted the CEO search were Phil Greer, who had engineered the initial investment by Bank of America in the airline, and Larry Lawrence, who performed similar work for New York's Citibank.

"To be perfectly honest," said Lea, "we sent those guys off on that assignment just to get them the hell out of our hair."

Serious talks were held with Hostage and Olsen, but neither was hired. The upshot was that Fred Smith stayed as chairman, with Lea's executive committee clinging to the reins.

By coincidence, just then Lea himself was in the midst of a routine physical examination in New York when his physician stopped a stress test and told him he could be in imminent danger of a stroke or heart attack.

Lea flew immediately to a cardiologist friend in Loma Linda, California, to undergo an angiogram. "My scare came just as Fred was going to trial. I remember talking to him by phone. I said, 'Well, I don't know whether I'd rather have your assignment or mine. But, anyway, good luck to both of us!' Lea came out okay; the West Coast doctors told him he "was just like Lionel train tracks—nothing wrong at all."

It was the opulent, old-fashioned kind of courtroom Hollywood adores for a set—a throwback to the 1930s, with tall windows and a high ceiling, the somber walls ringed with portraits of judges long dead, the musty atmosphere redolent of drama.

Splendid cast, too. The DA looked hard as nails. The stern judge was anxious—it being his first trial. The defendant was a young, handsome Vietnam hero who had forged papers to borrow $2 million, not yet paid back. The defense attorney reminded one of Jimmy Stewart and a few times stumbled over names.

United States District Attorney W. H. Dillahunty, nicknamed "Sonny" and sometimes called "General," began the prosecution by putting in the witness chair Union National Bank officers. He quickly established that the $2 million loan would not have been made except for the fake resolution that pledged collateral from the Frederick Smith Enterprise Company.

Defense Counsel Burch told the jury he would show that Fred Smith "had the implied authority" as president to act unilaterally for the Enterprise Company, and that he and Bobby Cox had many times signed each other's names to legal documents in various Federal Express financial transactions.

"One of the essential ingredients in criminal prosecution is criminal intent, evil intent," Burch recalled in our 1991 interviews. "And in the course of dealings that had existed between Fred and the family trust for several years, he had been given a perfectly free hand and had spent hundreds of thousands of dollars, always believing that he was it.

"He could do what he wanted to, and my defense was that in perfectly good faith he was just carrying on a course of conduct that had preexisted. He thought he was authorized."

On the stand Herbert Hall McAdams, chairman of Union National, whose bank was even then suing in Memphis to get the $2 million back, might have been irate and vindictive. Instead he displayed compassion for the defendant, which greatly distressed the DA.

The surprising nature of his feeling was shown in McAdams's responses to a cross-examination by Burch about Fred Smith's unexpected visit to the bank chairman's office on May 15, 1974.

> **Q.** Are you sure that Mr. Smith told you that he had any domestic difficulties at all?
> **A.** No. He had voluntarily, as I understood it, separated himself from his wife, sort of isolated himself. He seemed to be rather distraught. He even went so far as to talk about that he

was very upset about the whole thing. He even talked about jumping out of a window. And I said, "No, Fred, don't think that way. You've got to think positively." And I quoted him a scripture and suggested that he go home and read it. And he wrote me a letter the next day and told me he appreciated it very much.

Q. He wrote you a very nice letter, and he and you personally were on a very good basis, and are, aren't you?

A. Yes, sir.

It was the fact that McAdams testified he even then was on a "personally good basis" with Fred Smith that infuriated "Sonny" Dillahunty. "What no one has ever told you," Dillahunty said in an interview for this book, "is that I literally had the rug pulled out from under me. At the time the bank wanted something done toward prosecuting Fred Smith, his stock wasn't worth a dime, and by the time we got ready to go to trial it was way up. So the bank said, 'Hmmm, if we participate in sending Fred Smith to the penitentiary, we may hurt ourselves. . . .' So the testimony that was given at the initiation of the thing did a complete flip-flop."

In the first of our two interviews, McAdams said: "The prosecuting attorney was all for sending Fred to the penitentiary. I always liked Fred and thought he had a great idea. The prosecuting attorney got carried away with the case. You must understand that we were not pushing it."

When Union National discovered—a year after the event—that it had loaned money on false documents, it was required by federal banking regulations to report it at once to authorities. "Left to our own devices," McAdams said, "it was questionable whether we would have undertaken any accusations at all. We had no choice.

Union National's attorney, Griffin Smith, had advised the bank's board of directors to immediately report Fred Smith's forgery to the U.S. Attorney, the FBI, the Controller of the Currency, and to the bank's bonding company, or they might themselves be exposed to "criminal liability for concealing the commission of a felony." Such reporting, the attorney asserted, is required under banking regulations set forth in 12 Code of Federal Regulations, Section 7.5225, and by 18 U.S. Code, Section 4.

McAdams then said:

"When Mr. Burch asked me on the stand how I felt then about Fred, I could have answered, 'What would you do if someone had just stole two million dollars from a bank that you had just saved, and you were going to have to do it over again unless this loan is paid?'

"I didn't feel that way. I honestly didn't. There was no ill will at all from me. During one recess in the trial, Fred came out a door and we almost ran into each other. I shook hands with him and wished him luck, and we visited for a minute on a very friendly basis, and I walked on."

Burch brought out several times in testimony that once sisters Fredette and Laura Ann broke with their brother because of their fear the millions in the family trust would all be lost, they refused to ratify financial transactions he made in the name of the Enterprise Company that previously had been either ratified or tacitly accepted.

In questioning McAdams, the defense attorney also managed to show that he had a courageous client.

> **Q.** What did he say about the alienation of his sisters?
> **A.** Well, he said he had been alienated from his sisters, and those are my words not his, the "alienation." But what he did say was that he had made a mistake, and he was ready to take his—well, for whatever wrong he did, he was ready to take his punishment, or words to that effect.

In questioning witnesses, Burch dwelled on Smith's feeling he had the "implied authority" to bind the Enterprise Company in furtherance of Federal Express. The prosecutor, of course, objected.

In one such instance, Judge Terry L. Shell excused the jury and took the lawyers into his chambers to hear their arguments on the point. In this exchange, the crux of the case emerged:

> **MR. BURCH.** . . . the fundamental ingredient which is necessary under the Constitution to constitute a crime, and that is the *mens rea,* the guilty intent, the guilty mind. Now, things that are done by accident, by mistake, misunderstanding as to

whether they were true, the making of a false statement based on erroneous information from a lawyer, things of these sorts, are traditional defenses to those and almost every other offense that is prescribed by the statutes of the United States.

Now, here is the defense in this case, if Your Honor please. There is no question that Fred Smith signed that buy-back agreement, which is what I prefer to call it, and which it legally was. . . . He signed that, and in a legal sense it was not false because there was, based on the circumstantial background which involved the dealings with and for the corporation going back over many years, and the corporate history, there was implied authority for him to execute that buy-back agreement, and it was legally effective . . . just as good as if there had been seven corporate seals hanging on it.

Also, I expect to show that the corporation had for many years actually been run on the basis of unilateral decisions. I was about to show when I was stopped by the objection that Mr. [William] Richmond had on one occasion without any authority whatever borrowed $2 million for the corporation, come back and reported it and ratified it. That on another occasion Mr. Richmond had gone out unilaterally, without any more authority than I've got in the form of a corporate resolution, but the greatest authorization based upon the circumstances, and un-ilaterally sold over $6 million worth of the company assets.

I expect to show that on another occasion Fred Smith had delivered to the First National Bank in Memphis a set of buy-back agreements just like this, almost the same, for over—I'm saying a million, but it was either a million or two million—and paid off by the corporation without the slightest problem.

I expect to show that all of this was done in furtherance of the corporate purpose, which was to obtain money to keep Federal Express afloat and going, the corporation having had over a $6 million investment in it.

And I expect the jury to find either one or both of the following:

1. That based upon the circumstances then and there existing, the things said and done and with the corporation under the authority of being its president, acting in its behalf, having his prior acts ratified, that he was authorized to commit the corporation to the buy-back.

And failing that, if the jury should not believe that, 2. that he had a reasonable belief that that was so.

I want to show that Mr. Smith reasonably believed he was acting properly in this occasion . . . and that not only did he sign Mr. Cox's name under this corporate procedure, which was very informal and relaxed, but that Mr. Cox on many occasions had signed Mr. Smith's name about the corporate business, and that in truth and in fact, when Mr. Smith did sign this instrument, he was legally justified to do it; and in the absence of that, even if it should develop that he was not legally justified in doing it, he had reasonable belief that he was, which negates the *mens rea*. . . .

MR. DILLAHUNTY. Of course, I am required and want to see that this man gets a fair trial. I am not required, nor am I going to sit silently by and let them parade public relations on the stand about Federal Express, Enterprise, or any others, if I can prevent it. . . .

We are trying this man for making a false statement in his application for a loan with the bank, in that he said to the bank, "I've got three hundred shares of stock. The corporation agrees they will buy it back and pay up to two million dollars in default," which was false and fictitious. . . . We are not trying Federal Express or Enterprise. We are simply trying Fred Smith. Did he make a statement in an application to a bank to borrow $2 million, which he knew to be false? And from counsel's own mouth, these elements have been made.

This black ink that gets thrown out when the octopus gets in the corner is what's bothering me. And that's the reason why I made the objection. Frankly, I'll be honest with you; Mr. Burch was too fast. Most of it got out before I could get him down. But I want to prevent that from occurring in the future in this lawsuit.

Judge Shell, from the small town of Jonesboro and new to the federal bench, deferred his decision for overnight study. Next morning he gave the lawyers a "yes and no" ruling that did not materially affect the course of the trial.

By indirection he admonished them not to get the criminal case tangled up in the fact that when Union National filed civil suit in Memphis to recover the $2 million, that act in itself tended to show that even now the bank considered Fred Smith's spurious documents as legal and valid.

"You waved that skunk in front of the jury," Judge Shell told Burch.

By midafternoon of Tuesday, the second day, the prosecution had finished putting its witnesses on the stand. Dillahunty called neither Fredette nor Laura Ann to testify. Now began the defense. Burch called Smith to the stand.

Burch's experience had been that in criminal cases most jurors "get the idea pretty quickly as to whether a fellow is wearing a white hat or a black hat." He recalled years later: "Fred is a guy who's very easy to like, and as cases go, it was not a hard case."

The presence of one particular juror gave Burch a "comfortable" feeling. As he later explained: "He was a black guy. Dillahunty showed some slight reluctance, nothing overt, but I think he left the impression that he wasn't much used to working with black jurors. There was just a little nuance, but I was very interested in that juror because he had been a gunnery sergeant in the marines, and I knew he knew the kind of man Fred Smith was, and could relate to him. And that's the only thing I remember about any juror."

Burch began to lead Smith through a recitation of his family background, college life, and his Vietnam service, including a listing of his medals.

"What did you get the Purple Heart for?" asked the lawyer.

"Not being quick enough, I suppose."

When Burch asked about the genesis of his cargo airline, Smith said: "I became convinced that Federal Express had the potential to be a company of astronomical proportions, on the scale of American Airlines or United Parcel Service. . . . I think definitely in just two years, in going from zero in sales to a hundred million dollars, that my forecast wasn't too far wrong."

Explaining need for millions of dollars in start-up money, he testified: "I think it is very important to understand that Federal Express's success is also its nemesis in that it is very similar to a telephone company. I could go out and try to sell you a telephone service for a dime a month that would allow you to call Seattle. You probably wouldn't buy it because you've got to call Little Rock, New York, etcetera. So Federal Express required . . . this massive front-end money."

Fred Smith testified that the change in his sisters' attitude toward him and the venture was in part triggered by their divorces. "They had brought lawyers on with a vengeance against their husbands, and shortly thereafter they had brought lawyers with a vengeance on myself and the bankers at National Bank of Commerce."

The National Bank of Commerce trust officers were "as well as I, very naive" about the ability of White, Weld to come up with $20 million in capital, the witness said, adding, "Mr. Richmond said he'd stake his life on it."

Burch asked him to "tell it in your own words and skip the meringue" about his relationship with the family trust. Fred Smith said:

Here in this court it sounds like Enterprise is over there and F. W. Smith is over here. Almost fifty percent of the Enterprise Company is Fred Smith, either personally or in trust for me. And I felt at the time that I was Enterprise Company. It's as simple as that.

And I felt that both the sisters felt the same way. Both of them had written letters to the bankers who sat on the board, saying, "We support Fred Smith in whatever he wants to do." And the bankers were not taking much of an active role in any regard.

"So that we will know whether we are talking about pipe dreams and moonshine and hopes, what is the present status of Federal Express?" Burch asked.

"Federal Express Corporation is very much a thriving business," the witness responded. "As of last night, having checked this morning before I came over, we carried some 16,000 shipments, which would have been revenues of about $330,000. We also have about $40,000 a day in postal revenues. The company in October, which is our last monthly financial statement, made $841,000 net pretax earnings. We employ 1,856 people. We fly thirty-seven airplanes and operate into eighty-two airports in the United States. Our payroll is $26.5 million per annum."

On that note, the defense attorney sat down and the prosecutor began cross-examination. His first questions were whether the airline was broke at the time the $2 million was borrowed and whether Fred Smith was desperate, highly pressured.

"Mr. Dillahunty," Smith replied, "the financial pressures I have been under have never caused me to be irrational, and they compare to such a gnat with what I went through in Southeast Asia that I am not going to tell you that I was out of control at all."

But the DA continued to hammer away.

Q. Were you highly pressured?
A. Yes, sir, I was.
Q. Pressured enough that you'd do anything to get some money?
A. I wouldn't kill someone, no sir.
Q. No, sir, but you would submit a false and fictitious statement on a document to a bank to get it, wouldn't you?
A. Mr. Dillahunty, I have never denied that. I told you that at the grand jury, and that is correct, yes, sir.
Q. You did submit a false and fictitious document to that bank to obtain two million dollars, didn't you?
A. I submitted to the bank a resolution of the Frederick Smith Enterprise Company of a buy-back, which I fully believed that I had.
Q. But it was false and fictitious?
A. If you're saying that the meeting never took place, that's correct, and if you're saying that I signed Bobby Cox's name, that's also correct, yes, sir.
Q. Is the document false and fictitious?
A. Well, to my own mind, no, sir, because that buy-back existed and it exists to this day, and if—
Q. Was that document that you gave the bank on that date false and fictitious, sir?
A. If you would like to call me to say yes, I will say, "Yes, sir, it was."
Q. No, sir, I want you to tell us the truth.
A. I just told you the truth, Mr. Dillahunty.
Q. Was it false and fictitious?
A. The document did not represent an actual meeting of the Enterprise Company.
Q. Then it was false?
A. If that's your definition, yes, sir.
Q. Was it fictitious?
A. In terms of the buy-back, no sir. I felt that that buy-back existed, and I feel that it exists today.
Q. With all the testimony, you still think it exists?

> **A.** Mr. Dillahunty, to my way of thinking, you haven't proved
> that it doesn't exist.
> **Q.** To your way of thinking?
> **A.** Yes, sir.

The prosecutor brought out that Smith had five separate bank accounts, that Federal Express and Arkansas Aviation each had three, and that in 1974 there were numerous overdrafts, one of $147,000, and the defendant's personal account was down to $2,700.

"If you're asking if I run business on the float," Fred Smith asserted, "the answer is unequivocally yes, because that's the only way Federal Express survived for seven or eight months.

"You're trying to paint a picture that just didn't exist at the time, the same as you're trying to do with these checks."

"No, sir," responded the DA. "You have the brush, Mr. Smith. I'm not painting."

> **Q.** Incidentally, do you recall what you had in your Union
> National Bank account here in Little Rock at the time you got
> the two million dollar loan?
> **A.** Probably a couple hundred dollars.
> **Q.** Well, double it.
> **A.** Okay. Four hundred dollars?
> **Q.** Four hundred dollars.
> **A.** I was better off than I thought.

On the third day, Wednesday, Dillahunty continued his cross-examination. "Now these were things . . . that you did without telling Enterprise?"

"Mr. Dillahunty," Fred Smith answered, "one of the things, if I'm not mistaken, in the American system of jurisprudence the burden of proof is on you, and you haven't shown that I didn't tell them about the Union National Bank thing."

"Mr. Smith, I would ask you to wait and let's see whether the jury believes that or not."

The prosecutor asked about a $500,000 loan Fred Smith obtained from Worthen Bank on July 7, 1972, with another "buy-back" document to which he had also signed Bobby Cox's name, and why it wasn't formally ratified by the Enterprise Company board.

"There wasn't any particular necessity to ratify it," Fred Smith said. "It had been substantially paid down—to one hundred and fifty thousand dollars. There's not a single reference in the Enterprise Company minute book approving the investment structure of the Enterprise Company with six million dollars in Federal Express. Now that's incredible. If that doesn't show the loosely run nature of the corporation, I don't know what does!"

At the end of the prosecution's interrogation, Burch returned.

> **Q.** Are you sorry in any way that you went into Federal Express and have put your blood, sweat, and tears and everything you had into it?
> **A.** I am not. I am immensely proud of it.
> **Q.** And would you do it all again?
> **A.** I would.

By 11:45 A.M. of the fourth day, Thursday, final arguments had been made, Judge Shell had read his instructions to the jury, and the case was in their hands. While jurors have much latitude in deciding what constitutes "reasonable doubt," both in their minds and in the accused's, they must strictly follow the court's interpretation of the law and definition of terms.

In this case much depended on two words: "knowingly" and "willfully." In his charge, Judge Shell said the government was required to prove "beyond reasonable doubt . . . that . . . the defendant did knowingly make a false statement." He read these definitions:

> *Knowingly*—An act is done knowingly if done voluntarily and intentionally and not because of mistake or accident or other innocent reason.

> *Willfully*—An act is done willfully if done voluntarily and intentionally, with specific intent to do something the law forbids, that is to say with evil motive or bad purpose to disobey or disregard the law.

The charge also directed:

> If the evidence leaves the jury with reasonable doubt whether the accused in good faith reasonably believed the statement to be true at the time it was made, the jury should acquit the accused.

From the outset of deliberations, the jury was confused. They met for thirty minutes and then requested the judge to bring them back into the courtroom and again read his instructions, which he did at 1:25 P.M.

At 3:40 P.M. jury foreman John D. Baker sent a note by the bailiff asking Judge Shell to send them a copy of his instructions. The court declined that request but brought them back to the box and again read his charge.

Shortly after 5:00 P.M. came another note from Foreman Baker: "Could we possibly have the definitions of 'willingly' and 'knowlingly' as stated in the court's instructions?"

This caused Shell to huddle with the lawyers. Burch pointed out that "willfully," not "willingly" was in the charge and proposed the jury be brought back again to hear the charge a third time. Dillahunty asserted that was unnecessary, but Shell did it nonetheless at 5:20 P.M. and then sent the jury out to dinner. "Taking a walk and getting a little oxygen will be good for you. Sometimes that clears the mind when we have problems to work out."

Burch, Smith, and a cluster of friends sat patiently throughout the long deliberations. The lawyer looked unworried, confident of acquittal; Smith was subdued and pale.

Shortly after ten the jury foreman knocked on the door and sent word by the bailiff that the jury had reached a verdict.

At 10:10 P.M. Foreman Baker stood up in the box and said: "We, the jury, find the defendant, Frederick W. Smith, not guilty of the offense charged."

Smith jumped up and threw his arms around Burch. Dillahunty was stunned; he took the highly unusual action of asking that the jurors be polled. Each of the twelve answered: "Not guilty."

► ► ►

There remained the other criminal charge against him—the hit-run fatality in Memphis. But it was getting lost in the cracks of the police court.

When the case was first called on February 3, 1975, in division 5, city court, before Judge S. A. Wilburn, it was postponed to July 30. At that time it was again continued—to December 16, a date that came on the heels of the Little Rock trial. And on December 16 it was again continued, to February 17, 1976.

Finally, the hit-run charge was called for the last time on February 24, 1976, and dismissed on motion of the city prosecutor, thirty-year-old Reed L. Malkin.

Asked sixteen years later on what grounds the prosecution was dropped, Malkin, now in private practice in Memphis, replied: "Honestly, I don't know. I don't remember that case at all. You say Fred Smith was the defendant? I don't remember it. I'd have to guess there just wasn't sufficient evidence to prosecute on."

15 ▶ *FALLING IN LOVE AGAIN*

Although perhaps the really dark chapters in his life were behind him, Smith was still trapped in a continuing period of frustration and tension. In this ordeal he was buffeted by unruly challenges in his professional career; and, even worse, his private life began to shatter.

Federal Express had just been turned down by the CAB on a request to use DC-9s. The bigger planes were urgently needed for the long hauls, especially to the West Coast and New York and Boston. Art Bass lamented: "Falcons are flying wing tip to wing tip over the same routes in the same night, and this is holding back our market expansion and adding terribly to our flight expense." At that time the Falcon fuel burn was about $150 an hour.

Substantial savings were possible if FedEx could carry the whole cargo on one larger DC-9 flight.

That crisis threw Fred Smith headlong into a new battle in Washington, one he eventually won in stunning fashion. His singular campaign would in the end materially speed up congressional reform that gave all airlines relief from government regulation.

At the same time, Smith was waging war against what the FedEx people in Memphis called the "jackals of Wall Street"—the investors and lenders who had a choke hold on the Federal Express Corporation.

In his desperation for money to keep his FedEx alive, Smith and the Enterprise Company had imprudently surrendered more and more of their ownership shares, until now the investors and lenders held the whip hand—control of the board of directors and the ability to make ultimate decisions.

What galled Smith was that in these financings, warrants for the purchase of one share of class A common stock had been issued on a proportionate basis to the "jackals," which, if exercised, would enable the investor-lender group to take nearly all of the company away from the founder. If FedEx became markedly successful, he feared they would do that.

Fred Smith felt the banks were obligated to return the warrants on a "reasonable basis," but they refused. New York's Chase Manhattan was the most adamant. Smith complained about the whole group: "Greed seemed to get the better of them when they decided to renege on this deal. If pressed, this issue could be litigated, and be won. They took the warrants to allow a fourth financing had it been necessary—not as an 'equity kicker'—and there were too many participants to ultimately deny this." What he was saying is that he believed if the banks exercised their warrants they would violate national banking regulations, particularly the Glass-Steagall Act.

Smith went back to General Dynamics, where chairman David Lewis had always been friendly and sympathetic. He requested that General Dynamics again become his guarantor on a loan—$3 million for two years. He wanted $700,000 to purchase the warrants and $1.7 million to exercise them and the remaining $600,000 to pay off his personal loans made for FedEx.

At this stage his personal holding was only 8.5 percent of the stock in Federal Express, and the family trust was down to 0.4 percent. If he could buy back the warrants and exercise them, he would be able to own about 25 percent of the company he had founded.

General Dynamics turned him down on the loan. It was a blow that made him think of resigning. From the Madison House in Washington, D.C., in June 1976, Smith wrote David Lewis and Colonel Henry Crown asking that they consider him for a management position in either General Dynamics or Trans World Airlines. A copy of this letter was discovered in a little used storeroom in the

Memphis headquarters in 1981 by a historical researcher. The file did not show the Crown-Lewis response; it may have been considered the momentary whim of a terribly distraught man.

Roger Frock, who was then in the executive suite with Art Bass, cannot recall ever hearing of Fred Smith's effort to go to General Dynamics or TWA. "I wouldn't be surprised if Fred got discouraged from time to time. It was a very difficult period. I must say that most—ninety-nine percent—of the problems he bore himself alone, in that he did not basically make that an issue with the employees of the company. Most of them really didn't know the turmoil he was going through."

The strain affected his home life. Linda was a loyal, patient wife and good mother to their two daughters. But she was young and wanted a social life. Her family had always been part of country club circuit and the Brooks Art Museum set in Memphis; Fred was not much inclined toward that social realm. Some friends suspect that he still bore resentment that the Memphis elite had looked on his father as something of a "roughneck."

When Smith was not at his Federal Express desk or flying around the country on company business, he stayed at home to read. "I read about four hours a day," he told an interviewer.

Trying to break him out of his compulsive routine, Linda began to set a social schedule for them—certain dates and times for going to parties, out to dinner, and so forth, say friends who knew them in these days. Fred Smith did enjoy relaxing at tennis or playing backgammon when he didn't have a book open, but that was about his limit.

Joe Golden, who started as the pre-FedEx researcher in Little Rock, observed the growing strain and felt sad. "It was a shame. I always liked Linda." In the first weeks of his work, Golden lived in Smith's guest house, a garage apartment. They rode to work and back, sometimes in the big Lincoln convertible of Smith's mother, Sally Hook.

"I always thought in Little Rock," Joe Golden recalled, "he did not have enough fun. Because he was always thinking about— always, always thinking about the business. That's to his credit, but it's also not good for you in the long run."

In a way Smith tried to compensate for spending so much time away from his two young daughters by naming two of the Falcons for them—*Wendy* and *Laura*. That gave him the idea of naming all the planes after children of FedEx employees. Everyone was permitted to submit names, and the winners were drawn out of a hat.

Friends recall that during the early years when eastern investors were coming to Memphis to look over the air cargo fledgling, Smith would make a late call to tell Linda he was bringing guests for dinner.

"I never saw such an efficient impromptu hostess. She never let him down. She would have an elegant meal, and on her table would be sparkling china and crystal, with polished silver and fresh flowers," remembered one neighbor.

Although not a frequent visitor at the Federal Express offices, Linda was admired for her friendliness with the staff.

Rick Runyon, the designer of "that damned purple airplane," remembered being called back to Memphis by Bill Arthur to confer on a special project for Federal Express.

"We were walking down the street and we passed Fred's house as his wife was coming out. She looked and said, 'My God, is that Rick Runyon?' And I said, 'Yeah. How are you doin'?' And she said, 'You look . . . Come here. . . . You look like you haven't eaten in a whole day! You get in here right now!' And she went to the stove and cooked me a whole dinner. That's the way she was all the time. She hadn't changed."

Fred Smith & Company stormed Capitol Hill in the spring of 1976 to attack the Civil Aeronautics Act of 1938. They felt right was on their side, and that they could convince Congress to lift the hoary strictures that were stalling the burgeoning Federal Express.

But the troops from Memphis were naive, inexperienced. In the early going they seemed as clumsy as Don Quixote. Their goal was to get an exemption to allow use of larger planes. Two courses were open: apply to the CAB for a certificate of convenience and necessity as an airline; or get legislation enacted that would permit the CAB to issue special regulations for all-cargo carriers.

By this time FedEx dominated the air express market for packages weighing less than one hundred pounds, handling 19 percent. The old leaders, Emery and Airborne, were down in this category to 10 percent and 5 percent, respectively.

Smith was in a quandary about applying for CAB certification; FedEx was warned the commercial airlines would object violently and their lawyers could drag out the proceedings for perhaps five years. In that period FedEx would be stalled in acquiring the larger cargo jets it needed and would be generally handicapped in expanding to more cities. Smith feared that terms of the certificate could restrict the Memphis airline's present freedom to choose its routes and times for nightly flights.

FedEx might find it difficult during the certification process to raise prices; although the airline was finally making money, Smith felt profit margins needed to be increased. Net income for fiscal 1976 was $3.5 million and would climb to $8.1 million in 1977 and leap in 1978 to $20 million.

After two decades of study, Washington was beginning to feel that much of the government regulatory structure was obsolete and needed change, particularly the Federal Aviation Act, which stifled competition and protected inefficient carriers. Aware of this, the Federal Express board decided to try for legislative relief, with Smith as spokesman. He sought help of the Tennessee congressional delegation. Senator Howard Baker was in a position of considerable power as minority leader, and Senator William Brock was receptive and friendly.

The FedEx chairman readily told of his company's plight to any reporter who would listen and wrangled several appearances before congressional committees considering changes in the aviation laws.

Smith was brash and brave, telling one newsman: "The government doesn't have to give us a thing. All they have to do is get out of our way."

Appearing in April 1976 before Senator Howard Cannon's aviation subcommittee of the commerce committee, Fred Smith roundly roasted the commercial airlines for objecting to FedEx's application to use DC-9s.

"They think," he testified, "they are entitled to the traffic regardless of whether they provide as good a service or as cheap a rate; and second, that they were there first with the mostest and consequently it is their business, and I think that is a very unhealthy attitude."

Aviation law, he argued in his rounds of the congressional corridors, had been written primarily with passenger service in mind and thus ignored and stifled the cargo carriers. This was his theme in an appearance before a House aviation subcommittee chaired by Representative Glenn Anderson of California.

But Congressman Anderson was skeptical that Federal Express actually would get tied up "two to ten years" before the CAB if it applied for certification, and he asked what the airline had to lose. Smith replied:

Well, we felt we had a number of things to lose by asking for a certificate. We could easily expend half a million or a million dollars—and we are not a rich company. And then only to find out that the Congress had taken some of these reform measures—and we think you are going to take some of them, certainly as it applies to air cargo.

The second thing, Mr. Chairman, is that it has just been put to us very directly that you get your neck into that certification noose, and we are going to chop you up. And what I am talking about are the opposition counsel for some of the biggest carriers. And they will use the certification process as a weapon of and by itself to delay us from the needed solutions.

To counter any feeling in the industry or Congress that FedEx was seeking special privilege, Smith assured the subcommittee his

213

company would apply for certification, provided it was permitted meantime to accommodate its growth by flying larger planes.

At midyear bills were introduced in both the Senate and the House to accomplish just that, authorizing the CAB to "grant relief by exemption in certain cases." Attorneys for the commercial airlines immediately jumped on this proposed legislation as "back-door deregulation" and derided them as "the Federal Express Relief Bills."

These bills so infuriated Robert Prescott, founder and chairman of Flying Tigers, that he got out of a sickbed and came to Washington only weeks before his death to attack them viciously.

Federal Express, he testified, was a small outfit doing nothing particularly unique but was invading "the cabbage patch" that Flying Tigers had pioneered. "They are serving off-line points . . . at a very high price," he testified. "They now want to trade their motorcycle in for a Mack truck and get into the air-freight business that we are in."

Always a quick study, Smith had mastered aviation legislation. Not only was he now an expert on the law, but he was intense about his campaign for relief. "We had to put up with a lot of nonsense in Washington," recalled J. Tucker Morse, who was there as a FedEx lawyer:

> We were sitting in there with the majority counsel of the House aviation subcommittee. I had the Civil Aeronautics Act of 1938 in my briefcase. This young whippersnapper was lecturing Smith about the airline business. What amazed me was that you'd go into these subcommittees and meet these young guys who were purporting to be experts on the affairs of the subcommittee, and they didn't have a clue as to what was going on in the industry. They'd sit there and tell you how it was going to be, and this and that, and it was just incredibly frustrating.
>
> We were sitting there listening to this guy tell us about how the bill was going to be written and why, or why he didn't want to do this or that. The guy didn't have any idea of what he was talking about.
>
> Fred reached in my briefcase and pulled out the Civil

Fredette Smith Eagle, Fred's half sister, about the time she took him to court over his invasion of their father's trust funds. Once soul-mates, they have been cstranged for twenty years. (Courtesy Charlotte Smith)

Fred Smith's other half sister, Laura Ann Rohm, poses on May 1, 1989, with some of the sixty-five or so neglected animals she has rescued, at her ranch home outside Corpus Christi, Texas. (Courtesy *Corpus Christi Caller-Times*)

ABOVE LEFT: Memphis crowd on January 14, 1978, surrounds the first 727 to be obtained by Federal Express following lifting of government restrictions. (Courtesy *Memphis Commercial Appeal*)

ABOVE RIGHT: One of the expensive IVECO Z vans FedEx tried out is displayed by Mike Fitzgerald. (Courtesy Mike Fitzgerald)

RIGHT: This new wing of the Memphis superhub, shown under construction on April 28, 1980, is large enough to contain four football fields placed end to end. (Courtesy *Memphis Commercial Appeal*)

Fred Smith boards one of the original FedEx Falcons on August 30, 1983, to fly it to Washington, D.C., to be placed in the Smithsonian Institution. (Courtesy *Memphis Commercial Appeal*)

FedEx acquires a
still larger plane, the
DC-10. On March 29,
1980, guests line up in
Memphis to christen the
new cargo carrier.
(Courtesy *Memphis
Commercial Appeal*)

A limited view of the sort at the
Memphis hub on August 4, 1981.
(Courtesy *Memphis Commercial
Appeal*)

ABOVE: Fred Smith at Memphis jobs conference October 21, 1981. (Courtesy *Memphis Commercial Appeal*)

TOP LEFT: On August 11, 1982, his thirty-eighth birthday, Fred Smith (standing left) in a west Beruit command post of Israeli military force, posing with Moslem agent (third from left); Ira Lipman, his companion from Memphis; and (far right) Israeli colonel. (Courtesy Ira Lipman)

BOTTOM LEFT: Fred Smith with Pepper Rodgers, explaining their effort to get a National Football League franchise in Memphis, August 13, 1988. (Courtesy *Memphis Commercial Appeal*)

Nestled in a vale off a narrow road on the eastern outskirts of Memphis, the sprawling residence of Frederick W. Smith at 649 Sweetbriar Lane is enclosed by a fence and electronic gate and largely hidden by trees. (Courtesy Elzene Miller)

Aeronautics Act of 1938. He held it in the subcomittee guy's face and said "You don't know anything about this act!" Fred took his hands and literally ripped the book in half. And threw it on the table. "This is what I think of your arguments."

And I loved it. I've still got the book; it's a historical document. An effective ploy at the time. Fred is not any giant muscle guy, and this book was probably two hundred and fifty pages. He just ripped it in half and flipped it on the table. This guy just stopped—bug-eyed. It took strength, absolutely. I still marvel at the thing. It was just extemporaneous. Fred was just so frustrated in Washington, as we all were.

While lobbying hard in Washington, Smith mobilized all employees in a letter-writing campaign to their congressmen, circularizing all customers with a brochure called "Sometimes Free Enterprise Needs a Little Help" and dispatching top executives, including the chairman, to speak on the topic before civic and business organizations all around the United States.

Then occurred one of the stumbles over congressional turf and prestige that have so often over the years killed special legislation. This time it was rivalry between Senator Cannon and Congressman Anderson.

The House passed the bill in late September providing reduced air fares for the elderly and handicapped. When it came to the Senate for concurrence, Cannon said he intended to tack on the "Federal Express Relief Bill" as an amendment. Representative Anderson blew up. "No! No!" he said. "If that is done, I won't call it up in the House. It will just die!"

The Senate voted 73–0 to adopt Cannon's rider. But Anderson was adamant and left the whole measure cutting fares for the elderly and handicapped lifeless on the table when the Congress adjourned.

The troops from Memphis were crushed. Their hard fight, months of work, was all negated. They'd have to wait for the new Congress to convene in 1977.

A phone call from a boyhood pal, John Fry, in early 1976 changed Smith's private life. Fry was still running Ardent Studio, the record company they had launched while in high school. Fry's secretary, he said, needed a change of scene. Did FedEx have any openings?

Stacy Diane Davis Wall, twenty-six, made a striking picture stepping off the FedEx elevator on the third floor. Fred Smith's secretary, Charlotte Curtis, blinked at her midcalf skirt with large floral prints and stared, perhaps a little enviously, at her shoulder-length curly hair. "She had a lot of hair," Charlotte Curtis remembered.

Her arrival was a surprise, Smith having neglected to list her on his appointments, but she went right in—and straight to work. In a small room between the chairman's office and Art Bass's, she sat at a table piled with papers. Charlotte Curtis was not told her assignment. (Charles Lea recalled her job was to unscramble Fred Smith's expense accounts, to get them in shape for corporate accounting.)

She applied herself industriously and chatted with other third-floor girls about her background. She came from a musical family. Her father, Richard "Scat" Davis, was a trumpet player who had earlier toured with big bands and picked up his nickname from the musical movie star Johnny "Scat" Davis. It stuck even when he settled down in Memphis, playing at night in local clubs. Her brother "Buddy" was a guitar player with Target. At Memphis State University she fell in love with a rock band drummer, Larry Wall. They were married and divorced in less than a year, leaving her with a daughter named Stacy Denise.

Diane, a bookkeeper, had first worked at a firm that produced advertising jingles. Through her husband she'd met John Fry and John King and moved over to Ardent as secretary. Then she'd become general manager and worked nine to nine. "I'm crazy about rock music, but that job about did me in," Diane admitted. "I got an ulcer."

At Federal Express what Diane Wall got was the attention of the chairman.

Her mother, Kathleen Hammond Davis, a secretary in the Shelby County Sheriff's Office, said in an interview: "Fred and his wife were separated. He had an apartment in the Federal Express building, where he stayed. He was trying to get a divorce, and she wouldn't give him one. She knew he was going to make some money one day, you know, and she didn't want to let go. But they were already separated when Diane first met him."

Their developing romance seemed largely to escape notice. Returning from lunch one day, Charlotte Curtis found a new folder atop one of the file "stacks" that Fred Smith habitually kept around his desk. Scribbled on the folder was "Look at page 56." Curious, the secretary opened the folder, found a book on belly dancing and on page fifty-six an entrancing pose. Diane had chatted about taking belly dancing lessons. And when a chocolate pie mysteriously appeared on the chairman's desk, and little notes began to be passed, the secretaries and others recognized the obvious clues.

In a matter of months Fred Smith had a new secretary, Diane, and Charlotte Curtis was out finding another job.

Joe Golden, who worked in marketing with Bill Arthur, remembered pulling a trick on Diane and two other secretaries:

> They took a long lunch and called in to Bill Arthur and me saying they needed a ride back because their car broke down. I said, "Bill, I'll go get 'em." I was going to teach them a lesson. I went downstairs and borrowed a pickup truck that had hog racks on it—wooden sidings—and some hay in the back. I drove down to where the girls were, and the front seat was all loaded down with stuff; the owner was going camping that afternoon.
>
> I locked the doors and told them they couldn't ride in the front, had to ride in back. I drove the truck back to the security gate and jumped out and told the guard I had a load of hogs for the third floor. Then I just ran and left the pickup parked there.
>
> I didn't say a word to anybody, just went back to my desk. The girls were so embarrassed they figured the whole office had watched them climb out of the pickup. They started saying "Did you see what Joe Golden did to us?" and so forth.
>
> It wasn't long before Fred Smith walked into my office laughing as hard as I've ever seen him laugh. At that time I

didn't know that he and Diane had anything going, or even if they did at that time. But he just thought it was a hilarious thing to do. The funny thing was I never said a word to anybody. They told on themselves.

The boss-secretary romance, however, created a conflict that entangled at least one executive colleague, J. Tucker Morse. He could understand why Smith was attracted to Diane.

"First of all, she is attractive. She's smart. She was there—they were working very hard in that period, and I guess he came to rely on her. Other than that, I'm not going to speculate one way or the other. She was a capable person. I think he was intrigued by her intelligence.

"Fred spent a lot of nights in his office. It happened all the time. That was a very difficult period. The reason I'd rather not comment much on it is that I knew Linda extremely well and I knew Fred well.

"When all of the problems developed, Fred moved in with me. I was a bachelor then and had a house on Picardy Place, two bedrooms and one bath. It was not all that far from his house on Morningside, about a mile and a half.

"Linda told him to leave, and he didn't think it was advisable for him to move in with Diane at that point. He stayed with me for about ten days or two weeks, and I was kind of in the middle of all this. There were phone calls. You can imagine all the furor. I knew both sides, and it just wasn't any of my business, frankly.

"So I told Fred, 'Here's the key to my house. You can stay here as long as you want. I'm getting out. I'm going to Hong Kong.'

"And I did, with a couple of guys from New York. We went to Hong Kong and then on to Malaysia. Fred had moved out by the time I got back.

"You know, there were a lot of split marriages over there as a result of the Federal Express experience . . . the guys all working hard and in a very taxing environment. Unbelievable."

The romance continued in early 1977 when Federal Express was busily lobbying in Washington. So many staffers from Memphis headquarters were shuttling to the nation's capital that the company rented a town house in Georgetown for them. "The hotels were so expensive," explained Tucker Morse. On several trips Diane was part of the Federal Express contingent.

Although the Memphis hub operation was still suffering from having to double up and triple up on nightly flights to and from several key cities, Smith became more optimistic that relief in the form of larger planes was visible.

This was based on the belief that President Jimmy Carter had taken office with an intention of trying to weed out some of the bureaucratic restraints on efficiency and competition in transportation.

Those signs also were read accurately on Capitol Hill. Two bills to deregulate the airline industry were promptly introduced in the Senate and endorsed just a week or two later by the White House.

Arrayed against any change in the existing structure were the big airlines, Delta, American, TWA, and Eastern. United, however, favored change that would create fairer competition. Smith, of course, espoused total deregulation, calling it especially needed by the cargo airlines. In testimony at a Senate hearing March 24, 1977, the FedEx chairman unleashed another assault on "bumbling bureaucrats" and "government red tape."

Smith was worried that entrenched commercial aviation powers might manage to derail the legislative push for reform. He still felt it would take two to six years to fight through the regulatory maze at the CAB to get regular airline certification. Most board members favored filing an application right away, but he still held back.

In Washington interviews he admitted his lobbying efforts to gain relief had run up against tremendous odds, with practically the whole of the airline industry fighting deregulation. Still, he expected to win in the end. "We're like old Ho Chi Minh," he said. "They've got to kill us one hundred times. All we have to do is kill them once."

On July 29, 1977, Linda filed suit in chancery court at Memphis to end their eight-year marriage, asking alimony and child support for Sandra Windland Smith, born January 19, 1970, and Laura Fredette Smith, born January 5, 1972.

Termination of the marriage did not occur quickly. The parties held numerous conferences with the lawyers working on terms for settlement.

Smith and Diane were eager for the divorce to be finalized; as soon as it was granted they would be married. However, Linda Smith seemed in no hurry.

On Capitol Hill in this summer period things seemed more favorable for Federal Express. Congressman Anderson of California, who had killed the "Federal Express Relief Bills" in the last session, switched sides and introduced a House bill that would virtually guarantee automatic certification for the present cargo airlines.

Anderson's legislation would include what is called a "grandfather clause"—which specified that any cargo airline already in business would not be required to obtain a certificate.

"But what if something happens, and the Anderson bill gets caught up in some snafu, and there's no action?" Smith asked his congressional friends.

It was something to think about, they agreed. Senator Cannon did more; he acted. On October 20, 1977, when an unrelated House-passed transportation bill was called up in the Senate, Cannon tacked on an amendment covering all provisions of air cargo deregulation. It sailed through both chambers with no opposition and was signed into law by President Carter on November 9, 1977.

Under the changes in the Federal Aviation Act of 1958, Federal Express (and all other cargo carriers) could now use aircraft of any size. Further, CAB no longer could control pricing or market entry. "Hey! We're free to fly!" shouted Fred Smith.

At once Federal Express began to take advantage of its new freedom by going into the market to buy Boeing 727s. These jets could carry a 42,000-pound payload, which was five or six times greater than the capacity of the Falcons. Soon the Falcons would be retired, and 727s would give the company a more efficient and less expensive lift.

Charles Lea and his executive committee gave all credit for the Washington triumph to Smith—plus a $100,000 bonus.

Smith was now supporting two households. He was firmly commited to his secretary. From Paul Trout he had leased a three-bedroom two-bath house at 192 Dille Place for one year at $400 a month and moved in with Diane Wall and her daughter, Stacy. Only their most intimate friends knew they were linked romantically; the landlord, however, had the impression they were married, and neighbors recall that Diane Wall appeared "heavily pregnant."

She was, and the fact was confirmed when FedEx secretaries were startled to read in the *Memphis Commercial Appeal* vital statistics column for November 5, 1977:

Baptist Hospital
Births
Mr. and Mrs. F. W. Smith
192 Dille Place
boy, 2:52 P.M.

When they brought the baby home to the leased house, the landlord was unaware his tenant was the founder of Federal Express. "All I know is he paid the rent on time," Paul Trout said in an interview.

It was nearly two months later—just before Christmas—that a settlement was finally reached between lawyers for Linda and Fred Smith for an uncontested divorce on grounds of irreconcilable differences. The decree, granted December 23, 1977, gave substantial money and property to his children and ex-wife. The terms were spelled out in the *Commercial Appeal:*

The property settlement calls for Smith to provide for the children's education in private schools, to pay their dental and medical expenses and to purchase a "new 1978 medium-priced automobile" for Mrs. Smith.

She would take title to 7,500 shares of Federal Express stock, and another 15,000 would be put in trust for her and the children. Smith said the stock represents about ½ of 1 percent of that issued by his corporation. The corporation's stock is not traded.

Mrs. Smith would have custody of the children and own the couple's former home at 46 Morningside Park and its furnishings.

At first she would receive $27,000 a year in child support and alimony, but that would increase to $60,000 when either Smith had paid a debt to the Union National Bank of Little Rock or Federal Express issues more stock, but in any case within two years.

Not reported in the newspaper was one provision of the decree, reminiscent of similar marital strictures written into Smith's father's divorces: "The payments of alimony shall terminate upon wife's death or remarriage."

Now free, Fred Smith quietly married Diane Wall—but not in Memphis, where the marriage license would have been routinely published. Smith notified the landlord they were moving from the Dille Place house, and Paul Trout canceled the last two months of the lease. "They were getting a larger place," said Paul Trout. "I'm always glad to see young folks moving up in the world."

Fred Smith's first son was named Richard, for Diane's trumpet-playing father.

Raised in a strong Catholic environment, Diane Davis Wall Smith was anxious for a large family. In this second marriage Richard would be followed by Kathleen, Molly, Arthur, Samantha, and Buchanan (called Cannon). That required Smith to oversee a lively brood of nine children: daughters Wendy and Laura from his first marriage, Stacy from Diane's first marriage to Larry Wall, and their own six.

▶ ▶ ▶

The financial picture in Memphis had suddenly turned bright.

The bankers who had gripped Fred Smith & Company for four years realized they now held a growing giant that would soon break free.

On the critical issue of the warrants that Smith had been forced to give, they suddenly caved in and accepted fair terms for surrender. The warrant holders turned loose 444,641 shares for $5.25 each, plus $2.50 as the exercise price. For $200,000 Smith waived his first option and permitted Federal Express to buy 200,000 shares, while he purchased the remaining 244,641 at $5.25.

The First National Bank of Chicago loaned him $4.7 million, guaranteed by Federal Express. Of this sum, $1,284,000 went to purchase warrants, $2,934,000 to repay his creditors, and $428,000 (in prepaid interest) to the Chicago bank.

All of this financiering enabled the board to make a public stock offering. On April 12, 1978, FedEx shares were offered on the New York Stock Exchange at $24.

As a reward for their loyalty and sacrifice during the years of struggle, Federal Express employees were offered stock at a modest discount, and 56 percent of them requested a total of 635,000 shares! With only 220,000 shares allotted to this pool, they were issued on a pro rata basis.

The public offering was a success; a total of 783,000 shares sold, raising $17,539,200 in new equity. Certain stockholders cashed in, selling 292,000 shares for $6,540,800.

From now on Fred Smith & Company could stop looking back to see how close bankruptcy and disaster were on their heels.

16 ▶ *BACKWATER TOWN CRITIC*

During the end of the seventies and in the early eighties, both Smith's bank account and his personality were remade. He became something of a superman. His tattered fortune abruptly took a meteoric rise; this helped his self-confidence soar. His mien and voice became that of a seasoned self-satisfied businessman, ready to pass judgment on anything that happened in his hometown.

That didn't bother Wall Street. The stock of Federal Express Corporation, launched at $24 a share, within four months was selling for better than $47—and splits would have it in a few years worth something like $250. What the stock market wanted to know was not what Fred Smith was spouting off about local affairs down in Memphis, but how large the package count was in his growing fleet of purple airplanes that skittered across the country and what was happening to the FedEx bottom line.

The first profitable fiscal year was 1976, with net income of $3.5 million off total revenue of $75 million. Profit the next year grew to $8.1 million off revenue of $109.21 million, and in 1978 profit leaped to $20 million off revenue of $160.3 million. By 1983 the purple airplanes would bring in their first billion dollars, creating a net profit of $88.933 million! At that time the company was only nine years old.

Smith could be excused for crowing, but in 1978 when he began wholesale unloading of his personal views and business and political opinions on his fellow Tennesseeans, it didn't always please them.

"He was cocky as hell!" That is still the reaction in Memphis of a number of businessmen, politicians, newspaper people, and society figures who were interviewed for this book.

Fred Smith struck out in disgust at the Memphis image as a "backwater town." He would single-handedly straighten everything out and in the process jolt the southern river city out of what he perceived to be its plantation mentality.

Said chancery court judge Wyeth Chandler, the former mayor whom Fred Smith tried to unseat:

"I have no idea where that [Fred Smith's sudden activism] stemmed from. It may be that he's just one of these typical people who goes from a small town in the south to Yale or whatever and gets his brains jellied by liberal professors who want to make everybody feel sorry for what went on in 1720.

"We have a lot of those people around here. They get a lot of money—the Kennedys remind me of them. They went out and robbed everybody they could get their hands on, and then when they got all the money they'd need for the rest of their lives, they suddenly felt like the white man had been horrible to everybody. You know, the Indians, and the blacks, and the Italians, and everybody else."

Colleagues who shared the FedEx executive suite in 1978 speculate that Smith's outbursts about Memphis's shortcomings were triggered by antipathetic impulses. "You must remember," said Charles Lea, "that Fred was just emerging from severe trauma and embarrassments. Layer after layer of insult and injury were taken off."

Lea was referring, of course, to the bank fraud trial in Little Rock, the traffic fatality in Memphis, Smith's divorce and remarriage, and the lawsuit with his sisters over the millions in the family trust.

"I think he just became ebullient," said Lea. "Sure he got cocky. We had just made him CEO again, which he had not been. I think

Fred grew up a lot. The executive committee told him to go and get it—and he did!"

Art Bass believes that Smith—either from his gorging on the history of military tactics or his own natural combativeness—automatically responds to challenge, competition, or insult with an immediate counterattack.

"Count on it!" he said. "Every time!"

Perhaps the FedEx chairman was responding defiantly to the titters echoing through Memphis society about his office romance and the untimely birth of his first son, and from suggestions that he might be cut from the same "roughneck" cloth as his father.

If so, he did it with a vengeance.

The "landed gentry" came in for most of his assaults. He was singling out the city's business elite, for the most part executives from old-line pre–Civil War aristocracy, whom he accused of clinging to "the plantation mentality." In a number of speeches he hammered this group as "insular, extremely conservative, and exclusionary. . . . They claim to be broad-minded, but they are not."

Smith criticized Memphis for having a "police problem." Roger Frock recalled: "I think he thought the police were picking on the black employees we had, because they were stopping them when they were driving home from the hub. Saying what business did minorities have being out at that time of night. I know he was riled up about that for a while."

Just at that time Smith had been singled out as one of the ten best executives in the country's "medium-size businesses." The kudo was voiced by the *Gallagher President's Report,* a New York–based weekly newsletter to corporate executives.

He was cited "for bringing a $110 million miniairline from start-up position to $8.2 million net in five years through innovative distribution ideas plus 'public company' management style at a privately held firm."

Ironically, E. W. "Ned" Cook, the chairman of the Memphis Airport board, who had been largely instrumental on clearing the way for Federal Express to establish its Memphis hub, was named in the same report as one of America's ten worst executives.

Cook was cited for "$87.4 million loss in fiscal 1977 at $400 million Memphis-based agricultural products processor resulting in 41 percent decline in stockholders' equity to $70.2 million."

Memphis newspapers got really angry when Smith unleashed his scathing opinions in an interview in the August 1978 *Esquire,* which commended him as "a noteworthy example of the imaginative and aggressive entrepreneur who is still alive and throbbing in the South."

The article, by business writer Dan Dorfman, said at one point:

> I wondered about the city, which recently made national headlines when some angry firefighters, unable to land a new wage contract, ran amok by setting over 200 fires all over town. (And no new contract has yet been signed.)
>
> "Memphis is a horrible place," Smith told me. "There are serious structural problems when thirty percent of the people earn seventy percent of the income and seventy percent (primarily blacks) get only thirty percent of the income. You have a massive underemployed black population, and it's not because the jobs aren't there or the blacks don't want to work. The real problem is that powerful interests in this city want the status quo maintained.
>
> "It's a backwater town that's not very progressive in either business relations or race relations."

The *Memphis Press-Scimitar* dispatched a reporter to Federal Express headquarters to get an explanation of the label "backwater town," which unfortunately had been pinned on Memphis by *Time* magazine ten years earlier in the aftermath of the Martin Luther King assassination.

Like many subjects who give frank interviews, Fred Smith had thought better of his candor and claimed that in several instances he was either misquoted or misinterpreted.

"Obviously I'm a fan of Memphis," he told the local reporter, "or I wouldn't be here. But the city doesn't seem to be able to get its act together on the economic front."

The "horrible place" quote, however, "was taken completely out of context," Smith said. "Basically, what I was trying to get across to him was that Memphis has at one point in time (1968) had horrible, horrible problems centering around race. And the city still does have racial problems. And largely because of that there's been an ambience about the place—it's divided along racial lines (in elections). That is a very, very serious problem. Some spark is missing. The problem is the city doesn't have enough jobs."

The reporter asked what he meant by "powerful interests" wanting the "status quo" maintained in Memphis. "I can only conclude that there must be some reason the proposals don't get passed," Smith said. "In most of the financial packages, they eventually evolve into some sort of bickering between financial institutions. . . . There is a tremendous resistance to change."

The *Esquire* writer angered Smith when he questioned him about money and marriage.

> "Money doesn't mean a damn thing to me," he says. "I don't need a lot of money, and I don't spend a lot of money." Added Smith (who drives a 1977 Ford): "Money may be a way of keeping score, but a Rolls-Royce in the driveway is not."

Fred Smith told the writer "about a growing life-style he believes corporate wives will have to adjust to if they want to hold on to hubby. It sounded simply dreadful."

> It's hardly unusual for executives to work long, late hours in pursuit of fast, important company advancement. And most wives adjust to it. But Smith, who puts in a seventy-hour workweek and is often away from home a few nights a week, tells me the problem of absentee husbands is going to get a lot worse. He says time constraints on today's executives are reaching such proportions—both inside and outside the office—that the corporate wife is going to be forced to seek intellectual fulfillment through her own resources to a much greater degree than in the past. "And if she doesn't," he says, "you're going to have a problem marriage."

The *Esquire* writer described having drinks with Fred Smith "at his new $275,000 twelve-room house in the heart of Memphis," and apparently they engaged in an all-guards-down conversation.

"An executive at a growth company can no longer afford to tend just to his own business," says Smith. "He's got to put something back in the system, to get involved in local activities so he knows what's going on in the outside world. The day is over when you can insulate yourself; the system no longer permits it. That means the forty-hour workweek is dead . . . and the wife has to understand and respond to these pressures."

Does the new wife understand? "How do you feel about Fred being away one or two nights a week?" I asked Diane, a tall, attractive brunette.

"You mean three or four nights a week sometimes," she snapped back. "No, I don't like it. So I try reading more, writing, painting. There's also the children (from their previous marriages) to take care of . . . and I'm teaching dancing. It's not easy, but I try."

Smith nodded his approval as he sipped a glass of Dom Pérignon in his backyard. "You have to be absolutely brutal in the management of your time," he explained defensively. "And remember this company is really just getting started."

Perhaps, I thought, if Smith were present at the creation, he might have asked God to add an eighth day.

For a man who did not fancy Rolls-Royces and to whom money didn't "mean a damn thing," Fred Smith suddenly found himself on his way to becoming one of the Fortune 400.

In fiscal 1979 the FedEx chairman was paid $200,000, which put him in the top echelon of Memphis executives. His pay was above two leading bankers, National Bank of Commerce's Bruce Campbell (at $160,000) and Union Planter's William Matthews (at $186,400), and slightly under First Tennessee's Ron Terry (at $211,236). However, he did not come close to Cook Industries' "Ned" Cook, who earned $440,834.

Federal Express finally became lucrative for its start-up executives. The year the CEO made $200,000, President Art Bass's pay in cash and cash-equivalent remuneration was $426,329. Also getting more than the boss were executive vice-president Peter S. Willmott ($337,560); and senior vice-presidents J. Vincent Fagan ($266,520) and James R. Ridemeyer ($258,968).

What made the pay envelopes of these subordinates so heavy was a stock purchase arrangement of the mid-1970s, established long before the company went public. FedEx sold 384,638 shares to certain officers for $625,923 and loaned them most of the money to buy the stock at 4–6 percent annual interest. The average price in those dark years for Federal Express was about $1.60 a share, after adjustments for the subsequent public offerings and splits. The difference between the issuing price and the average open market price of the stock—over $20—was reflected in the executive pay column.

Like many plutocrats, Smith found himself at odds with the tax collector.

In September 1978 the IRS hit him with a personal income tax bill for the years 1972, 1973, and 1974 that came to $634,912.51, including penalties. This centered chiefly on a dispute over how much profit Smith made on the purchase and sale of 466 acres of farmland in De Soto County, Mississippi. The government contended that he realized a long-term capital gain of $1.1 million; he reported instead an "ordinary" gain of $17,945.

When he couldn't reach a settlement with the IRS, he appealed January 9, 1979, to the U.S. tax court.

Smith might have had more such disputes with the tax collector if he hadn't pulled off another of his stunning congressional coups in 1978. It is still talked about, and marveled at, among his close friends. Charles Lea recalled: "Fred went to Washington in 1978 and spent a lot of time working to get a rollback on the capital gains tax from 49 to 26 percent. Of course that has to originate in the House Ways and Means Committee, which has thirty-seven members. It is almost impossible to get a majority vote in that committee. But Fred got one of them to draft a measure and then worked and worked to get signatures. He needed nineteen, but he was still one short of a majority. Finally he presented his case to Representative Harold Ford of Tennessee, a young black guy, and was able to convince him that the tax rollback would be good for entrepreneurship in general and Tennessee in particular. He got Congressman Ford to sign as the nineteenth and got it through Congress even though it was opposed by the secretary of the treasury and the White House. We all called it the 'Frederick Wallace Smith Relief Act.' "

The lower capital gains tax, of course, saved him several million dollars on the appreciation of his Federal Express stock.

His earnings in 1982 came to $51 million, according to a *Business Week* survey, making him America's highest-paid corporate executive for that year. For that he could thank a Wall Street rally that sent FedEx stock prices soaring, permitting him to cash in stock options that provided all his income except for $414,000 in salary and bonus.

Still in his thirties, Smith might have been dismissed by Memphians at large as an erudite gadfly. He wasn't, not even by entrenched society, for the obvious reason that he had created a business that brought Memphis great national attention and prestige, his financial clout was becoming heavier and heavier, and he had created hundreds of badly needed jobs—reasonably good jobs—for local citizens.

Knowing his voice would command attention. Smith decided in 1979 to try to help give Memphis its first black mayor, and he vigorously pushed the candidacy of W. Otis Higgs, Jr., a former criminal court judge who had already run unsuccessfully in 1975.

At an integrated Higgs luncheon on Beale Street, Smith made an emotional appeal for Memphians to respond "Yes, we can" to the challenge of making the city more progressive.

"Contrary to our own thoughts about ourself," Smith said, "Memphis is a viable, productive place." Federal Express commissioned a survey by independent researchers, he said, that found Memphis an ideal city for industry to locate. "Workers here are more productive and have a lower absenteeism rate than any other metropolitan city." Even so, he said, the "backwater" image persisted; and he blamed lack of leadership for the label.

In backing Higgs, Smith trampled a long family relationship with former Mayor Wyeth Chandler, son of his father's lawyer, confidant, and social mentor. Chandler was upset by Smith's support of Higgs. Recalling the events of a decade earlier, he said in a 1991 interview:

I really didn't know him. He had come back to Memphis. He had put together this company, which is a good company. But that doesn't make him wise in the affairs of man, you know. That just makes him able to run a good company, to make one good business guess.

He never gave me any help or hindrance. Never asked me for anything. I helped him, as a matter of fact, when I was on the city council. I worked very hard behind the scenes to give him all that airport property out there so he'd have a way to conduct his business. But he never knew that, apparently, or cared about it.

And I don't know where he was getting his information from. I know that he has always been some kind of a zealot on civil rights. Where he got that from, I don't have any idea.

Later on he worked with me trying to get a professional football team here, and was very cooperative. Gave me his plane a couple of times to fly to Chicago and St. Louis.

I didn't know anything about Fred Smith's politics. To me, he's always been kind of weird. When he backed Higgs, he didn't know Higgs from Adam. All I know is, I went out to his place [Federal Express] and campaigned, and I'm sure I got ninety percent of the people who worked for him. They voted for me. They couldn't have cared less what he thought. Higgs ran twice against me and lost both times, and then went back to practicing law and did reasonably well. He's not really a bad guy.

The city [government] was a great help to Fred Smith. He had a good deal on the airport property. He had one councilman, Lewis Donelson, who was trying to ram it through city council, and Ned Cook, a bigwig here, was his ramrod at the airport. I don't know whether he ever gave me any credit for helping him or not. I always had the feeling he thought his people were getting things done without my help, when in fact Cook or Donelson couldn't do a thing without me.

I was hurt—not hurt, but I was kind of amazed that here's a man who comes into the city that we all worked for, everybody in government worked diligently to do everything we could to help him, and I feel like I'd been part and parcel of that. The next thing I know I'm running for mayor and he's out there backing my opponent.

It may have been based on race. He had never sat down and talked to me a day, a minute, about what I'd done, about this, that, or the other. How I felt about it or anything. And making statements our government was hidebound and I was a plantation mentality sort of guy. It just amazed me. I don't mind anybody who sits down with me and says "How do you feel about this, that, and the other?" And then they say "Look, I'm against that. And I want to get out and beat your butt!" That's fine.

I have always thought in my own mind that it was nothing so personal against me as it was just a way he could express he was not a southern redneck—he was an educated, up east liberal.

Smith continued his civic activism, attacking the influx of "parochial, very doctrinaire" rural whites; the blacks who mistakenly saw "each and every issue as a civil rights battle"; and the patricians, the "landed gentry."

The politicians were running for cover, and the businessmen largely were sitting on their hands, he announced. But all was not lost. At an ecumenical luncheon at Catholic High School on October 30, 1978, he saw reason for hope.

"The leadership has got to come from the religious community," he said. "It is the only element that has credibility and nonpartisanship." But thus far he'd found the city's clergy "far too timid in recognizing the tremendous marketing opportunities that exist in this city" for their leadership. "Memphis needs a religious community that calls it like it is." But he didn't let the preachers forget their past misdeeds, pointing his accusatory finger back to the strikes by police and firemen.

"There was no excuse for those strikes," he said, "yet I did not hear the religious community standing up and making themselves heard. . . . This city is desperate for your leadership. . . . Please do not let this city down by failing to take on this challenge. . . . Put on that marketing hat and go out and sell a little bit."

For months the Memphis newspapers had given the Federal Express chairman's broadsides serious and lengthy coverage. Now the *Commercial Appeal* seemed to feel it was time for him to back off a trifle. A few days after the Catholic High School speech, the newspaper printed this editorial:

MR. SMITH'S MEMPHIS

Frederick W. Smith, board chairman and chief executive officer of Federal Express, is solidly on the record these days about Memphis and the problems which are peculiarly its own.

It appears, at least, that he cares. The same cannot always be said for his peers in what is generally defined as the business community.

In Smith's latest recitation, given before a local ecumenical conference, it is easy to agree that Memphis has suffered from the parochial attitudes of citizens black and white, and from a "landed gentry" which tends to be "insular and exclusionary." The facts of our contemporary history make all of that fairly obvious.

We would quarrel, however, with Smith's apparent conclusion that new, more active and progressive citizenship is beyond the capacity of any in this city, save the clergy. . . .

That brush is too broad. And some of his strokes with it are faulty. . . .

The point is, Memphis is a big and complex city. Too big and too complex to pin all its hopes on any one of its many resources.

Nobody should count any of us out.

But nothing daunted Smith, and even the *Commercial Appeal* was forced to concede in mid-1980 that he had become "the town's best attraction around the civic club circuit."

He was the only multimillionaire in Memphis who could get away with it.

Lewis Nolan, a bright *Commercial Appeal* reporter who kept close tabs on Federal Express, observed that Smith "is considered wildly antiestablishment in some quarters. His driving around town in a Federal Express van or dented station wagon does nothing to assuage that perception. Smith was summarily booted off the board of directors of the Memphis Area Chamber of Commerce last year for playing hookey."

Failing to show up for meetings, or being late, was not uncommon for Smith. Charles Lea recalled waiting in vain for him to arrive in San Antonio for a long planned weekend. Fred Smith's excuse for not showing up: "I had to take my daughter to the dentist." In New York, late for an important meeting, he told J. Tucker Morse: "I couldn't find my socks." (That may have been true, because colleagues say he came to a top-level meeting at Chase Manhattan Bank wearing no socks.)

In the summer of 1980 he was described as by far the most visible executive in Memphis and also one of the most interesting. Covering a Fred Smith speech at the posh Summit Club on the thirty-third floor of Clark Tower, Nolan noted the audience "laps up his jabs and jeers," adding:

> Doubling his allotted podium time without losing the attention of a single listener, Smith characterizes the Memphis power structure as "three billiard balls. They roll around the table and occasionally crack into each other, then go their own ways."
>
> The first is the one he is most intimate with, the group he calls "the landed aristocracy." He says many are his childhood friends whose family wealth is based on agriculture. Any actions to enhance the economic growth hold little personal appeal for them.
>
> The second is what he terms the "parochials." This Anglo-Saxon group embraces the famous Puritan work ethic and fundamental view of the Bible. But it also has the Puritan intolerance for outsiders and those who would change the status quo.

The third is the civil rights leadership, which has found it in its best economic interest to exploit along racial lines those issues that are not racial in nature. He gave as an example the willingness of black elected officials to depict the now settled United Furniture Workers strike against Memphis Furniture Manufacturing Co., as a struggle for racial equality. In Smith's reality, the basic issue was the value in the marketplace that workers add to products which must compete in many parts of the country.

Coming up to grip his hand afterward are some of the city's most wealthy and influential businessmen. They are members of the Economic Club of Memphis, who that night elected iconoclast Smith their president.

"Fred, what do you think about . . ." "Say, Fred, I really enjoyed . . ." "We've not met before, Fred, but . . ." "Fred . . ." "Fred . . ." "Fred . . ." And so it goes, here and elsewhere, as the peripatetic (that is the kind of polysyllabic word he favors) Mr. Smith makes his public speaking rounds.

The Memphis media found that Smith's messages developed a sameness, reminiscent of those given by political candidates. But they seemed to work. He unabashedly gave the identical speech to both the Rotary Club and the Better Business Bureau, yet neither seemed to mind. "His biggest lectern asset," wrote Nolan, "is fresh honesty. It isn't just his wealth, position, or even personal magnetism that gives an aura of excitement to most anything he says. This town is full of people who wished they had listened earlier to the young man's plans for starting up the single largest venture capital deal in United States history.

"This time around, he has the ears of many. They love to hear him, but one wonders if they are truly listening."

In 1979 Smith plunged unexpectedly into big-time politics by becoming national finance chairman in the presidential campaign of Senator Howard Baker, Republican of Tennessee.

Political columnists were confused because they had considered Fred Smith a Democrat, a supporter of Jimmy Carter in 1976. "That's not particularly true," he explained. "We've [Federal Express] supported various candidates. I would say I'm much more independent than anything else. I believe more in betting on the man."

He said he would basically recruit a good state finance chairman to raise a sufficient amount of money to conduct the primaries. "I don't anticipate that to be an impossible task," he said.

But in August, only four months after taking the job, Smith quit and was replaced as Baker's chief fund-raiser by Ted Welch of Nashville.

No seasoned politician, he had discovered painfully that he could not handle the monster of a task. He offered the traditional excuse for stepping down—too busy with his own business affairs. He told the press: "I have just not been able to spend the time on the situation that it really requires, although we raised him [Baker] some money."

The brief experience in national politics was a sort of inspiration. Smith began to develop an idea that he might like to take his own fling as a candidate for some high office.

But for now that was only a vague possibility for sometime in the distant future.

He really was too busy with his own business affairs to do much of anything else.

17▶ DRAMA AT MIDNIGHT

On a chilly midnight in late 1980 Smith whizzed past the runway lights at Memphis International Airport, parked at the Federal Express hub, and headed straight for operations chief Mike Fitzgerald.

"What's the lift look like tonight?" he asked with repressed anxiety.

"Big," said Fitzgerald. "Damn big. High nineties—maybe one hundred thousand."

"Can you handle it?"

Fitzgerald, a sunny Irishman, gave the boss a waggish look. In his mind's eye he could look back seven years to the incredibly disappointing tiny package count at the start-up. (He recalled: "I could have sorted everything the Falcons brought in those nights in the back of my station wagon.")

For most of 1980 Smith had been a frequent midnight visitor, fearful the hub operation was dangerously overloaded. Any minute now this corner of the airport would explode with frenetic action. As usual, the Federal Express planes were flying in time-sensitive packages from all corners of America. Except for these flights, Memphis Airport was asleep for the night, with no commercial traffic scheduled. Fitzgerald's crew at the hub was under a tight deadline. They had a "window" of roughly three to four hours in which to unload the incoming planes, sort the cargo, and reroute all the packages back out along the "spokes" to their overnight destinations.

"Oh, don't fret, Fred," Fitzgerald said. "Our boys will do the job."

Smith relied on the expertise Fitzgerald had acquired in his earlier career at UPS. It had been up to Fitzgerald to design the hub—a long and fairly narrow building at 2837 Sprankel Avenue—one thousand feet by two hundred fifty feet, with a roof forty feet high. A network of moving conveyor belts snaked around the interior, going at different speeds—some fast, some slow, up and down, several making seemingly impossible right-angle turns. At various junctures the higher belts rolled past slides where packages could be diverted to another section of the sort. All this movement was meant to deliver cargo to workstations where sorters looked at the address and sent the shipment on by new belt circuits to be containerized again for the outbound plane that would take it on to proper overnight destination.

Outside, on the edge of the darkened asphalt aprons, were docking areas for the incoming fleet. Dropping from the night sky, now that Fred Smith had won his deregulation fight in Congress, were not only the Falcon fan jets, but much larger and more efficient aircraft—giant McDonnell Douglas DC-10s and Boeing 727s and 737s. When the pilot of a 727 shut down his engines, the ground crew could unload him in eighteen minutes. That meant taking out eight tent-shaped aluminum containers, each as large as a small living room, setting them on lowboy trailers, and trundling them quickly into the hub building.

For efficiency, the hub had no doors. The ends and sides, of course, had a number of huge portals, but these were covered by thick dangling plastic strips about a foot wide. Mainly these flimsy barriers were intended to help keep out the weather, but on winter nights the hub was usually cold. Tractor drivers pulling a string of trailers loaded with cargo containers would pause at the strip "door" long enough to honk a warning, then barrel on through.

To keep the army of sorters keenly aware of their deadline, giant clocks were positioned around the hub—counting down the minutes. Zero hour was 2:30 A.M.—when all sorting was supposed to be completed and the cargo loaded up for its outbound flights. The clocks were first started at 11:00 P.M. and then reset at 12:30 A.M. for the final two hours. Sorters could see a giant red pointer. If it pointed down they still had some minutes until deadline; if up, they were behind schedule.

Incoming containers were dumped on two parallel conveyor belts that trundled the separate packages slowly through a crew of thirty or forty, who scanned the address label and snatched packages off the line and put them on one of the destination belts moving behind them. There were five of these conveyors, and they moved slightly faster.

"One of these belts, for instance, would be designated to carry all packages for Illinois, Indiana, Wisconsin, Pennsylvania, and Ohio," said Fitzgerald. "Another would take all cargo for the Northeast, another the Southeast, and so on. Those packages would then travel the high-speed belt to a secondary sort, where they would come down a slide, at whose foot were more sorters ready to make a further breakdown—for example, putting everything for Chicago on one conveyor and cargo to handled by Peoria on another."

At first the hub was far too large. But with the package volume beginning to grow with the fury of a prairie fire, the operation had been experiencing strain for months.

Many a midnight Smith came out to do his homework, trying to unravel more of the mysteries of this end of the business. In particular he was trying to comprehend the specific make-or-break points in the sort mechanism and to see for himself that all was going well not only with the planes and the packages, but also with people.

"When Fred came out to the hub," Fitzgerald said, "it was not to check belt speeds or production levels. He was out there waving the colors and talking to people. He has a great knack for going around and making sure that what he was being told was true—like people in the hub are happy.

"His philosophy was—and it was good—that all senior vice-presidents worked in the hub on certain nights, loading and unloading, and so forth, and preferably on nice cold nights. So they could get the flavor of what the hell was going on."

This night some of the purple birds were already aloft for their pilgrimage home. The plane from Binghamton, New York, had arrived at 10:15 P.M. From the east and west, forty-seven others would follow. Not every pilot would arrive on time. Things seemed to happen, little glitches. Any delay of a FedEx plane reaching Memphis put an emergency strain on the hub. And the hub operation itself was not immune to accidents and snafus.

"When an aircraft comes in late," Fitzgerald recalled, "you just put a lot more bodies at the job and force speed. We had that happen all the time. They came in late because drivers were hanging out to the very last minute to get the very last package from a customer who had to have it on the plane; and we were very accommodating. So you learn to live with that."

Weather was often a problem—but rarely in Memphis. "The hub would be crystal clear," said Fitzgerald, "But New York, Boston, and Chicago could be up to their hips in snow. So much of that delay had to be overcome with sheer manpower; a lot of it was accomplished with the rescheduling of aircraft. But in terms of some wild thing happening, it was just every night!

"Belts would tear and go off the head rollers. A carton of paint buckets might break open and fall off the conveyor and splash other packages. Somebody would hit an airplane with a forklift, which put the aircraft down—and it seems they waited to do that until after the airplane was already loaded! Those kinds of things happening."

Even on the night Fred Smith was worrying about overload, relief was on the way. Not unexpectedly, the boss had ordered construction of a new "superhub." It was three times as large as the present facility, enclosing almost eight hundred thousand square feet under one roof, and more sophisticated than the first sort building, which was a simple gravity-driven operation.

Within a matter of weeks, by the early part of January 1981, the new structure would be finished and the nightly sort operation would be transferred to the larger, faster, high-tech hub.

For its time, the original hub was extremely efficient. In his years at United Parcel Fitzgerald learned a lot about belt speeds and what production levels men could achieve in the different sort stages. In the first (or rough) sort, one man could handle about a thousand packages an hour. That meant, given a three-hour work span, it would require a crew of thirty to complete the primary sort, if the lift was ninety thousand.

"The first is rough and fast," Fitzgerald said. "The secondary took a little more study, and the tertiary, the third sort, where you are down to the areas of a city, for instance, takes even longer. So your production levels, your manning levels, are obviously based on the complexity of the job."

The pure mechanics of the sort operations were of limited interest to Fred Smith. "His involvement in this was less of a technical nature in terms of discussing how many pieces per hour could go through a hub, although he would do that," said Fitzgerald. "He was a quick study, and he was up on all terms of production, especially in tying production to service levels, to make certain it was actually productive.

"On the other side of it he watched closely that things were not done in the name of expediency that altered or injured our approach to the treatment of people. He was kind of our watchdog.

"He wanted to know, for instance, how you put large numbers of people into a building and it remains a good place to work. How do you feed them? Not everybody is part-time; you have large numbers of people who are full-time, overlapping, people coming in by aircraft. How is hot food provided? What is the quality? He's not going to sample the soup, although he did that, too. But these are considerations that we would keep in mind, and he just made sure that we did. Locker rooms, bathroom facilities . . . How are you going to make sure that with such large numbers of people our messages are going out clearly and that we have good interactive reaction with them?"

In the early 1980s, growth in and of itself—whether fast, as it was, or slow—became a major problem. Finally, it was necessary to alter the concept of one hub to serve all spokes of the system. Sticking with that scheme led to a bottleneck.

"We developed regional hubs," said Fitzgerald, "and made other adjustments. We simply had to bleed off volume from the Memphis hub, for three big reasons. First, you can only get so much freight through a window, a time window. That's a fairly short window they have in Memphis. So if you can effectively bleed off volume that they don't have to handle there, your productivity levels are better. You can take stuff that never should have been put on an airplane and reduce loading time, sorting time; it just doesn't have to fly.

That's a basic rule in distribution—if it doesn't have to move, don't move it."

Fitzgerald illustrated this point by singling out packages originating in New York City. "Let's say freight coming out of LaGuardia Airport will have some merchandise that ultimately ends up being served out of Newark Airport. Under the old scheme you threw everything into the airplane, flew it to Memphis, and sorted and sent it back to Newark, because there wasn't enough Newark volume to make it worthwhile bleeding it off and sending it by truck.

"Now as the volume grew, and you watched your package flows from point to point, you'd see LaGuardia is generating three hundred packages served by Newark. You have the pickup drivers keep them separate in their truck, sort it all out, and put them on a FedEx truck going to Newark. That would keep three hundred packages out of the hub. You might send another two hundred to Albany by truck. If you multiplied those kinds of numbers across the country, you might pull out of the Memphis hub several thousand packages that never had to go there in the first place."

In time a central hub grows too big and unwieldy. "You get a monstrosity," said Fitzgerald. "The dynamics of that many people and packages in one place are just not worth the management it takes to do it. Too difficult to do. It's the same at United Parcel Service. They have some number in their mind that whenever the volume in one of their hubs reaches that, they put up another hub, located geographically away.

"You don't have great masses of people all milling around in same general area in the same time frame. You are trying to supervise the people, keeping your relationship with them meaningful, because the work must get done and the employee is a part of the process, not just cattle that you are herding around.

"My opinion is that it's not a worthwhile task to try to get all kinds of people under one roof, simply because it's in one place."

The phenomenon of Federal Express was under rather steady surveillance from the Memphis's largest daily newspaper, the *Com-*

mercial Appeal. One feature writer captured much of the color, tension, and drama of the hub in a December 28, 1980, story.

> Not until, after 11 P.M. does the hub come totally alive. Furiously alive. Frantically alive. If commerce has lifeblood, it may be passing through: human organs, vital spare parts, and urgent documents. The hub is the heart, and the packages must be pumped through. All of them.
>
> Tonight 91,301 packages will be handled by Federal Express. Some of the packages may come from San Francisco to be sorted in Memphis and shipped to Los Angeles. It sounds crazy, but it works. Crazy doesn't seem to bother Frederick W. Smith, the company founder. Crazy may be genius, and so it is that most city-to-city deliveries whisk through Memphis as part of the "hub and spokes" concept that allows Federal Express to dominate the overnight package-delivery business. Its 18 million shipments inside the United States is larger than that of Emery Air Freight, the world's largest freight forwarder, and is more than the combined shipments of the next four largest such companies.
>
> Of the tens of thousands of packages handled nightly, only about 150 will discredit the company's promise of "absolutely, positively, overnight" delivery by noon the next day. Officials claim the odds of a package being lost, stolen, or damaged while in company hands is 4,500 to 1. One odd package from the handful of failures apparently contained seat belt buckles: the buckles are scattered on the concrete floor inside the sorting building.
>
> Most of the sorters are part-time employees, and many are college students. They move the packages, not throw them. Among the parcels passing through are poisons, flammable concoctions, and radioactive substances; also included in the swarm are computer programs and laboratory specimens.
>
> Among those last, for instance, may be tadpoles. One employee says such a package broke open one night, bringing home another reason for care in handling: esthetics.
>
> Also vividly remembered along the odd-size package conveyor is an eight-foot-long bright green pickle.

Almost anything can be urgent to someone, somewhere.
And so the pickle moves tonight, too.
At a price.

The reporter is fascinated by a flood of packages rising on the conveyors as the clock counts down. "Ninety-eight, ninety-seven, ninety-six . . . Incoming conveyor belts must make right-angle turns, something that defies physics and the laws of inertia. Inside the sorting arena at the corner of an incoming belt, a man works against physics. He uses a pole to prod packages that hesitate in the 90-degree turn. He stands on a platform six feet above the floor and prods. He looks like a lumberman working a log jam. . . . One large box breaks loose and falls eight feet to the floor."

United States Customs officials are on duty. Their job is to examine parcels arriving from Federal Express agents in Canada or from some overseas freight forwarder. FedEx has its own desk on the far side of the building for shipments requiring special paper-work—radioactive materials, poisons, and corrosive substances. Even money comes in on the purple-and-white birds—locked in bulky purses. Mostly this is Federal Express cash; it is unloaded in a wire cage and put in a safe.

Nearby a crew mans a special rewrap desk, keeping a sharp eye for busted packages they will repair or for others they are able to intercept before they come unglued.

A speaker announces that the sort will be finished at 2:40 A.M.—ten minutes after the arrow shifts from pointing down to pointing up. Some conveyor belts have broken down tonight; three planes arrived more than thirty minutes after they were scheduled to; two will be that far behind schedule in leaving.

Above the conveyors, above the sorting hands and moving belts, managers eye the flow and issue directions by radio. They are like gods on their platform; their hands move dials, and movement begins/ends/slows/speeds.

The arrow shifts. The sort is almost over.

By the routes they came, the packages will not return. New routes and new pilots are their destiny. New planes.

Now the clock reads 3:45 A.M. One by one, the last planes leave. The hubub stills.

The heart stops.

The wonder is that it could ever be started.

In comparison with United Parcel Service hubs, the original Federal Express sorting center was, as Fitzgerald said, "really a hub in miniature. It wasn't all that big. But it certainly was more time-intensive than any UPS hub." United Parcel's truck-hauled traffic never got trapped trying to go through a three- or four-hour nighttime "window." But later on, that criterion underwent abrupt and decided change when UPS plunged into the overnight air freight business, trying to compete with FedEx.

The advent of the Memphis superhub gave Federal Express the ability to move between half a million and seven hundred fifty thousand packages a night.

Said Fitzgerald: "It represented a quantum leap for us from a belt, labor-intensive, straight over-the-ground conveyor hub that had multiple belts and slides. The superhub got into container handling, with elevators bringing packages to the workstation, with scanners and automatic diverters. As packages moved along the conveyors, the sorter could use a keyboard that would trigger an arm coming out of the side of the channel of a belt and push and nudge the package to a specific slide or discharge point. And that could happen two hundred fifty feet down the line after the guy keyed it in. It was that sensitive; it would count the packages and get the right one.

"That kind of technology existed in the marketplace, and what had to be done was to take it and adapt it to our specific needs. The credit for that goes to Mike Basch [another former United Parcel veteran who was recruited by Smith]. He headed up the superhub task force. He did a remarkable job."

Most of the FedEx sorters were students from Memphis State University. Fred Smith & Company copied their hub personnel tactics, along with many other proven techniques, from United Parcel Service.

"It was a fairly simple thing to do," said Fitzgerald, "if your work is located near a university, military bases, or even high schools. UPS learned a long time ago to have a large number of part-time workers. They all supplement their income by that. They are by and large an easy force to work with. We especially wanted college kids, and made every effort to get them into other jobs where they could learn more about the company. Then when they graduated we could often hire a college graduate with about two years of practical experience with our company."

There developed a down side, however, to the "college kid" syndrome that disturbed Smith and prompted him to correct the problem with his typical innovative thinking.

As he recalled: "In our cargo terminal here in Memphis we were having a hell of a problem keeping things running on time. The airplanes would come in and everything would get backed up. We tried every kind of control mechanism that you could think of, and none of them worked.

"Finally it became obvious that the underlying problem was that it was in the interest of the employees at the hub—they were college kids, mostly—to run late, because it meant they made more money. So what we did was give them all a minimum guarantee and say, 'Look, if you get through before a certain time, just go home, and you will have beat the system.' Well, it was unbelievable. In the space of about forty-five days, the place was way ahead of schedule. And I don't even think it was a conscious thing on their part."

Of many nights at the hub, the one that Fitzgerald remembers most vividly was "a real pain in the butt—our first bomb scare."

One night in the late seventies, Federal Express operations office got an anonymous telephone call, with a startling message: "A bomb is planted in one of your airplanes. It is going to blow up tonight." End of call.

"I was at the hub that night," said Fitzgerald. "So was Art Bass. The aircraft had already come in, and the hub was humping along. The trouble was the caller never said it was going to blow up in New York or Toledo, or anywhere else. So the whole fleet would be effectively down.

"So Art and I began working on strategy, with the help of the pilots. All the aircraft were gone over, as best we could. Security was alerted. We did everything we could—which really wasn't much.

"Now it came down to one question: What do we do?

"We had the merchandise to get out. If we shut down the hub that night, I think we could have expected to receive a similar anonymous phone call a night—forever!

"So it was critical, as to just what we did. Obviously we didn't want to put anybody in danger. Our security officer said whoever took the call had heard that voice before—and the guy sounded like a kook.

"We made another check of all the airplanes. Some pilots said, 'The hell with it! Let's go!' Some were on the fence, and some were kind of reluctant to fly. So we gathered the pilots—we had about thirty planes then—and enlisted their thoughts. What do we do? We listened, and the talk went back and forth.

"Then Art and I spoke to the pilots and said, 'We're convinced about this, we've done this and that, and we'll fly ourselves with anybody here. You just name it, tell us where to go, and we're on the plane. That's how confident we are!' That went a long way to quieting things down.

"One of the pilots was flying down to Florida, and he said, 'Come fly with me.' And I did, to Jacksonville and then on to Miami. Art went with somebody to Chicago, I believe.

"Did any pilot refuse to fly that night? No, not a one. That was when we were in a truly pivotal state of our growth. We couldn't afford to have a massive service interruption. There was a lot of customer skepticism at that time about the airplane hub. 'Why are you taking my package to Memphis? I'm sending it from Albany to Newark, and you are taking it to Memphis. What the hell are you doing that for?'

"We tried to explain that, but I assure you it is not easy for the average person to understand that. So it was critical that we protect the service, as well as at the same time truly not endanger any employee. But I can tell you we would have had a rash of those calls for a long time had the hub shut down.

"I don't take anything away from Fred Smith on this. He just wasn't at the airport that night, and we didn't feel we had to communicate all kinds of stuff to him. Art was president, and I was senior vice-president."

18▶ *OUT OF A HIGH-TECH BRAIN*

In the few years surrounding his fortieth birthday, Smith burst forth with a new round of creative thinking, decision making, advice giving, and action. In what struck some close colleagues as a mad flurry, he launched bold—and sometimes desperate—new ideas. Several of these ventures were flops; at least one was a disaster that cost millions. Even so, he marched forward, headstrong, un-inhibited, sure of his own judgment.

In the process he pitched overboard many of the entrepreneurs who had gambled their careers on his idea and helped him rise in the air freight industry. (It must be noted that most of these men departed millionaires.)

And he kept the Federal Express reins in his own hands, exploit-ing his vaunted personal touch in something of a one-man show that impressed customers and competitors alike.

It is questionable whether he could have found the peace and freedom necessary to inspire this fresh spate of invention while having to defend himself against accusations that angered and threatened him.

The lawsuit in which his two half sisters accused him of robbing the family trust, wrongfully signing away their share of the millions left by their father, was a dagger at his throat. Smith seemed destined to be brought again before judge and jury—in civil court this time—to account for his financial machinations in his struggle to launch Federal Express.

Lawyers on both sides of the dispute prepared in the spring of 1976 for trial by taking sworn depositions from Smith and his sisters. These private proceedings developed into brutal confrontations and indicated a public trial would air sensational allegations that might be harmful to the image of FedEx.

The sisters' counsel accused Smith point-blank of usurping Fredette's and Laura Ann's shares of the estate in collusion with certain bank officers for his sole benefit.

Fred Smith exploded. He had accused Fredette of being "disloyal" when she'd first brought in lawyers, and now he shouted that she was guilty of telling "a direct and unconscionable and absolute lie."

In fierce language he also attacked one of his sisters' lawyers, Robert Molloy, for statements he allegedly made to attorneys for Chase Manhattan Bank in New York, one of the financial backers of Federal Express.

Molloy, Smith said in his deposition, made it a point to contact the Chase Manhattan counsel "and screamed and yelled at them and told them that he was going to enjoin the financing, which would have meant the bankruptcy of Federal Express, and the sisters took on very much an adversary relation, and the rest of the investors said to hell with the Enterprise Company. . . ."

Smith conceded that Federal Express at that time owed banks and other lenders about $45 million and that the debt would have to be repaid before the money he had taken out of the Enterprise Company trust could be returned.

To the sisters that looked like a long wait. All they wanted essentially was to have again in their hands the money their father had left for them and his grandchildren. For Fredette that would be close to $6 million, for Laura Ann about $4.25 million.

The lawsuit moved slowly until late 1978, when negotiations began to settle out of court.

Fredette Eagle contends that a summary filed in the chancery court of Shelby County by one of her lawyers, James W. McDonnell, Jr., compellingly showed a series of misdeeds in manipulation of the trust funds. This, she believes, frightened her brother and bank officers and made them so certain they would lose in a trial that they decided to offer a settlement, which her side accepted.

The suit was dismissed on January 9, 1979. Documents filed in court show Smith agreed to buy out his sisters' interests in the Frederick Smith Enterprise Company. Details were kept secret, but presumably Fredette and Laura Ann got what they considered their fair shares of the original trust. The National Bank of Commerce resigned as trustee of the estate. Fredette established a new trust in Bankers Trust Company of New York, Laura Ann moved her inheritance to Union Planters Bank of Memphis, and Smith transferred the remainder of the Frederick Smith Enterprise Company to First Tennessee Bank of Memphis.

To buy out his sisters' interests in the Enterprise Company, Smith could not simply write a check for the $10 million or $12 million required. But he was no longer strapped for cash—or credit. By this time Federal Express was generating annual revenues of almost $300 million, which created a 1979 fiscal year profit of $21.4 million. On the strength of that financial picture, Smith obviously had no trouble financing the trust buyout.

Former executives of Federal Express familiar with the settlement asserted that Smith, because he was angry at some of the plaintiffs' attorneys, was not inclined to be generous, and what resulted was a bad deal for the sisters.

"As I see it, they walked away and left several million dollars on the table," said Charles Lea.

Not all the new ideas came from Smith. They flashed from a broad spectrum of thinking—from new uses for high technology to the most mundane aspect of the business, such as the color, fit, and feel of employee uniforms.

Serious consideration was given to using the daylight down time of the large fleet of airplanes by establishing a commuter airline out of Midway Airport at Chicago, only 491 miles north of Memphis. That would not at all interfere with the nighttime duties of the purple-and-white birds. The proposal called for using nine 727s of the quick-change type that permitted slapping seats into the cargo holds.

In the final analysis, however, the accountants at FedEx determined there was not enough potential profit to compensate for the hassle involved.

It made sense to his colleagues when Smith suggested that the high-speed Concorde could be a means of getting international time-sensitive packages across the Atlantic. And they were not surprised that he dashed off to Europe to take up the plan with the British and French governments.

The *Commercial Appeal* likewise applauded the scheme, editorializing as follows on November 1, 1981:

PURPLE LIGHTNING

The story of Federal Express Corp. is the story of what can be done with ideas, energy, venture capital, and some daring. We won't know for some time whether the company can strike a deal with the British and French governments to lease supersonic Concorde jets and make overnight package delivery a global service, but everything in its short history suggests that eventually there will be a way—absolutely, positively.

The visions of Fred Smith and Art Bass and the other people who have written this success story happened to include a sea of high-priority freight and a fleet of fast aircraft roaring off in the night, headed everywhere. But, in fact, the same measures of innovation and resources and courage would probably have made them equally successful in men's clothing, fast food, or video games. Or something that no one has yet thought of. Isn't their example powerful encouragement for others here willing to challenge convention and able to take risks?

What greater strides might Memphis make if the model of those Falcons, 727s, DC-10s, and maybe Concordes were applied to the city's natural economic resources? For example, what bold concepts are there waiting to be tested in agriculture?

The prospects are as exciting as any that Memphis can contemplate as a city.

Federal Express's reach for Europe can do more than boost that company's own markets and profits. It can do more than provide new jobs where they are badly needed. Important as those things are, to a locally based business and to this community, the real promise is that it could set a pace for the whole commerce of the city and move it into the coming new world economy. That's where we must be before the highest of our ambitions can be realized.

Think of it. Legal documents, financial papers, engineering work, medicines, computer chips—the urgent business of a nation—assembled in Memphis every night for transport to London, Paris, Rome, Frankfurt, Amsterdam, Brussels, Luxembourg, and Milan. All in a purple blur, at twice the speed of sound. . . . Now we know that Mach 2 is not only the speed of a supersonic jet, but the lesson of a lifetime.

The Concorde plan proved too difficult even for the wizards of Federal Express. But Smith came up with something even bolder— the idea of hauling bulkier and slower freight through the skies in dirigibles. His startled senior executives thought he was joking. To go along with the gag, they found an artist who whipped up a surprise present for the boss—a painting depicting triangle-shaped blimps hovering over the sorting hub at Memphis International Airport.

Smith didn't appreciate their humor. He said in a statement at the time: "We believe there may be a future for lighter-than-air transportation for Federal Express, but that application is in the late 1980s at the best. But we will make a decision in the next six months on an investment in a small airship for the learning process and for public relations."

Fred Smith managed to win over FedEx president Art Bass. Their thinking had been triggered, of course, by the realization that the sixty-million-dollar Memphis sorting hub was basically in use just four or five hours a night—and could become a second profit center if the facilities were also put to daytime use. The airships, whose majestic slowness would be counterbalanced by lower shipping charges, could potentially use the hub during the day—for packages that could wait two or three days. With ton-mile efficiency approaching that of trucks, Bass suggested an airship could move many thousands of packages across hundreds of miles at a fraction of the cost of jet cargo liners.

Smith's research showed the football field–size *Hindenburg* was able to carry two hundred fifty tons at ninety miles an hour before its spectacular crash in 1937. (At the time he was having this brainstorm, the biggest plane in the Federal Express fleet was the DC-10, which could carry only fifty tons.)

Art Bass and the boss, however, had in mind a design much different from the traditional zeppelin. They considered the airship best suited for their purpose would be a vector-shaped, positive buoyancy vehicle. Such a design, admittedly untried, would eliminate problems of locating a huge mooring facility near the airport. It would also make loading and unloading much easier. The design would allow for speeds in excess of one hundred miles an hour, compared with the blimp's top speed of fifty-five. The vehicle would land and take off from the ground by pumping helium or possibly forced hot air out of a container. Engines would burn cheap natural gas in such a configuration, yielding an economy that no other mode of transportation could approach.

Adding dirigibles, of whatever configuration, to the FedEx fleet would not be easy, Bass readily admitted. "We already have modern technology that is capable of producing an airship far beyond the *Hindenburg*'s limitations," he said. "The Soviet Union faces enormous costs in maintaining railways across the Siberian wastelands, and they are now experimenting with airships thought to have a lift of more than two hundred tons. Our whole program is fraught with problems—mooring, weather, and crossing the Rocky Mountains. We step back and say what kind of an airship would solve these problems. We don't know yet, but we'll find one, even if we have to make it ourselves."

Federal Express, however opted to not build a dirigible. Instead it went to a couple of companies already in the business—Goodyear Tire, which operated a fleet of promotional blimps, and a British firm, Airship Industries. The latter had an idea it could build a blimp that would lift two tons for around $2.5 million.

Like so many of Fred Smith's ideas, this was another that never came to actuality.

Smith believes, however, that the key to successful innovation is constantly to subject problems to every angle of scrutiny that can be thought of, with the idea that "unless you are trying to defy the laws of nature," some risk-taking way will be found to solve the problem.

As he explained in a 1986 *Inc.* interview with Robert Tucker:

The problem of fog, for example. Since the invention of the airplane, people have been looking for a way to fly through fog. And the solutions all went in the direction of creating systems that eliminated the need for the pilot to see, in the favor of machines that "see."

As a result, you now have these very complex systems that bring the planes in using lots of on-the-ground electronic equipment, and the damn things are always breaking down.

So we kept looking at the problem. It wasn't our biggest problem, but since our goal has always been to improve our service, to be able to offer absolute guarantees on overnight deliveries, it was an important problem to try to solve. And we would not take no for an answer. We even went to Paris to look at the big machines that blew fog off the runways there. They cost twelve million dollars apiece. Not right.

Then, one day I was on a plane with a bright guy who worked for us, Charles Brandon, and he was reading a magazine article about the air force using millimeter-wave radar to take pictures through clouds. And all of a sudden Charles looked at me and said, "You know, what we ought to do is try to see through the fog."

In other words, put the pilot back in the loop, which was 180 degrees from what everyone else had done. Well, to make a long story short, it's absolutely feasible to see through fog. We've just authorized thirty-five million dollars to put the first parts of the components in our planes. And I guarantee you that by 1990, none of our big planes will ever be stopped from landing because of fog.

And as ancillary benefits, our pilots will also get a warning system for wind sheer, and we'll enjoy slightly reduced costs for things like tires and brakes.

Federal Express worked several years to create such a "magic window." Prototype equipment manufactured by California's Flight Dynamics Corporation was tested on 727s flying into Memphis. The device centered on an inertial platform and laser ring gyroscope operating a "heads-up display" by which the pilot could see reflections of instrument readings while looking out the windshield. But FedEx engineers, dissatisfied with results versus high cost, put the idea on the "back burner."

Meanwhile Memphis International Airport installed on one runway what is known as "Category 3" equipment, which permits airliners to land in essentially "zero-zero" visibility, making FedEx's home field on a par with any in the United States for bad weather operations.

With "auto land ILS," FedEx pilots land even though runway lights do not appear until they are down to thirty feet. "You don't touch anything," explained Speed McLain, FedEx's chief 727 pilot. "The equipment lands itself, keeps itself on the runway once it gets on the ground. You can't see enough to do that yourself, so you rely on the instruments."

Wind sheer rarely adversely affects Memphis flights—though it is a major problem at Denver—but a doppler radar ring around FedEx's home field was installed in 1992 to provide a wind shift alert. And Federal Express engineers again took up their study of the old "magic window"—a new approach using infrared imaging.

As the incident with Brandon illustrates, Smith was normally receptive to ideas and schemes suggested by his associates. But there could be a risk involved, according to Frank (Francis X.) Maguire, who joined Federal Express in the mid-1970s and for a decade played a key role as senior vice-president of industrial relations.

"You had to have your facts in hand," said Maguire. "Sure, he listened to people who worked around him. I think Fred Smith will be the last one to tell you that it was all his idea, that everything that ever happened around there that was good was his.

"I've seen a lot of people go into his office, and I've never seen anybody thrown out. They might have come in there with some ideas that they authored, but when they came to the mountain Fred never let his ego get in his way. He always listened. Fred Smith is one of the best managers or gatherers of information I have ever seen.

"I worked in the executive offices of President Lyndon Johnson during the War on Poverty, and Fred ranks right up there with guys like [Robert] McNamara, [Sargent] Shriver, and Mr. [Hubert] Humphrey. Many times I have thought how great it would be if we had more managers who could process information. Now Fred has good opinions. He's a bright man. He's got very sharp ideas."

Maguire was in awe of Smith's appetite for reading material. "I defy anyone to go up to Fred and ask if he has read a certain book and hear him say no. He reads and reads. Quick reader. This man can thumb through a book and come out with more specifics in that book! I don't think his would qualify as a photogenic mind. I do know he reads all the time. I used to go to him as senior officer of personnel and training, taking a book hot off the press, and say, 'Fred you need to look at this.' And he would say, 'Just finished it.' "

Smith is not given credit, says Maguire, for another vital talent. "He's a world-class expert in time management. He processed things that came to him immediately. You never had to wait around for decisions from Fred. Put it in writing [an inclusive report topped by a one-page summary], put it in the system, and you'd hear back— often the very next day.

"He listens beautifully. But I'll tell you what, you better have your bags packed when you go in there. You better have your facts."

In describing the "secret" of the phenomenal success of Federal Express, Smith credits intuition or strong gut feelings, as well as pure luck and good timing—all coming together "right on the curve."

To him, innovation must be viewed from two sides—demand and supply.

"Pogo, the cartoon character, pointed out one time that the way to be a great leader is to see a parade and run like hell to get in front of it," he told his *Inc.* interviewer. "There's a lot of truth to that. I don't know of many innovations where somebody just sort of dreamed up an idea out of the clear blue and went off. . . . There are usually some fairly discernible trends available for a long time indicating a demand for a product or a service. And the time to act on that—to get in front of the parade, if you will—is when that demand, and the technology to meet it, begin to converge."

Smith cited as his classic example of such a convergence the start of *USA Today* by Gannett Newspapers. "We've been a national society in America for about twenty-five years now, largely as a result of television, but it is only recently that you could describe anything like a market for a national newspaper. And that's because there was only recently the technology available to send the copy via satellite to print sites all around the country quickly and inexpensively. So there was the convergence of societal change or expectation, and a technology that allowed someone to fulfill it. Al Neuharth, Gannett's president, was one of the first to see it."

Gannett's losses were horrendous because of the *USA Today* start-up, Fred Smith conceded:

> But I think he's going to prevail—and that gets me to the supply side of the equation. Remember, he didn't have to start *USA Today* to pay the dividends and turn on the lights. But I think he was aware of the threat to his existing business, Gannett's local newspapers. There is, to one degree or another, a death cycle under way with the local papers.
>
> The TV gets you the news faster now, and has more or less coopted the trendy, glitzy part of the news. And for more in-depth discussion of the issues, there are many other vehicles that do it better. So what the local newspaper is left with is the births and deaths and marriages and the latest stabbings and the stupid machinations of local politicians. So long term you've got to say that, other than as a direct-mail advertising medium, the papers have lost much of their rationale.

It's at that point that the innovator says to himself, Now's the time that I ought to take a risk. I see the threat on the supply side. I see the opportunity on the demand side. And, oh, by the way, I'd like to do something new and useful and important. And when all of that happens, that's when organizations tend to innovate.

Smith estimated that throughout the eighties he spent at least four hours a day reading—newspapers, magazines, books on management theory and flight theory, and journals on the latest technological developments. He sponsored a lot of market research, but when he began brainstorming on "large-scale innovation," he found he relied quite heavily on his own vision, backed by assimilating information from many different disciplines all at once.

"Particularly information about change," he explained, "because from change comes opportunity. So you might be reading something about the cultural history of the United States, and come to some realization about where the country is headed demographically. The common trait of people who supposedly have vision is that they spend a lot of time reading and gathering information, and then synthesize it until they come up with an idea."

That, precisely, happened to him.

It became more and more obvious that Federal Express must have the ability to track "at every moment" every item their system was transporting. "And when we got to thinking about it," Smith told *Inc.*, "it looked as if it were impossible—never been done before. At that time I had been reading some very different types of things about the grocery business and the price performance of computers. Well, one thing led to another, and we began to look into using a version of those bar codes that are on soup cans to give a number in sequence to every package. It turned out to be a very good idea. And that one little innovation, probably more than almost anything else, has led us to be able to say 'Absolutely, positively' on television, because without it we could not have controlled this organization. It would have been impossible to take millions of items every night and deliver them with the reliability we do."

An opportunity for several weeks of intensive reading was thrust on Fred Smith while recovering from surgery on his back, necessitated by the flare-up of a Vietnam shrapnel wound.

He picked up a two-volume autobiography of Dwight Eisenhower and discovered what he considered a "perfect example" of the role of "luck" in terms of success.

"I mean, Dwight Eisenhower in 1940 was a soon-to-retire lieutenant colonel with a respectable but not particularly outstanding military career. But it just so happened that he turned out to be the right person in the right place at the right time. And most important, he had the right skills, mainly the skill to force coalitions. And then he built on that opportunity, and those skills, to go on to be president of the United States. Well, my guess is that there are probably a thousand Dwight Eisenhowers at any point in time. And Fred Smiths, too. So it's the confluence of things that determines success.

"Timing? Yes, very important—knowing when to really go, and when to sit on the sidelines. Once you decide to go, certainly serendipity plays a big part in it. But I think timing is often more important than luck.

"In my case, for example, the idea that is Federal Express 'absolutely, positively' would not have worked five years before we did it, for many reasons. And five years later the market would have been so clear that somebody would have served it in one way or another. And that is probably true of most start-up organizations."

Smith found it difficult to abandon his idea of flying bank checks to cut down the costly float time, which had been rejected by the Federal Reserve System. But in late 1981 "First Express"—owned by First Tennessee Bank of Memphis—undertook that service for a number of banks across the country, hoping to take it national and using, of course, FedEx planes for transportation and a four-hundred-thousand-square-foot section of the superhub for sorting facilities.

A few months later Federal Express "began kicking the tires" on a scheme to establish low-power UHF television stations to distribute business information, asking the Federal Communications Commission for permission to operate in fifteen cities. Frank Maguire said it was very much a tentative plan and might be dropped. The stations would broadcast first-run movies in the evening. During the day, TV clients with decoders could receive business information they'd pay a fee for; the movies would be free.

Reading about high-tech devices that warned ammunition plants of severe storms, Federal Express spent $300,000 to install a similar system at Memphis International Airport. Three sensors, located on towers around the airport, feed weather data to a computer, which analyzes it and predicts the probability of severe lightning and also shows when storm conditions begin to dissipate.

In 1983 Smith considered getting into the business of building boosters to launch satellites for worldwide communications, through a three-way partnership in Space Transportation Company, a New Jersey firm. It was an idea that put the Memphis company in competition with bigger, more powerful companies. On closer study Smith abandoned that effort.

An abandoned military flying field in Illinois caught Smith's fancy. It had excellent runways, aprons, hangars, and administration buildings. On top of that there was a collection of barracks and officer houses. Why not move his entire administration and hub operations from Memphis? When the news leaked out, Memphis authorities were dismayed. Smith ultimately canceled his "company town" plan, for several reasons. But he remembered the effect of the mere suggestion; as a result he dropped subtle hints about leaving any time city officials were slow in approving Federal Express requests.

One of Smith's most unusual ventures was as corporate sponsor of a dirt-track race car. Often he joined the spectators at the speedway just across the river in West Memphis, Arkansas. Another racing buff was his mother; Sally Hook had a startling, and she hoped prophetic, dream in which she saw a car bearing the Federal Express purple colors win the Indianapolis 500.

By chance, Alvin Jeffrey, the Little Rock mechanic who became chief of FedEx ground maintenance in Memphis, built race cars as a sideline. He was someone Smith was comfortable with, and they often talked over coffee at the hub office or at impromptu bacon-and-egg breakfasts at the Jeffrey house.

"He wanted to be a farmer," Jeffrey said, "He said he would do the work, and I could manage. He was very interested in farming back then. He was always talking, too, about doing the small packages with blimps. He was way ahead of his time. Always reading. My wife and I would be invited to his house, and usually he'd greet us with a book in his hand. He'd come up with good ideas. There wasn't anybody in the company who'd match him. They just didn't think fast enough."

Fred Smith began "aggravating" Jeffrey about "going big time" with his race car—"NASCAR and Indy." Finally they decided to run in the "World of Outlaws" national sprint car circuit, ninety races coast to coast, with a budget of $180,000 and Sammy Swindell, then a young professional, as driver.

The venture rattled the executive offices. Frank Maguire was involved. "Jeffrey frankly just walked away from his job and made his whole life that one stinking race car," said Maguire. "it was soon brought to the attention of Mr. Smith that there were double billings going on, and all kinds of things. Mr. Smith felt betrayed by a very dear personal friend.

"I want you to know it was a very tough day when Fred called me in and asked for my judgment on this thing. I told him it was certainly not a significant piece of the business we are doing. 'I'm going to say this is strictly your personal call. I don't see any value to it. If you were to tell me to make the decision, I wouldn't do it. But if you say you want it done, we'll do it the best we can.'

"There was nothing of an essential nature to the business. But Tuck Morse [the early-day corporate attorney] went in and went nose to nose with Fred. They closed the door, but I sat in the room and I just loved it.

"Tuck was against it, and he told Fred to just stuff it. It was beautiful, and the thing I liked about it and the thing I respect about Fred was, when you close the door and you were with one of your senior vice-presidents, you were free. You didn't get killed for telling him what you thought. And Tuck told him in no uncertain terms.

"What was wrong? Let's delete the expletives. First of all, Tuck didn't think it was worth a damn from a promotional standpoint. He felt the image of Federal Express and outlaw racing cars was counterproductive. And he said, 'Wouldn't it be great for us to be famous . . . all these couriers rushing around the streets pretending they are So-and-so in a race car?' Tuck made a lot of good points. And he said, Besides, it's not a major sport.

"He really went after Fred, and Fred got hot. And Tuck got hot, and they went at each other. It was really beautiful. Red faces. Fists slamming down.

"You know, Fred had no use for people who didn't tell it like it is. But it boils down to this, and Smith says, 'I want to do it, and we're going to do it! Do you understand me? Would you like me to explain it?'

"Tuck Morse looked over at me—and my regard for him went through the ceiling because it would have been easy for him to just wimp out, but when he left, he stopped by the door and pointed his finger at Fred and gave him those famous lines—'Someday you will be sorry!'

"And Fred was sorry. He decided we'd made a mistake, about a year later, and pulled the rug. He called me in and said, 'The A. J. Jeffrey deal is dead.' I said, 'Okay, boss, I'm glad you finally woke up.' It didn't shake Fred. He says, 'Hey, I made a mistake, okay. Next?' "

(Giving his side of the debacle in a 1991 interview, Jeffrey, curiously, voiced no bitterness but said Federal Express hurt him badly with the IRS by reporting all the "sponsor money" as personal income to him in addition to his $56,000 annual salary. Because he was unable to pay a huge tax bill, Jeffrey said, the IRS took his home and about $100,000.

"I didn't even fight it," Jeffrey said. "I'll tell you why—Fred said, 'Don't worry about it. I'll take care of you.' I ain't never bothered him. If that's the way it's gonna be, that's the way it is." Jeffrey said he was never accused of making "double billings—not whatsoever." Frank Maguire, Jeffrey said, "doesn't know what he is talking about. Why, I did all the work myself. The IRS audited the whole deal, and they said I had one of the best records on something like that in this part of the country." Jeffrey said he was not out of work long; he landed a "good job" at the Nike shoe factory in Memphis.

Smith showed Frank Maguire another aspect of holding corporate control. Maguire had a pet project he couldn't get through the budget process. He had talked to Smith about it two or three times—unsuccessfully.

As senior personnel officer, Maguire usually stuck his head in the boss's door to say good-bye as he left every Friday afternoon.

Smith appeared to be in an unusually good mood.

"Listen," Maguire blurted, suddenly inspired, "you got a minute?"

"Frank are you going to talk about that thing again? Just hold it. . . . Before you say anything, come over here!" Smith got up and pulled back his chair. "Sit down here," he commanded. Maguire sat, and the chief gently pushed the chair up to his desk. "I want you to lean forward on that desk."

Maguire did.

Smith moved around to the front of the desk and stared hard at the personnel officer. "Okay, Francis, tell me one more time why we should do what you suggest."

Maguire gulped and stammered, "Fred, I really want only one thing."

"What's that?"

"I want out of here."

Smith said, "It looks a lot different from there, doesn't it?" He smiled as Maguire got out of the chair.

Maguire, recounting the incident, recalled: "I said, 'Hey, Fred, it's all yours!' It was the most profound lesson in management I ever received. Because what looks so clear to the senior officer of personnel doesn't always look that way to the chairman of the board. When I sat there and looked across his desk, I saw the financial community. I saw the stockholders. I saw the employees. I saw the customers. I saw the budget department. It was like . . . I sat in that chair and realized how overwhelming it was!"

Over the years Fred Smith has tried to remain one of the most "private" public figures in America. He is basically shy, and it pains him that he has become a celebrity. He tends to rebuff outsiders, particularly the media; but for a decade or so he was quite accessible to employees. Pilots he had known for years thought nothing of stopping by his open-door office and perching on the edge of his desk to talk about flying experiences or their families. He often dropped into the hub at night, where he called many sorters by name. The same familiarity existed with the mechanics on the flight line, the dispatchers, and the secretaries and clerks. It was a ritual that any courier who racked up ten years' service could hop in the jumpseat of a Federal Express plane and fly to Memphis and have an "anniversary breakfast" with the chairman of the company.

Of course, the sheer growth of the company, and the monumental demands on Smith's time, eventually made that ceremony impossible. He has tried, however, to retain close rapport with the people in the field, and most observers believe that he has.

One business reporter covering a speech the chairman made to six hundred Federal Express employees at the Riverfront Holiday Inn in Memphis observed: "Scary. After he finished, the entire group was ready to go to war at I-240 and I-40 [the interstate intersection near Federal Express headquarters]. Powerful. Emotional."

In the same vein, Heinz Adams, an early-day executive, said: "If Fred Smith lined up ten thousand employees on the George Washington Bridge and told them to jump, 99.9 percent would jump. That's how much faith they have in him."

Fred Smith purposely tried to retreat from public view, but only after a two- or three-year media splurge that put him on the cover of numerous magazines and made him the subject of featured articles in the leading business publications of America.

In the late 1970s the business press was captivated that their calls were put through to him; now they are routed through the PR department. Smith regularly turns down requests for interviews from network television and national magazines. When *Time* magazine was reportedly considering him for "Man of the Year," their reporter was unable to talk to him.

Smith explains: "As a company gets bigger, you have to be a lot more cautious in what you say and how you say it. Part of the reason the company is successful is that as it has gotten bigger, I've changed my role. You can't manage a two-hundred-and-fifty-million-dollar company like a one-billion-dollar company. It would be disastrous."

Smith decided he should be the principal spokesman for the corporation and passed those instructions on to Frank Maguire. "He felt for the benefit of the company," said Maguire, "he needed to be the sole spokesman for big publications like *The Wall Street Journal* and *The New York Times,* because he was very concerned that the national media accurately represent what we were doing, and he was, of course, convincing and very credible.

"I let about three slip by, because he wasn't available, or I didn't go to the extent to find him. And I heard about it! 'Frank, I thought we had an understanding. . . .' He was definitely irritated. My times with Fred were not all happy and gay; but, again, I can tell you this: the man was very patient and very understanding."

Inquiries at Federal Express for anything about Fred Smith are carefully screened and answered briefly and with hesitation. His travel plans are never announced, and when he is out of Memphis his home is patrolled by security men.

He bristled when reporter Lewis Nolan asked if he would agree to being described as a recluse. "Oh, heavens, no. But I'm not a social lion, either!' He asserts he has never developed a taste for personal publicity and would prefer his name never appear in print.

It surprised many when he made an appearance on the Tom Snyder television show in 1980 and fielded sharp questions from reporter Jessica Savitch. Later, as he was for the first time making the *Forbes* magazine list of the four hundred richest Americans (with an estimated $400 million), Smith let Bill Moyers bring his Public Broadcasting System crew and cameras to Memphis for his "Creativity" series.

Maguire, as overseer of the corporate image, was in the middle. "Bill was in and out two or three times and flew to Chicago with us to see Fred address the Young Presidents Organization. Our small corporate jet was crowded, but Bill had found a cameraman who could wiggle his rear end over the seat and get a camera there. Bill Moyers, as I recall, asked Fred, 'Is your total drive and commitment to the establishment of Federal Express a result of the anguish'—I forget the exact word he used—'from Vietnam? Are you spending this energy'—which everyone admitted was unbelievable, because the man had boundless energy—'are you doing this in any way to reaction to feelings that you harbor from Vietnam?' And Fred looked at him and said: 'Yes indeed!' "

In 1980 Dr. Robert A. Sigafoos, professor of business and economics at Memphis State University, wrote Smith asking his help in writing a book about the Federal Express phenomenon. "I wrote an outline of what I intended to do, and a résumé with the fact that I had been a management consultant for twenty years to the largest companies in America," he said.

"Fred probably thought I would take a Harvard Business school approach and bring out all the innovations his company had introduced. My outline went down to him. I called once. They said, 'Mr. Smith has it and will get back to you.' "

Weeks later Sigafoos, fifty-seven, with degrees from Penn State and Indiana University, was at his MSU desk at 10:20 P.M. "just absolutely ass dragging" after night classes, when the phone rang.

Smith didn't even introduce himself. "Professor, you still want to do that book?"

"Sure!"

"Okay, come out and see me tomorrow morning."

The professor went to Smith's office and was asked to explain again what he wanted to do. He repeated what he had written in his outline.

"All right," said Fred Smith, "I'm going to have to think about it a little more. I'll let you know."

A month later, six months after this first approach, Sigafoos was in a Memphis hospital for hernia surgery when he got word from Memphis State University that Smith had written a letter approving the project.

It took Sigafoos nearly a year to get rolling. "The first six months I was overwhelmed by meaningless stuff," he told me. "It took a while to figure out what was important and what wasn't." The PR man who set up his appointments was moved to a new job, and his replacement, "afraid of his own shadow," began stalling. Sigafoos complained to Smith, who promptly wrote a letter to all executives. "He said, 'Give this guy free access, grant him interviews, have anything he wants. . . .' And for the next two years they forgot about me. I was out there one, two times a week."

In search of 1972–1973 records, Sigafoos was admitted to a locked back room. "It was a god-awful mess. They had wooden filing cabinets from back in the 1890s. I don't know where he got all this crap. But in there, in no order whatsoever, were manila folders—some tied with rope, some loose—just a clutter.

"I spent a week in there, just sitting on the floor, hoping to God I'd find something, and I did find several key letters. There were lots of plans, diagrams of planes, lots of stuff of no interest. He probably wishes to hell he'd burned all that."

The book, *Absolutely Positively Overnight!*, was published in October 1983 as 190-page softcover by St. Luke's Press of Memphis. By back trailing the intricate financing and delving into some of the personal drama, by interviewing Smith, his executives, and many former associates, the professor crafted an interesting and revealing business book.

But his product made Smith explode.

"I'm not his favorite guy," says Sigafoos:

He was furious with me. Told his employees not to buy the book. And he took a couple of mean digs at me. I think I've got him analyzed pretty much. That's why he's so bothered by it. I don't think he ever had any idea that he wasn't a perfect individual. I think his own personal assessment of himself was far different from what an objective observer would come up with.

Now I'm writing a Civil War–type book; I think I would like to write about people who are dead, and not have to worry. Smith, you know, is a tough guy. After my book came out, there was a time or two when I went home late at night that I'd look up and down the alley. Because he was pretty sore at me.

I know he was upset about the mention of the word *fraud* used in that Little Rock trial. . . . He said the word *fraud* was used in the pejorative sense, that perhaps I should have used "Title 18 Federal Criminal Law," but the newspapers used the term *fraud,* and this hacked him off, I guess.

At that time I suspect he had political aspirations. He's really a cocky guy, and I think he dismissed this fraud trial from his mind. And then when the book came out, he suddenly realized, "My God, he's telling the world I was on trial for fraud!" And anybody looking at his record if he tried to run for office could bring that out. So I suppose that is why he put the blanket over me—just ignored the whole thing completely.

Feeling he'd written a creditable book, Sigafoos had expected favorable reaction from Federal Express people. "When I got none, I began to think I was not only persona non grata, but I was considered a kind of traitor in Memphis for saying these things about this wonderful company. I don't think I said anything bad. You set any public figure on a pedestal, you usually see some flaws.

"I gave a favorable report on Fred Smith and Federal Express. The guy did pull off a miracle. He should receive accolades for that effort, but somehow or other they didn't see it that way.

"It was somebody like Frank Maguire told me Smith only wants to hear good things. He's talked himself into believing he's a wonderful member of society. But he's just as rough-and-tumble as any other guy who's successful in business. They've all done things, I'm sure, they're sorry for."

In an interview in late 1991, the professor, from his retirement home at Eureka Springs, Arkansas, showed some compassion for Fred Smith.

"I imagine the poor guy is under great stress now. The company is getting beat up right and left. They're in a lot of competitive trouble, I believe—not doing well in the international market. United Parcel Service is just running circles around 'em—trying to, anyhow."

19 ▶ ESPRIT DE CORPS

The growth of Federal Express began to frighten Smith. He was afraid that for several reasons, his company might get swamped by the accelerating rise in package volume, stall, and collapse into a tailspin from which it could not recover. But on the other hand, he was overjoyed by the FedEx "miracle." At the outset he had hoped that Federal Express might eventually peak at about $100 million annual revenue. Yet in less than a decade it seemed quite clear that it would be a billion-dollar-a-year business.

The organizational structure, pieced together by more or less haphazard whim over the years, alarmed him. It had been made too decentralized; the lines of authority seemed flabby. Worse still, he saw abundant signs that his senior executives were not working as hard as they did in the early days, perhaps even turning soft and lazy.

The worst thing that could happen, in his view, was that the vital esprit de corps might be lost. That eager spirit was the heart of the company's success. It must be nurtured and preserved; everyone in the executive suite must extend himself to maintain the one-for-all and all-for-one rapport with the pilots, the couriers, the station agents, the sorters in the hubs, and the mechanics and crews on the line.

This was the situation that engaged the chairman's attention in the late 1970s and sent him into deep contemplation of examples and ideas he had burrowed out of his constant reading of history, business theory, and military tactics. In addition he was moved to consult with a variety of outside experts, seeking an even wider range of opportunities and options.

The result was that over a period of four or five years he instituted a rash of extreme—and risky—shake-ups that sometimes left executives and employees reeling with surprise and occasionally jostled his company by an expensive failure.

At nearly every turn in the development of Federal Express there was some reflection of Fred Smith's love for the military. He apparently drew inspiration for what he termed his "corporate philosophy" from a speech General Douglas MacArthur made on May 12, 1962, at the United States Military Academy at West Point. MacArthur, on that occasion accepting the Sylvanus Thayer Award for service to the nation, reminded the cadets several times of the words inscribed on the academy's coat of arms—"Duty, Honor, Country."

The ring of that motto appealed to Smith, who came up with this credo for Federal Express:

> "PEOPLE—SERVICE—PROFIT"
>
> Our company always balances the needs of employees, our customers, and our shareholders, considering each in making plans or policies. We always consider the effects on our people first in making decisions, recognizing that if we take care of our employees, they will deliver a superior service which our customers will, in turn, utilize. Only by making a surplus or profit can we insure our company's continued existence, future opportunities, and our employment.

As far as employee relations went, there had been a fortuitous dividend from the era when Federal Express was just managing to escape bankruptcy. The "us against the world" mentality developed a close-knit employee bond, a camaraderie that helped the company through its toughest days.

Smith and his senior colleagues were smart enough to build on this affinity. From the outset the communications going out from the executive suite to the rank and file stressed one main theme—"You are part of a dynamic corporation that cares about each one of you." In effect, the employees' personal welfare and the company's were the same. Which was one way of saying that how profitable the company could be depended on the degree of efficiency and productivity of each employee.

One basic step to enhance morale and motivation was establishing a "no layoff policy." That was Smith's way of trying to convince all employees that the company would take care of them, barring any uncontrollable financial debacle. In other words, they had a lifetime job.

Further, the company policy was "promotion from within," which offered advancement opportunities to reward loyal hard workers. Wages were competitive—certainly high by Memphis standards—and Federal Express added a handsome profit-sharing arrangement. Now at the start of the 1980s Federal Express had grown to nearly ten thousand employees, operating almost four thousand trucks. And the money was rolling in—annual revenues in the half-billion-dollar range and profits of $50 million or more and climbing.

At this juncture Federal Express's corporate thrust was principally along three lines:

1. employee training and motivation to enhance productivity
2. an intensive marketing campaign to create broad-scale awareness of air express and to further increase volume
3. an investigation of all new technology that could be adapted to improving or expanding FedEx operations.

Smith had a distrust of labor unions. He saw no need for them at FedEx and feared if the company were unionized, the first after-effect would be a lessening of the esprit de corps he had worked so hard to establish.

In the early years labor leaders made four or five attempts to unionize FedEx employees. All were beaten back. Pilots, because they were generally looked on as prima donnas and some objected early on having to help unload their planes, were the first target. The unionization attempt was made by the United Pilots Association, an offshoot of the Air Line Pilots Association. But Smith personally debated the union organizers and warned his fliers that being forced into a contract could break the company and that the pilots, in the end, would be losers. Commercial pilot jobs at that time were not easy to come by, and the union was rejected.

The Teamsters, who had United Parcel Service and most other air transport companies organized or partially organized, made three runs at FedEx mechanics and field employees. Management fought back, with effective reminders that FedEx was a close-knit employee-oriented company that practiced "sharing the wealth," promoted from within, and in effect offered lifetime jobs under its "no furlough policy."

Though none of the initial union organizing efforts succeeded, labor leaders kept a close eye on Federal Express for signs of worker unrest. Management, by strict attention to the potential threat, kept workers, in the main, satisfied and the unions out. In later years union organizers launched new campaigns to sign up pilots and ground crews; but their efforts were still unsuccessful.

Efforts to enhance the "We Are Family" theme that FedEx vice-president James A. Perkins's personnel department instituted did not entirely succeed, owing in part to the "promotion from within" policy. To fill many new middle-management positions necessitated by the rapid growth, FedEx frequently advanced employees who had never received any special managerial training. Some of the new managers had been initially hired right out of high school or college. They, of course, were not seasoned as "bosses." Clashes and conflicts began to erupt; a large number of employees resigned. When this trend became apparent, the company moved quickly to identify and eliminate the miscreants.

Smith established a new code, which was posted on every office wall—a "Guarantee of Fair Treatment Policy." This established an open door between workers and managers, where their conflicts could be addressed before going to a higher executive level. Employees were also given wallet cards setting forth the grievance procedure.

Smith designated one of his long-time colleagues, Ted Sartoian, to circulate through the various facilities as a roving ombudsman to gauge employee satisfaction. The chairman warned managers that they would be closely monitored and those found mistreating the help would be fired.

"Managers must grow with the job," Fred Smith said in an April 1981 memo. "Substandard performance in the management ranks cannot, and will not, be tolerated for any sustained period of time. The necessity of teamwork in our operating environment prohibits unrealistic and unwarranted egos. To condone either fault would be to begin an inexorable slide toward mediocrity—the fate of most large corporations."

Executives were alerted to any detail that contributed to maintaining company morale. For instance, company president Art Bass, on one of his routine night visits to the hub, discovered there was neither paper towels nor toilet paper in the men's room.

"Right then I marched over to the executive offices and had all the towels and toilet paper moved out and put over in the hub," Bass told me. "Then I went in early next morning to listen to our top people complain. One thing about it—it got their attention!"

Despite management's concern, there was still friction between worker and boss. Federal Express twice distributed employee questionnaires to gauge attitudes about their treatment by the company. Two responses disturbed the officers.

Did the employee have "confidence in the fairness of management," and did his or her job seem to be leading to the kind of "future" the worker wanted?

One-third of the FedEx employees gave a negative response to both questions.

275

As a means of rewarding couriers or mechanics for some action beyond the normal call of duty, the company began handing out vouchers for "a dinner for two" or some other honorarium.

Smith wanted a more distinctive token of appreciation, however, and found it in his marine experience. He remembered being impressed when the navy, to commend a unit for exemplary performance, would hoist the "B" and "Z" flags for "Bravo Zulu," meaning "Job well done."

He had hundreds of replicas of the "Bravo Zulu" flags printed, stickers about the size of postage stamps, which were liberally handed out to FedEx people who did something special on their job.

In addition to livening up the company newspaper, Smith felt the need for regular contact between executives and the far-flung employees in the FedEx stations and courier vans and loading docks. He found a vehicle in what became known as "the family briefing." Initially, small teams of corporate officers would annually leave Memphis to report directly to employees and their families at a picnic or luncheon, usually on a Sunday afternoon. The company made a concentrated effort to be candid about Federal Express progress, problems, and prospects.

These sessions managed to reach most FedEx cities in a matter of weeks and were well received. Frank Maguire, who was then the vice-president overseeing this effort, recalled: "We would gather not just the employees but their partners in big clusters in significant places around the country. Started on a yearly basis, and then it became semiannual. We would tell them everything that was going on within the company. We would cover the issue of where we had been, where we are, and where we're going. And it got to be such a force in the company that in 1977 we hired an outside television firm to handle it by satellite. We had forty-seven cities on the line. Boy, were we proud of that! Now, of course, they can do a live feed every day on the Federal Express satellite communication network."

Maguire credits Smith for seeing the necessity of keeping the employees informed on corporate values and visions. "Here's what I would say Fred Smith did. He recognized that we had a corporate communications crisis. He decided to build our corporate culture on three things: shared vision; shared knowledge; and shared responsibility. And that's what he did. I'm sure I helped substantially, because before I left the company Fred gave me a plaque reading 'To Frank Maguire, who not only taught Federal Express to communicate, but to have a heart.' You know the old saying, what you do speaks so loudly I can't hear what you are saying. I think Fred observed the first time he met me that I really did care, and I did. I'm not a financial officer; don't ever let me be the person in charge of your operation. But if you want to get a significant goal accomplished through other people's energy, I believe very strongly, as does Lou Holtz, there's nothing you can't accomplish if you just get enough people to care."

However much the Federal Express chairman might worry about the awesome future impact of high technology and computer development, in this period in the history of his young new business, his primary concern was with old-fashioned values and virtues. And that meant the organizational chart—the lines that connected the chief executive at the top to the troops in the field. And especially how the word filtered down through vice-presidents, managers, and supervisors—clearly identifying the official responsible for making decisions, issuing orders and seeing they were carried out, and handing out merited rewards and imposing necessary reprimand or punishment.

The boss himself was primarily an idea man. He did not have years of experience as a trained manager. He had learned by doing and by reading the best books he could find on business theories.

As a result, he was inclined to experiment with a variety of organizational schemes. When one trial-and-error setup did poorly, the chairman abandoned it, often abruptly and usually by unilateral action. However, he finally sought outside help from the business school experts.

Frank Maguire was his go-between in bringing in the professionals. The first was Benjamin Trego, who operated a think tank with Charles Kepner in Princeton, New Jersey, with whom Maguire had formerly worked. Dr. Trego flew down to Memphis to confer with Smith, Art Bass, and the chief financial officer, Pete Willmott.

"It was quite impressive," Maguire recalled, "to sit in on this conference with someone who is a recognized world-class strategic planner. He took us through this process of strategic planning. Fred listened quietly and made appropriate comments. It was very interesting because Trego would ask a question, obviously anticipating he would get an answer that would not be on target, but Fred would give him the answer that was right on target.

"Next day from Princeton came an overnight package for Fred Smith, and it was Ben Trego's new book on strategic planning, which was on the best-seller list of business books. It had an inscription, 'To my new friend, Fred Smith: Like bringing coal to Newcastle. Regards, Ben Trego.'

"Did they ever get together? No, no need to. Everything Ben Trego was telling the rest of the world, Fred already knew."

Later a New York–based expert named Paul Lanier was brought in as a consultant, and from talks with him Smith detected flaws in the Federal Express method of operations—and a drift that imperiled the company's ability to successfully handle its rapid new growth and complexity.

The shake-ups in the executive suite began with Roger Frock, who, starting in Little Rock as general manager, remained second in command for nearly four years. Abruptly, in February 1975, he was demoted to senior vice-president and Art Bass was elevated to president.

Bowing to investor demands to increase the ten-thousand-a-night package count, Smith sent four senior vice-presidents—Mike Fitzgerald, Wes Terry, Tucker Taylor, and Frock—into the field to head regional divisions that were supposed to streamline FedEx by bringing management supervision closer to field personnel and the customer. It hadn't worked out. In many cities salesmen were trapped by necessity in answering the phone or delivering packages and were thus unable to sell. Both the telephone system and the tub files used for customer records were hopelessly old-fashioned. That led to installing a computerized system known as "COSMOS"—customer-oriented service management operating system.

Three years later Smith decided decentralization had been a mistake. He abolished the four regional centers and pulled the lines of authority back into Memphis corporate headquarters. In February 1978 he drafted an aggressive memorandum titled "Managing Federal Express, or 'Holding on to the Tiger's Tail.'" The field divisions were structurally defective and "not true profit centers." His memo said: "The staff resources available at the regional level are about as analogous to the current corporate staff as the Boy Scouts are to the Marine Corps." The company's new approach, he asserted, would be to do a few things well rather than many poorly, which he felt was currently the case.

There was a sting, and an implied threat, in his message, which was co-signed by Art Bass. The new order "will require greater specialization, more mutual trust, and significantly more professionalism. . . . There is no place here for those who cannot, or will not, recognize this fact nor for those who cannot, or will not, adjust to this reality."

Smith summoned the four field commanders to Memphis to explain the new setup. But, apparently anxious for a confrontation, he took them to dinner the night before their formal conference and summarized his plan. He startled the executives by asserting that he had decided on his own to go with a new multimillion-dollar centralized phone system that had been hotly debated for months in the company.

Roger Frock's notes of the meeting disclose that he and others protested that Smith acted unilaterally.

"A decision has been made," Smith thundered. "I am never going to hear another question about the centralized telephone system. Never! Period! I don't want to hear any more backbiting on this."

The debate turned snide when Fred Smith expressed surprise that Frock, with an MBA from Michigan, couldn't understand him. "One of three things is getting in the way of your understanding: emotions, personality, or compassion. Everyone has got to understand that these three devils stand in the way of constructive solutions to these problems."

When the criticism continued, Smith snapped back: "You guys sit around and think you are going to contribute a lot of policy formulation in certain areas that you think you have expertise and prerogatives in, but the facts of the matter are, you don't have either the information or the energy, or the time, to make the input. And I see it over again and again. You are offended when the policies come out and you don't feel like you were consulted. Most of the input has been verbal, less than cohesive, lacking in quantitative data, and it is a symptom of a company three years and one hundred fifty million dollars ago.

"And I am telling you, if we don't get on some more organized basis, all of this esprit de corps and rah, rah, rah is going to shift like a goddamned counterweight. So many companies have been exactly the same place before, and we have now got to systemize this monster or we've got to get some people in here to systemize it."

There had been heated clashes before. The old hands usually fought it out with the boss—and then forgot it. But the climate was changing rapidly inside Federal Express. It was becoming one-man rule—and there was no question which man.

The start-up executives were no longer willing to put in the grueling sixteen-hour days, nor were all of them comfortable in the new MBA atmosphere. Smith made it apparent that he felt some were now overpaid.

In this frame of mind, Smith suddenly rented six thousand square feet in an office complex six miles distant from FedEx's airport headquarters and, most unusual for a transportation company, established his own think tank.

Called Advanced Projects and Research Group, it was a place of calm in contrast with the normal frenzy at the airport. Amid plush carpeting, mirrors, and modernistic furniture was a system of functional project rooms. They were walled with blackboards and cork boards that held schematic drawings. There was one direct connection with the airport headquarters—remote terminals tied into the mainframe Federal Express computer.

Office gossip dubbed the ARPG the "turkey farm." Translation: "the place where there's an ax and a chopping block."

To the "turkey farm" as chief of staff went Art Bass, then forty-eight, who had been squeezed out as president in the fall of 1980 and moved to the relatively unimportant post of vice-chairman of the board of directors, with Peter Willmott elevated to president.

Bass put the best face possible on his new assignment. In a *Fortune* interview he conceded most of the initial executives were "undisciplinable" entrepreneurs. "You cannot be caught up in the intense environment of day-to-day operations," he told the *Memphis Commercial Appeal.* "You have to get out and have your mind somewhere else to make the future visible." He told the newspaper his role was to "provide the corporate horsepower to give researchers time to think through and evaluate the practicality of their ideas without worrisome middle managers peeping over their shoulders."

First on the ARPG agenda was Smith's idea of using dirigibles for heavy freight. Another was the extremely difficult "magic window" that would permit pilots to see through fog. The "turkey farm," whatever its true purpose, was a costly venture, eating up about 2 percent of the FedEx budget.

Significantly, the most senior top officers assigned to the project were old hands who had quarreled with Smith and were out of favor—among them Roger Frock, Mike Fitzgerald, and Tucker Taylor.

The "turkey farm" marked the end of Bass's career with Federal Express. On March 9, 1982, he announced he would resign because "the company has reached a point in its stability and growth that it has made it more interesting for me to look somewhere else for the kind of entrepreneurial challenges I've always been involved in."

Behind similar statements, the other top officers who had been shuffled off to the research department were gone within about a year. In ten years Bass had picked up about six million dollars' worth of stock, and the other "turkey farm" retirees left as millionaires, too.

By the end of 1984 Federal Express dominated the domestic overnight air express industry, taking in $1.72 billion a year, far ahead of number two United Parcel Service with $675 million. Next came Purolator Courier, $590 million; United States Postal Service, $500 million; Airborne Freight, $305 million, and Emery Air Freight, $175 million.

It was at that point Fred Smith led his company into a painful and expensive error—ZapMail.

Smith long had wanted to find another innovative new venture that would push FedEx into the ranks of America's corporate giants. The rapidly emerging telecommunications field caught his eye at the beginning of the 1980s.

Facsimile transmission would be that venture.

As Smith saw it, as fax machines emerged they might cut into the use of FedEx overnight letters; but if the company was already heavily into facsimile transmission, no revenue would be lost, and much could be gained—a switch from airplanes to satellite communication for moving legal documents, architectural drawings, reports, and the like.

And instead of overnight, Federal Express could deliver the item in two hours!

Smith insists ZapMail was not his idea alone. In an interview in June 1984 with *Inc.* magazine, he said: "When we were making the decision we used things like a consenser, a device with two knobs that you put around the table where there are twelve or fourteen people. You can vote yes or no and as to the insensitivity of your feelings. So in developing our strategy, we used a lot of those methods to surface things."

For a man with a rational mind, it is surprising Smith would invest millions of dollars—"bet the company," some said—on a decision made by a Ouija board, even though he did brag about often making decisions on his gut feeling.

He did not foresee the coming explosion of fax machines, that there could be one in every business office by the time he would get his ZapMail rolling. His concept was faulty—because basically it was tied to transmission from one FedEx office fax machine to another FedEx office, which required pickup and delivery at both ends to serve the customers. There was a whole roster of miscues on FedEx's part. But what ultimately defeated ZapMail was that for $300 or so anybody could buy his own fax machine and save money on transmission without having to depend on FedEx couriers.

Fred Smith struggled for nearly three years to make ZapMail pay out and abruptly on September 29, 1989, admitted defeat. *The Wall Street Journal* called it "a megaflop."

In its short life, ZapMail racked up a pretax loss of $326.8 million—and operations were phased out with a pretax write-off of $357 million.

20 ▶ IN SEARCH OF ADVENTURE

Moving cautiously through the African bush, Smith experienced the same fascination with warfare that he had discovered a decade earlier in the jungles of Vietnam.

This exercise was different from his marine combat experience in Southeast Asia; now he was only "playing" soldier, an observer of the revolution in Rhodesia. Yet accompanying a "stick"—a five-man native patrol—he was in danger. The bullets were real. Guerrilla "terrorists" were up ahead, hidden near a kraal, shooting in his direction with their AK-47s. He was out with these government soldiers for the excitement of it. They fired back with machine guns, though they could not really see their enemy.

This episode took place in 1978. The civil war that was to turn Rhodesia—a nation with 6.6 million natives and only 230,000 whites—into the new black-ruled country of Zimbabwe was at its height. It was almost a man-to-man war. In the last four months 1,100 people had been killed.

By odd circumstances, this conflict had drawn Smith to warring Africa from his business-oriented, serene, peaceful—and safe—life in Memphis. Instigator of this adventure and his companion on the visit to Rhodesia was Memphis attorney and friend, Lucius Burch, Jr.

"I had this money from selling my lodge in Ireland," the lawyer explained:

It was like finding it in the road. I hadn't done a day's work to get it. So I was looking for a place to put that money at great risk, and if it hit I'd really have something big out of it. It looked like Rhodesia was such a place.

War was going on, and it began to look like Bishop Abel Muzorewa was going to come out as head guy in the government. And I knew about Muzorewa.

He was born in 1925 into the Manyika tribe, eldest of nine siblings, and aspired early to the clergy. Muzorewa was sponsored by the Methodist church and came to the United States. I knew about him from Nashville because he attended Scarritt College there, and got a master's degree.

So Fred and I went over to Rhodesia. And Fred liked to go out with the government patrols at night. Just for the fun of it. It wasn't attractive to me; it was bad enough as it was. The guerrillas would come around shooting at the houses, putting mines in the goddamn roads, and everything. But Fred enjoyed that. He'd go out with the soldiers on what they called "sticks"—four- or five-man patrols.

He stayed in Rhodesia as long as he could. But he had a baby on the way, and he had to go home. I remained over there a month or more. The sort of life he led in Vietnam, I think, was something that was congenial to his nature.

Fred did the same thing later over in Israel, when they had the fighting in Lebanon. The last big one they had. He went over there to go around with the Israeli guys, flying some, I think, watching the operations.

Indeed, Smith surfaced in west Beruit in the middle of fierce hostilities on his thirty-eighth birthday, August 11, 1982.

This adventure had a prosaic origin years earlier. The FedEx chairman was given an award at a dinner in Memphis by the international Jewish fraternity B'nai B'rith in the spring of 1979. Smith told the dinner chairman, Ira Lipman, head of a Memphis security firm, that he wanted to visit Israel. Lipman offered to take him.

"He didn't get around to it then," said Lipman in an interview for this book, "what with having all those children. But we finally settled on 1982. We left Memphis on August 9, just after Israel invaded Beruit—the war was going on. We didn't tell our wives we were going into the battle zone until later."

Smith and Lipman were flown by the Israeli army to west Beruit and spent several hours in a bunker during an artillery and bomb barrage.

The love of flying was common to many of the FedEx officers, and when he became chairman of the executive committee, Charles Lea tried to impose some rules about it.

"The first thing I did when I went down there was to say, 'I know all of you guys are pilots—none of you are going to fly.' So I grounded everybody—Fred especially. Absolutely. I said, 'I've got enough worries and enough concerns without this business crashing into the ground. The last thing I want to do is wake up some morning and read about one of you guys buying the farm on your own wing.'

"All these guys were very competent pilots. All of them. And they love to fly. But the plain vanilla facts were we had a desperate situation on our hands, and I just didn't think it wise to have any of them flying around in any of this hardware that we had, or what they could lay their hands on. I was afraid the rule was going by the boards, but it certainly was one I was very determined about when I got there."

Smith was fascinated by the World War II military planes and later bought a surplus AT-6 (two-passenger advanced trainer), which he often flew with his executive assistant, Byron Hogue, who had been a marine fighter pilot in Vietnam, for—as the Memphis newspapers reported—"high-altitude frolicking."

Occasionally on company business the chairman took the controls of a Federal Express plane, and even then he could not always resist a little stunt or two. A Little Rock attorney recalls going along on a business trip when Fred Smith was flying one of the Falcon jets.

"I was standing up in the cockpit," the lawyer said, "right behind Fred's seat. I was holding a cocktail glass that was pretty full. Fred looked around and sort of grinned, and said, 'Just hold your glass steady. I'm going to do a barrel roll. Don't worry. You won't lose a drop!'

"It surprised me, that force of gravity. That Falcon rolled over real easy. When we were upside down I thought sure I'd spill my drink. But Fred was right. I didn't lose a drop."

In 1982 Smith got a strong desire to own one of the most spectacular planes World War II produced, the British Spitfire. He found that movie star Cliff Robertson owned one and managed to buy it from him.

"Oh, yeah, that's when he got rich," Charles Lea recalled. "I know Fred bought this airplane and had it reconditioned and flew it around a good deal. It was a high-torque fighter, and I kept telling him, Make sure you've got your foot on the right rudder. When you take off the torque from the prop is very substantial, and if you haven't done it for a while, you can really get a big surprise."

Though from time to time mentioned as a potential shoo-in for elective office, Smith denied any interest in politics. "That is not something I would enjoy. To be a good politician, you have to say many of the same things over and over again. That's boring. You also have to modify what you say before different audiences."

Despite the lack of interest in running for office, he told the *Memphis Commercial Appeal* that he thought he could have "an impact on the country," particularly in the way the Defense Department spends money, and he confided to close friends that he could see himself as secretary of defense. While he had never apparently discussed the matter with Ronald Reagan or George Bush, he evidently did contemplate it enough to place conditions on his possible service, telling the newspaper:

"First, I would have to be comfortable leaving Federal Express and believe there were two or three things that needed to be done in government that I could do. Or there would have to be a national emergency."

In a 1982 feature article on his life, the newspaper observed:

> Smith talks about the "natural camaraderie" that developed among members of frontline outfits. "It is a small,

enclosed fraternity. There were only four hundred thousand who saw any real conflict. The rest of the country did their own thing. There is a real bond there."

He keeps in contact with a number of his war buddies. Some are in a variety of occupations; others have risen quite high in the military service. From time to time there have been whispers about the company and its security-cleared executives cooperating with the nation's intelligence community.

The company's research into the potential "magic window" system of electronic vision, for example, has obvious benefit to the military.

Federal Express does a huge volume of time-sensitive shipping for the Defense Department. . . . As for Smith, he smiles a Cheshire grin when asked about the Central Intelligence Agency making use of Federal Express, saying, "Even if it were true, I couldn't talk about it."

In contrast with his normal penchant for privacy, Smith played out in the public spotlight one of his most unusual adventures or diversions—pursuit of a pro football franchise for his hometown.

Long before Smith got personally involved, Memphis began trying in the late 1960s to land an expansion berth in the National Football League. The river city came up short, making the final five but losing out in 1974 when new franchises were awarded to Tampa Bay and Seattle.

Its pride stung, Memphis began courting the new United States Football League, a second-best operation at the most. Multimillionaire cotton merchant William B. Dunavant, Jr., bought the USFL franchise in 1984 and promptly launched a team known as the Memphis Showboats. But Dunavant's team lasted only two years, losing between $12 million and $15 million, and the league itself disbanded.

Cast adrift was the Showboats' colorful coach-manager, Pepper Rodgers, who had become acquainted with Smith because of the FedEx chairman's participation on the periphery of the pro football scene. They became friends and talked about the possibility of a partnership to seek an NFL expansion franchise.

"We called them the Memphis Odd Couple," said Mike Fleming, former sports writer for the *Commercial Appeal* and later a television reporter. "They had met at parties and sports events. Pepper is crazy, very outgoing and colorful—all the things that Fred is the exact opposite of. But in December 1986 they became partners, forming Mid-America Football, Inc., with Pepper as president, to try to get an NFL franchise—of course with Fred's money. It was expected to cost about one hundred million dollars."

Memphis was intrigued by Rodgers's irreverent behavior, which helped bind his relationship with Smith. They first met in Memphis at a formal dinner party and struck up a conversation. The name of Dallas Cowboys quarterback Danny White came up. Smith described White as the son of Supreme Court Justice Byron "Whizzer" White.

Rodgers brashly spoke up, "No, he isn't."

Smith shot back, "Oh, yes, he is!"

"No, I'm telling you White's father is not the guy on the Supreme Court."

"Yes, he is."

They decided to settle it with a wager.

"We'll put your name on the side of one of our planes if you're right," Smith vowed. "If you're wrong, you have to agree to let me stand in the middle of the field during a Showboats game and announce to the crowd that I know more about football than Pepper Rodgers."

By now the dinner group listening to the give and take was leaning forward on every word, Mike Fleming wrote in his newspaper.

"You may know more about sacking packages than I do," Rodgers said, "but this is football. You got a bet."

Rodgers ultimately proved to be right, but, he says, with a laugh, no Federal Express plane yet carries his name.

The football coach later got revenge of a sort. As master of ceremonies, he was introducing Federal Express executives at an employees meeting. "This man," Rodgers said, "was a great athlete in high school. Smart. The women all liked him. He was even more outstanding in college, and the women all liked him. He was outstanding in social circles and was president of his senior class in high school and in college. Now he is recognized nationally as a truly outstanding individual."

Rodgers paused for effect, making sure his audience had digested the glowing account.

Then he added the kicker: "Well, enough about me. . . . Now let me introduce Fred Smith."

The crowd howled, and Fred Smith joined in the laughter.

Mike Fleming observed: "It was a daring move for Rodgers, one that very few might attempt. But it was testimony to the relationship that was formed between them."

The Odd Couple had several things going for them—great local pride and interest in professional sports, a lot of goodwill in the National Football League because of previous contacts, a sizable regional market, and a suitable pro football stadium, the Liberty Bowl.

But Memphis still faced a struggle—and aggressive competition, especially from St. Louis, Baltimore, Charlotte, North Carolina, and Jacksonville, Florida. Said Fleming:

> Looking back, you can see Fred's heart was never really in this thing. Oh, sure, he wanted to help bring Memphis an NFL team. But that's not anywhere close to the things that drive him. He doesn't get up in the morning thinking about pro football.
>
> Pepper used to tell me it was like finding teeth in chickens to get him to go to NFL meetings or do the necessary things. Fred doesn't like big crowds, doesn't like the limelight. He saw more and more what the NFL owners were— not his cup of tea. He just couldn't stand people like Victor Kiam of the New England Patriots.
>
> Fred is not apt to kiss ass. That's what you have to do as part of the process. He never was comfortable doing that. His

life is really Federal Express. He got in the NFL thing
because he thought it would be great for the city, and it
would be sort of our ultimate salvation, bringing the community together.

Basically, the NFL owners, virtually all older, were "enamored,
even in awe" of Smith because he had made such a huge business
success so quickly, said Fleming. "With Fred, we had a good chance
for a franchise. When I was around the NFL they all spoke of him
with the same reverence they reserve for Pete Rozelle. No one ever
spoke of Fred except in some glowing way. He had this almost
mystique about him. They really respected him for what he had done
as a businessman."

Still, local political squabbles developed over the project. It was
going to cost the taxpayers $700,000 to complete construction of
forty luxury skyboxes at the Liberty Bowl Memorial Stadium. Some
city councilmen muttered that that would give a windfall profit to the
NFL partners and dragged their feet, stalling the skybox completion.

That, among other factors, began to sour Smith on his great
National Football League adventure.

"Fred didn't want to hurt Memphis," said Fleming, "but he never
liked dealing with politicians. In his business, when he makes a
decision, he has people carry it out. Just do it. Down at City Hall he
just couldn't handle all the haggling and bullshit and controversy
about those luxury boxes. Finally he just got fed up with the whole
thing."

Fleming became fairly close to Smith, frequently played tennis
with him, and was one of the few Memphis reporters with his private
phone number. "I'm proud of the fact that I got through to him when
nobody else here [at the paper] could," the sports writer said. "I
didn't take advantage of it. He knows that I ain't gonna call and ask
how his backhand is. I've always thought the world of the guy. He
became more and more isolated, and just got tired of talking about
the NFL, and would fend off the questions to Pepper."

The Odd Couple—or rather the monied partner—handed Memphis such a stunning jolt on February 19, 1991, that the news took up
the top half of the *Commercial Appeal*'s page one.

With Rodgers slouched on a pew behind him, Fred Smith stepped before a microphone in the Memphis City Council chamber and read a long statement saying he was abandoning his effort to buy a NFL franchise but would lend his support to somebody else to do it.

In a quiet tone, the FedEx boss sharply criticized the council for "misunderstanding" his motives, saying that his Mid-America Football, Inc., partnership planned to use skybox revenue (about $200,000 a year) only to pay Rodgers's salary and to pursue the NFL quest.

"I would also point out in passing that I have never received a penny from Mid-America Football. Quite the contrary, I have provided all funding for the organization except for the money earned from exhibition games."

His abrupt decision to drop out of contention for an expansion team and concentrate on Federal Express affairs drew favorable comment from financial analysts. Typical was this observation from George G. Morris of Prescott, Ball & Turben: "What we are used to at Federal is a direct result of Fred's charisma. When things get tough, as they have been for Federal for the last several years, it takes more and more of that time and effort. People drive this economy, and people drive individual companies and motivate people."

After Smith's announcement, the Memphis City Council voted to go ahead with the forty skyboxes, and fifty-eight-year-old William Dunavant, despite his failure with the Showboats, promptly decided to go after the NFL franchise, teaming up with his thirty-six-year-old second cousin, Paul Tudor Jones II, a Memphian and Wall Street commodities trader.

"The financial experts tell me that there's money and then there's liquidity," Fleming said:

> If you are liquid, you are potent. William Dunavant is what they call liquid. He's got tons of money that's cash. Cotton transactions are basically handled in cash money. [Dunavant's firm has just made a $200 million sale to China.] Billy has got enormous wealth in the liquid area.

Fred, one banker told me, is not nearly as wealthy as Billy Dunavant because most of his assets are tied up in stock he got when Federal Express was formed. So let's say the franchise would cost one hundred million dollars. Dunavant could write a check for it tomorrow. Fred would have to cash out a lot of his stock to get that amount and, capital gains tax being what it is, would probably come up with only seventy-six million. So he's not really in the ballpark with Dunavant.

But in my opinion Dunavant has a problem with the NFL because he owned the USFL team here. Those guys have minds like elephants. I'm not sure they're going to forget USFL. Billy Dunavant has a much bigger ego than Fred has. He's a worldwide cotton guy, but he had gone through divorce court and had some local problems. It could be difficult for him to get approval of NFL owners.

The lure of a challenge was what first prompted Fred Smith to go after the NFL franchise, in Mike Fleming's view.

I think he hates to be told he can't do anything. Lot of people said Memphis couldn't ever get an NFL team, too many guys before have tried it. I remember him saying one day, "That's the worst thing you can do—tell me something can't be done!" He wanted to do this, even though he knew he was going to have to swallow a load himself, and bad stuff. I think he wanted to show that it could be done.

But Fred is a proud guy. I believe he came to the conclusion that the NFL was going to bypass Memphis. So in effect, if they bypassed Memphis, they bypassed Fred Smith. They say the NFL picks the city first and the owner second. That's bullshit. If they were going to pick Memphis, it would be because of Fred Smith, not whether our city stacks up with most other cities in any number of categories—per capita income, economic growth factor, and so on.

Fred just finally decided to turn all his attention to Federal Express. He really wants to leave a lasting monument. I think there is some truth to the story that he wants to exceed his father's business achievements, to prove something—

whatever. He's a guy who's really conquered the mountains. He thrives on a challenge.

The fact that Fred Smith had aborted his plan left mixed reactions and some confusion in the sports world. Pepper Rodgers said the NFL hunt "is still moving full speed ahead." But Danny Sheridan—a CNN and *USA Today* pro football analyst who had earlier predicted Baltimore and Memphis would be added to the NFL in 1993—considered it a shift into reverse. "I won't say it was a death blow—but Memphis is a much longer shot now."

Al Dunning, sports editor of the *Memphis Commercial Appeal,* remained optimistic, writing:

Frederick W. Smith didn't accumulate all those airplanes by guessing wrong or misreading signs.

So when the president and chief executive officer of Federal Express Corp. says Memphis is still a hot contender for membership in the National Football League, it's wise to take him at his word. Few if any participants in the Great NFL Franchise Hunt are likely to be better informed than he is.

Yet when Smith declared himself out as a potential team owner Tuesday, early reaction was that Memphis's NFL chances had just taken a torpedo in the boiler room. Smith's personal prestige and the likelihood that he would own the franchise had been regarded as Memphis's No. 1 advantage in the NFL expansion derby. With Smith out of the owner-ship picture, the perception here and elsewhere is that Memphis has lost much of its clout.

It needn't be that way.

For one thing, Smith made it clear in his address to City Council that he will remain an active player in Memphis's drive for NFL status. He said he can be even more effective now that he has made clear he isn't lobbying for person-al gain. He said, "It has never been my intention to be an NFL owner." He emphasized that his pursuit of an NFL franchise has been on behalf of his hometown, not his per-sonal fortune.

With Smith continuing to beat the Memphis drum, about all that has changed is his role. Booster instead of proprietor . . . which is what he now says was his intent from the start.

All other situations remain as they were before— including maps of the United States which show Memphis perched in a large hole where the closest NFL team is about 400 miles away.

So if expanding to Memphis was a good idea last week, it remains so today.

21▶ THE NAKED MADONNA

People in Memphis smiled when they read about Diane Smith's 1982 Christmas present to her husband, a painting of herself in the nude.

It was not her first naked portrait; she had already given him three others, also as Christmas presents.

That she had been painted in the nude was actually nothing to be ashamed of or embarrassed about. Smith, however, was stunned that this secret was out and mortified that Memphians were laughing about his private life.

Curiously, although Diane Smith was beautiful, the paintings of her naked were not meant to inspire salacious or lustful visions. Quite the contrary. Diane had them patterned after the ancient religious *Madonna and Child* portraits. In each portrait she was shown holding her own newest baby.

Diane Smith herself made the disclosure when interviewed by the *Commercial Appeal* for a feature on what wives of Memphis VIPs were giving their husbands for Christmas. The story said, in part:

> Gifts for men at the top—men whose annual incomes fall into six and sometimes seven figures—are tough to buy for, their wives can tell you.
>
> But people who want to know more about Memphis's leading executives would do well to study what the women

who know those executives best—their wives—got for their husbands for Christmas.

Men of money and power are flesh and blood, after all, and have to be concerned about what to eat, to wear, and to read, and to be entertained.

Did they get offbeat gifts? Practical? Arty? Luxurious?

Some of the wives told all in pre-Christmas interviews.

"Fred wants his own jet, but that's a bit tough," said Diane Smith, wife of Frederick W. Smith, chairman and chief executive officer of Federal Express.

"He likes history and especially likes to read about kings. So I had another Royal Worcester porcelain of Alexander the Great shipped from England. Last year, John Tigrett hand-carried a Worcester sculpture of Richard the Lion-Hearted from London. Our little boy is named Richard."

She said she would also give him a nude painting of herself and their 6-month-old baby, Arthur, by artist Joe Lear. "This is the fourth nude painting I've given him of myself with our babies—first with Richard, then Kathleen, Molly, and now Arthur. They're very lovely and very discreet. I will also give him bins of books because he's into computers and satellites—futuristic topics.

"And I always give him a joke gift. Last year I gave him a case of peanut butter because he loves it and says it's the only thing that got him through Vietnam. This year my joke gift will be his own gymnastic equipment, which I have hidden outdoors in the poolhouse."

She said he wouldn't get his own jet this Christmas. "But Fred acquired actor Cliff Robertson's Spitfire this year, and Cliff's pilot is checking him out on it. There are only 40 Spitfires left from World War II, and we bought one which is in the crates and will take 19 months to put together in London."

The reporter, the late Alice Fulbright, also interviewed Mrs. Kemmons Wilson, Mrs. Maceo Walker, Mrs. J. R. "Pit" Hyde, Mrs. William Dunavant, Mrs. Lamar Alexander (wife of the governor of Tennessee), Mrs. Bruce Campbell, Jr., Mrs. Norfleet Turner, Mrs. Ron Terry, Mrs. John J. Shea, Mrs. Dick Trippeer, and

Mrs. William B. Tanner. Their gifts were more prosaic and not as unique, ranging from wood figurines and smoked salmon to jeweled cuff links and dining room chairs.

"I was delighted Diane Smith told me about the nude paintings," Alice Fulbright said in a 1991 interview. "I don't know why she volunteered that. She's kind of an airhead. She should have known better. I understand Fred got real upset because Federal Express people were drinking it in. She'd eat up the publicity; but he sat on her."

Of the many Federal Express executives interviewed for this book, only the former vice-president of industrial relations, Frank Maguire, said he had seen the nude portraits—and he found them in good taste.

"Those paintings were just beautiful," Maguire said. "And there were not . . . I mean, there was nothing offensive about them at all." They were, he said, on the style of the Old Masters like Rapnael and Leonardo da Vinci, portraying the incarnation of mother love and childish innocence. "I mean, the one I saw was not even . . . It was like a chest, a portrait shot. I don't known why people got so excited about this."

Smith, he said, was furious about the news story, "because he knows that people think in terms of nude pictures of someone like Marilyn Monroe. They don't think in terms of the *Pietà* and *David*. They don't understand that."

In his family and social life, Smith has largely surrendered leadership to Diane. Though he was raised a Protestant, she enrolled their children in Memphis's upscale Catholic schools—the girls in St. Agnes Academy and their sons in St. Dominic School for Boys, located adjacent to each other on Walnut Grove Road on the east side of Memphis.

Fred and Diane Smith rule a household of ten children. "All boys," he often quips, "except seven girls." He has two from his first marriage to Linda: Sandra Windland Smith, born January 19, 1970, and called "Wendy," and Laura Fredette Smith, born January 5, 1973. Diane has a daughter from her marriage to Larry Wall: Stacy, born February 14, 1970. Their first child is Richard, born November 5, 1977, followed by Kathleen, called "Leenie," Molly, Arthur, who was born May 27, 1982, and Samantha, Rachel, and Buchanan, named for his steamboating paternal grandfather and in the family called "Cannon."

Said one of Smith's several cousins: "I understand there was some level of outrage somewhere along the line about how many children she was having, and he was furious. My God, she seemed to have a baby every five minutes! It was embarrassing. She's supposedly a devout Catholic. That was part of her attitude on birth control. But, you know, there is a limit. I don't care how rich you are, there are just so many children you have time for."

Sally Hook, Smith's mother, was greatly upset, friends say, by his second marriage, which came as a surprise to her. She frequently deplores his scant social life. But she sees in him the same kindness and consideration for children that big Fred Smith had. "He's just like his father," she said. "I have never seen a man who has as many children as he has, and as busy as he is, who gives so much time to his children. He took his little boy Arthur to England with him. This child can read like I don't know what. He loves the stories of the different presidents. He names them in order, and Thomas Jefferson is his favorite."

When former president Ronald Reagan made a luncheon speech in Memphis in the fall of 1990, Fred Smith took eight-year-old Arthur to meet him.

Mrs. Hook continued, "My son doesn't like shooting big game . . . but they go bird hunting. He goes to their soccer games when he's home. He's just a man who gives of himself to his children."

The Smiths live in an upscale section on the east side of Memphis, near the I-40 freeway, on a winding road, Sweetbrier. Their contemporary house, originally located on a one- or two-acre lot, is now even more secluded because Smith bought two or three adjacent vacant lots. They have added several rooms onto their house, turning the exterior into a combination of brick, stone, and wood.

In the back is a large playground—described by a friend as "a real playground, not like a home, but with swings and stuff like a municipal park, and a lovely pool, and tennis courts." There is also a separate guest house, which Smith's mother occupied in the winter of 1991–1992. (She had sold her condominium in Little Rock and had her furniture in storage while looking for a suitable house to buy in Memphis.)

In recent years metropolitan Memphis has developed other residential sections with houses that are considerably larger than Smith's, but real estate people estimate the market value of the Smith property at around one million dollars.

To maintain their privacy, the residence is not listed in the Memphis telephone directory. However, the unpublished number does gradually get passed around. (One of his brothers-in-law gave it to me.) So Fred Smith changes it every two or three years, his friends say. Like many wealthy families, the Smiths have concerns about kidnappers and maintain security at their home, a topic they prefer to not discuss.

On the social scene, a Memphis socialite who attended a wedding reception in December 1991 at the Hunt and Polo Club summed up the Smiths' contrasting styles:

> Fred is a very introverted person. Hard to talk to at a party. He never acts like he's having a good time. He never smiles, and his wife is very vivacious and so outgoing. She loves to dance; I believe he did dance with her once at this party. But he seems happy to just sit off in a corner somewhere.
>
> When you see him at a party he is very quiet. It's like his mind is off in another world, and I'm sure it is. Anybody who has such a wonderful business mind is probably thinking all the time on business. I don't know if it's that or just his personality.
>
> They were at the big zoo party in the fall, the fund-raiser. She's just real active in a lot of things, but he goes along acting like "I have to do this because I'm her husband."
>
> On the dance floor, everybody was laughing and talking, and I looked over where Fred was sitting, and I said to my

husband, "Honey, you know what—he's got a stone face."
And I'm sure that's just his way. I'm sure if you talked to
him, he'd be friendly. But I told my husband—and this is
horrible—"You know, honey, the worst thing that could
happen to me would be to be seated next to him for two hours
at a dinner party."

The fact that his father was unable to join the Memphis Country
Club rankled Smith, and he never applied for membership. Instead
he joined the most exclusive of Memphis clubs, the Hunt and Polo
Club, whose membership is limited to one hundred twenty-five. He
also became a member of the University Club, chiefly because of its
excellent tennis courts.

Diane Smith has an active social life with a group of women
friends, one of whom is Pat Tigrett, wife of financier John B.
Tigrett, a director of Federal Express and one of the partners in
development of the trouble-plagued Pyramid convention and sports
complex just opened on the Memphis riverfront. In her own right,
Pat Tigrett is a noted fashion designer. For a portrait of Diane and
the ten children, a copy of which Sally Hook proudly displays, Mrs.
Tigrett created elaborate silk-and-brocade matching costumes for all
of them, including pantaloons for the boys.

Over the course of a year, however, it would be surprising to find
either Diane or Fred Smith in the social column more than twice or
thrice. In many respects Memphis remains an old-fashioned society
town where southern traditions going back to the Civil War remain
alive and respected. Debutantes still "come out." Much is made of
annual selection of the "Maid of Cotton." And every spring at Mardi
Gras time there is a real competition for the honor of being selected
king and queen of the yearly Carnival Memphis. Usually these roles
are inherited from "royal" families whose grandparents or great-
grandparents were at least princes or princesses in the pageant.

The Fred Smiths do not cater to these affairs, though the Earl
Smith side of the family provided a duchess and at least one princess
for the Cotton Carnival.

Nor does Smith care for golf. Too many people are involved, and
a round of golf steals too many hours from his day. He hates crowds.

He told reporter Lewis Nolan that it annoys him when strangers or friends come up and ask him to give a Federal Express job to some relative.

Tennis is his game. Says Mike Fleming: "He enjoys tennis because he can play it quick and get a lot of good exercise. It's not like golf; he doesn't have to take a lot of time. He has his own court at his house, and plays at Hunt and Polo and the University clubs. He has a real big serve, and his forestrokes are fair. He couldn't go out on the tour—senior tour—tomorrow, but he loves it, and he's competitive. We have played four or five sets at a time, or half a day. It depends on what he has going on. He would play all day if he could get somebody to stay out there with him. I've done that. He'll wear your ass out. And he'll be the last one to leave."

Despite numerous fights with local politicians, Fred Smith seems to have largely avoided any lasting local feuds. In 1991 Memphis elected its first black mayor, former city schools superintendent Willie Herenton, but no activism by Smith or the company was visible in the campaign, even though Smith had campaigned for a black candidate in 1979. However, Federal Express's veteran personnel director, James A. Perkins, a black, accepted a post on the new mayor's transition team to review the hiring of city employees.

Perhaps his most distressing rupture is with his half-sister Fredette Eagle. They haven't spoken since 1972, but she has attempted to patch things up. Fred Smith rejected the overture she made through Lucius Burch. During interviews for this book, she told me: "I would like to reconcile with Fred. Neither of us intended the other harm. He was desperate and so was I, and we did what we had to do. We did not act out of spite or vindictiveness. We are both equally guilty. It is so sad the family got ruptured that way."

Despite their rift, Smith continues his friendship with his sister's former husband, Bryan Eagle, who heads a major electronics company, and with their son, Bryan III. When the boy graduated high school, Smith gave him a summer job helping devise a computer program at Federal Express and let him stay as a guest in his home.

Said Bryan III: "He told me, 'Just one thing. Don't mention your mother, and we'll get along fine.' He gave me a shotgun. It's hard for a boy to be mad at someone who gives him a shotgun. It was a fine summer."

Fredette Eagle said when in 1991 her son sought some business and financial counsel, Smith directed him to the right people.

There seems no residue of ill will between the other half sister, Laura Ann Smith Patterson Rohm, who was also a plaintiff in the lawsuit challenging Fred Smith's manipulation of the family trust. There is no contact, either.

After two marriages ended in divorce, she closed her real estate business in Denver in 1983 and moved to the Texas Gulf coast, where she took up a new career as "animal humanitarian." At the large home she bought two miles outside Corpus Christi, she established a refuge for abused and neglected animals.

She took in stray and wounded cats, dogs, goats, burros, rabbits—even baby opossum and chickens and quail. It grew into a large—and expensive—operation, that included fenced pens, electrically heated shelters, even a laboratory. In December 1991 she was caring for eighty dogs and sixty cats and kittens alone.

A reporter from the *Corpus Christi Caller-Times* was impressed that Mrs. Rohm, a tiny woman in her mid-fifties, only five two and weighing ninety pounds, had hired an assistant and kept her "animal hotel" spotlessly clean. "Rohm maintains her own animal dispensary," the newspaper reported. "She uses a microscope to test for worms and other diseases and gives the animals all their shots and medication, except rabies shots, which by law must be given by a veterinarian. The dogs are kept bathed and dipped and well fed.

"She keeps meticulous records on her inmates, recording their characteristics, history, and medical record in a book. When they are put out for adoption, she said, she thoroughly checks out the new owners to see if they will give the pets a good home. With each animal goes a full chart of how to care for it."

She is fond of all animals and once in Dallas had a most unusual pet, a large tarantula. "I called him Crazylegs. He had a good personality."

One of her sons, John Frederick ("named for my father") Patterson, came to Corpus Christi as a minister for the Unity church. He escorted her to the 1991 meeting of the Coastal Bend Veterinary Association, where she was honored as "Humanitarian of the Year."

Laura Ann Rohm said she is estranged from her brother. "I doubt if he would know me if he saw me. No, I hold no bitterness; but then I don't think he cares to have anything to do with me. He's happy with where he is, and he's happy with his life. I'm not going to have any feelings one way or the other. I don't believe in the Hatfields and McCoys, and I hold no malice toward my brother, who is, I suppose, the dynamic charismatic person. I don't know him."

Fredette Eagle has not kept contact with her half sister. When told about the animal refuge, she expressed approval, adding, "I'm really pleased to see that Laura Ann is trying to do something useful with her life."

Smith has often been involved in personal family business—not only on his father's side, but with his mother's relatives and his wife's.

In March 1988 his second cousin, Earl Smith III, was killed in an auto crash in Memphis. Known in the family as "Little Billy," Earl had been made wealthy by inheriting the bulk of his grandmother Estelle Smith's Toddle House estate. Married at seventeen, he attended Oxford University in England and became a seminarian, expecting to be ordained to the Episcopal priesthood.

However, while back in Memphis under an assumed name in a drug rehab program, he left the hospital, wrecked his automobile, and was killed at age thirty-seven. His wife, Tommie, and their seven-year-old daughter, Kelli, were in London. Fred Smith took charge. Among other things, he recovered from the police department Earl's clothing and effects.

Even so, his actions were resented by several family members, including the victim's sister, Lindsey "Sissy" Smith Brady, a commercial photographer in West Palm Beach, Florida.

"At first it seemed like Fred was being real nice and helpful," said Lindsey Brady. "Then he was sort of ordering us around, and I had to say, 'Excuse me, Fred, this is my brother, not yours. I think we can handle this situation.'

"My sister-in-law, Tommie, was not well. She had to come all the way from England, because that's where they were living at the time. And when she got to Memphis, she was practically a basket case. I think his original interest was to handle it all for her. Tommie wasn't able, but it was my mother's and my job to handle it, and we were able.

"It seems he made some decisions beforehand that really weren't his to make. Like going to the funeral home and picking out the coffin, and that kind of thing. Ordering flowers that we didn't need; because he was a priest, though not ordained, his coffin would be covered by the church's pall, not flowers. But we didn't change the coffin."

However, an aunt, Margaret Repkoff, said: "It was all just a big mess because Fred had gone out and bought clothes for Earl to be buried in, and Tommie called Fred and said she was bringing something from London she wanted him buried in. Fred did everything. He kept stuff out of the paper. He arranged for the funeral at Calvary Episcopal Church right in the midst of the Lenten programs; the priest there didn't know the Smiths at all. When we came out of the mausoleum, Fred seemed to feel a little bit out of it. I went up and hugged him and said, 'Thanks for everything.' I think he did a good job."

There was some confusion, too, about whether Earl III would be entombed in the Smith family mausoleum in Forest Hill Mid-town Cemetery. Said Lindsey Brady:

My brother and I hated that place. All the children were taken there every Christmas and Easter, and we swore to each other we wouldn't let the other be buried there. I wrestled with myself about letting him be buried there, but it was so difficult not to be. The Fred Smiths believe they own it. I always felt half was theirs and half ours. Sally was upset when my brother was buried there. I don't know why. There are eight crypts. On their side there's big Fred and three blanks, and on ours Earl, Estelle, and Earl the Third, and one empty. I don't know exactly how we got in there; I guess Fred Junior gave permission.

Fred sort of backed off, and wouldn't talk too much after that. . . . I don't know, sometimes it seems like I'm a little too open and a little too honest. Fred's very reserved and very reluctant to even like some of the funny things about the family that the rest of us think are kind of humorous.

For instance, Fred mentioned to me that Fredette's son, Bryan Eagle the Third, lived in a Memphis apartment building called Kimbrough Towers. Well, all of our fathers kept women in the Kimbrough Towers at one time or another. All of us had known that all of our lives.

I said, "You mean to tell me Bryan is living in the Kimbrough Towers?" And he said, "Yes, why?" "You mean you don't remember all the women who were kept there?" He said, "I guess I really had forgotten that." He didn't find it amusing or ironic or anything. . . . I just don't know.

Three years after the death of Earl Smith III, his forty-year-old widow, Tommie, married William Dunavant, Jr.

Two of Diane Smith's three brothers have jobs at Federal Express in Memphis. Kevin Davis is a senior mechanic, and Buddy Davis is a professional musician on weekends and a logistics assistant in the FedEx warehouse operation. Brother John, a graduate of the Air Force Academy, is stationed in Phoenix, Arizona, and was assigned to AWACS duty in Saudia Arabia in Desert Storm.

Two of Diane's three sisters live in Memphis, Denise Dunavant (no relation of the William Dunavants) and Dana Brandon. The other, Donna Thomas, lives in Montana.

"I was in the music business until I was about thirty," Buddy Davis said in our interview.

I played guitar in a band called Target. We had two albums out in 1976 and 1977 on Herb Alpert's label, and all of a sudden we found our manager was stealing from us.

Diane and Fred got some attorneys for us, and we started a big lawsuit out in California. Our lawyer was a friend of Fred's, William Carter. He is an ex–Secret Service man, was a bodyguard for LBJ, and is an ex–Federal Express attorney. Now he's in music law in Nashville and represents Tanya Tucker and people like that.

We didn't win, and it made me have to get out of music full-time. I still play weekends with some of the Target guys. But when you have children and are buying a home, it's rough. I was working at the railroad during the day and I got a job at the FedEx hub at night, starting at the bottom. My brother, Kevin, came out of the air force and started at the bottom as a mechanic and worked up. We had to earn our way.

Buddy Davis said he sees Diane and Fred Smith about once a week and gets along well with his brother-in-law. "He really came through like an older brother during Daddy's coma. He really came through like a champ for us, coming to the hospital [in March 1990] and still carrying on all his work at Federal. And he had an uncle [Sally Hook's brother William Wallace] dying of cancer in one hospital and my daddy dying of a stroke in another. And he kept making the rounds."

Diane Smith's mother, Mrs. Richard "Johnny" Davis, decided to retire at the end of 1991 from her position as secretary in the Shelby County Sheriff's Office—but had no desire to land a new job at Federal Express.

"Oh, no," she said, laughing. "I'm just going to enjoy my twenty-three grandchildren."

22▶ *THE FLYING TIGER CRISIS*

Expanding Federal Express worldwide became in the 1980s Smith's newest dream, and he diligently sought ways to achieve that goal quickly.

His best hope seemed to be to acquire the legendary Flying Tigers, the world's largest carrier of heavyweight cargo, whose thirty-nine planes—half of them 747s—generated annual revenues of around a billion dollars.

In 1984, when Smith saw Flying Tigers begin losing money, he approached its parent, Tiger International Inc., with an offer to buy all or part of the cargo line. Turned down, he set out to build his own global network, first acquiring a Minneapolis package courier called Gelco Express, which served eighty-four countries. Smith expanded his overseas network with acquisitions in Holland, Britain, and the United Arab Emirates.

But this pace was too slow for him; he was convinced FedEx would not prosper by the year 2000 if it did not deliver worldwide.

He continued to believe the solution would be to buy Flying Tigers, chiefly for its delivery routes with landing rights in twenty-one countries, acquired over forty years. Federal Express would then become the world's number one air cargo carrier, using its own planes for package delivery overseas, no longer required to contract out this portion of the business to other airlines, and also able to crack the heavy-freight market.

Founded by a daring band of World War II fighter pilots, Flying Tigers had been modestly profitable. Then came heightened competition, acquisitions that proved troublesome, and unionized pilots that brought steeper labor costs and eventual losses. Every possible expenditure was deferred, and its equipment deteriorated.

New executives were brought in; management squeezed workers for wage concessions. As costs went down, profits rebounded and the company earned $89 million in 1988 on revenues of $1.4 billion. Even so, trouble loomed ahead, mainly increasingly stiff competition and the need for costly aircraft repairs that had been put off.

Saul P. Steinberg, a New York financier who had a 16.5 percent stake in Tiger International, notified Smith in late November 1988 that Flying Tigers was for sale.

At Federal Express Corporation headquarters secretaries were sent scurrying to collect all the latest on Flying Tigers—computer printouts, charts, annual reports, confidential memos. Smith stayed past midnight, poring over the data, weighing the gamble, deciding whether it would pay out, designing his offer. A FedEx insider remembers it like this:

> Fred finds out through the grapevine, it didn't take a great deal of trouble, that Flying Tiger was in serious trouble. He gets all his ammunition. Something on the company, assets, the whole thing. Sits around and analyzes it. Calls the Tiger CEO. Proposes a meeting with him. No attorneys. No secondary people. Just Fred and this guy.
>
> Fred goes in and makes the proposition. Up or down. This is it. No haggling. Final. You'll never see me again if you don't take this. No counteroffer. This is it! Again, he really had the guy by the balls.

The perhaps truer scenario indicates Smith was fearful hesitation might rob him of his chance at this prize. Steinberg cannily let it be known that if an offer was unacceptable, he might buy the other 83 percent of Flying Tigers for himself. Then, too, competitor cargo carriers might bid against FedEx. Smith heard that United Parcel Services was considering doing so.

Smith rushed in with his offer—whether or not on a take-it-or-leave-it basis—of $20.88 a share. Flying Tigers took it. It was about $6.00 a share above market price, meaning FedEx was paying about $880 million.

The Federal Express chairman was convinced he had made a brilliant acquisition. Wall Street, at the moment, seemed to agree; within a month FedEx shares rose ten points to about $55.00 a share.

But that was only the beginning; the marriage of the air cargo lines was destined to encounter myriad troubles—so severe that by 1992 analyst Paul R. Schlesinger of Donaldson, Lufkin and Jenrette described it as possibly Smith's "fatal step." He added: 'I think he was outsmarted, hoodwinked, whatever, by Saul Steinberg."

▶ ▶ ▶

At the time of the Flying Tiger Acquisition, Federal Express was a $4.6 billion-a-year success story at home, the nation's largest overnight carrier, responsible for more than 45 percent of the U.S. market. But trying to crack the world market was proving expensive; losses on overseas operations came to $75 million by the end of 1989.

At the same time domestic earnings turned sluggish, and FedEx's growth rate in the U.S. market slacked off from 58 percent in 1984 to 25 percent in 1988. The volume of domestic package and document shipments suffered from the boom in facsimile machines and a price war to fend off the United Parcel Service's push into overnight deliveries. As overnight letters declined, FedEx was forced to concentrate on moving boxes—precisely the "back-door trade" that lower-priced UPS traditionally had led.

The Federal Express long-term debt, highly leveraged, was ballooned two and a half times by the merger. At $2.1 billion it became far more vulnerable to economic swings and possible downgrading by investment monitors. But at that time the equity market showed no concern about FedEx's ability to pay off its loans.

The consolidation confronted Smith with half a dozen dangerous and unexpected challenges, but he faced them upbeat. One analyst warned: "This merger will have to be handled like two porcupines making love: very carefully. Federal is playing big casino, with big risks."

Smith disagreed, observing: "It's a big challenge—no question. I don't know that it's a bet-the-company move. We get a lot of hard assets with this acquisition." That certainly was true as far as foreign landing rights are concerned, in the view of David Guthrie, who follows FedEx for Morgan Keegan & Company, Inc., Memphis. "Fred was afraid somebody like UPS was going to come in and buy it. The most valuable things that Tiger had was all those route authorities, those you essentially can't duplicate by just going in and applying for them. Take you fifty years to get all that stuff." Smith knew that; until he got Tigers, FedEx had only five foreign slots: Montreal, Toronto, Brussels, London, and Tokyo. But the Tokyo slot was limited; FedEx couldn't use Tokyo for jumping off to anywhere else in Asia.

But some of the assets—namely several of the twenty-two giant 747s—came up short, at least in a layman's eyes. Part of the Flying Tiger fleet was almost unusable because of neglect. Many of its 747s needed fast reconditioning to meet Federal Aviation Administration maintenance deadlines. FedEx had to promptly spend an estimated $100 million above the purchase price to repair fuselage corrosion and structural defects and otherwise bring the Tiger aircraft up to United States government requirements.

Smith was not deceived on the 747 defects, in Paul Schlesinger's opinion. "Fred had already decided that long-term the 747 was not the plane he needed; but they came with the deal. In the whole scheme of things that extra one hundred million dollars is more than a rounding error, and it's not walking-around money. But it's not the difference between success or failure."

With the merger, Federal Express acquired 970 Tiger pilots, who were unionized, with legal seniority rights. Fred Smith, from day one, had promised his pilots, now numbering 1,000, that nothing would ever disturb their seniority. But in combining the two airlines, he had little choice. As much as he hated unions, particularly the Air

Line Pilots Association, he had to renege and create a single senior-ity list, bumping down hundreds of his own fliers to give slots to incoming union pilots who had more years in the air.

The reshuffling of personnel necessitated by the merger, as well as the worldwide business downturn that reduced overseas flights, created an excess of pilots, a large number of whom were paid just to sit around. That gave no solace to the Federal Express aviators. They protested vigorously about Fred Smith's "treachery" in diluting their seniority, and they began lobbying each other to unionize themselves and reject the "family" dogma he had successfully preached.

Besides the new pilots, FedEx absorbed an additional 5,500 Tiger ground workers around the world. This influx, far out of reach of the congenial Memphis "family" atmosphere, posed a forbidding challenge. Would they and the pilots dilute the vaunted Federal Express entrepreneurial spirit, built on the cornerstone of Fred Smith's paternalistic "no layoff" philosophy, all aimed at creating and maintaining the premium of customer satisfaction?

Federal Express encountered intense competition at home and abroad. Smith looked at UPS as his strongest domestic challenger. Largest package delivery company in the world, now headquartered in Atlanta, and management-owned with 252,000 employees, UPS grossed $15 billion annually, with earnings of $700 million in 1991. Its ubiquitous brown trucks deliver some 11 million parcels daily, accounting for 85 percent of income. UPS didn't inaugurate air service until 1982, but by the time FedEx was swallowing Flying Tigers, UPS had a main million-square-foot hub in Louisville, with satellite hubs in Philadelphia and on the West Coast, and a fleet of 99 jets and 240 smaller airplanes.

UPS had plunged into international air cargo, buying eight small-er air freight companies in Europe and one in Hong Kong, boasting it could deliver by air or ground in 175 countries and territories. Smith knew UPS, with $7 billion in virtually debt-free assets, was financially superior; it could suffer losses abroad to gain a foothold much longer than could FedEx.

Smith had to battle two other airlines already entrenched in the global market. DHL International, privately held and based in Brussels, carried 40 percent of the continent's express traffic and 60 percent of all U.S.-bound express packages, with same-day service across the United States and between London and New York. In business since 1969, its 190 airplanes served 188 countries. To counter FedEx inroads, DHL beefed itself up by tie-ins, with Lufthansa and Japan Air Lines getting priority on cargo space by selling each a 7.5 percent interest.

TNT, the other major player, was a $4.4 billion Australian conglomerate, with a worldwide presence not only in air freight, but in truck lines in the United States and Europe.

Also competing anew for domestic and overseas freight, major airlines took advantage of the fact that passenger fares paid most of their costs, permitting relatively cheap rates for cargo under their feet in the plane's belly. Going after a bigger piece of international freight, the American Airlines cargo president asserted: "Passengers won't ride in the basement. So I have excess capacity, and that's how I price the cargo."

A negative view of the merger was taken by freight forwarders all over the world. Flying Tiger had generally confined itself to moving cargo from airport to airport; freight forwarders were the independent agents who handled customs, paperwork on most of the goods in transit, and local deliveries.

Federal Express specialized in door-to-door small-package handling, and the forwarders feared it could begin to do the same on heavy freight. When forwarders, whose influence on overseas customers is big, complained that such a move would put them out of business, Smith tried to appease them by limiting FedEx to freight weighing 150 pounds or less.

"Our plan is to totally integrate the two companies," Smith told the press, "and to make sure we keep Tiger's customers happy." But many forwarders were not mollified. It would be fairer, they argued, to set the FedEx limit at thirty pounds, since the average package they handled weighed fifty pounds. One industry consultant told

Business Week: "Right now many forwarders had rather use a barge than Flying Tiger."

Smith countered that because of his reliable, on-time service it was still to the forwarders' advantage to use Federal Express. Even so, many agents who used Tigers exclusively began to cut back, scattering shipments on several airlines. In 1992 many forwarders still shied away from FedEx.

There was an ironic competitive complication with United Parcel Service; it had been using Flying Tiger to deliver packages to countries where UPS held no landing rights. That business dried up rapidly as UPS gained its own route authorities abroad, such as permission to fly six times a week into Tokyo.

Smith conceded that he encountered unexpected problems in his foreign expansion. His pocketbook was hit hard by, among other things, higher fuel costs. He claimed his rivals also were losing money overseas. DHL and TNT denied it; UPS, while admitting losses, said cost of its global expansion was "investment" and the overseas operations were targeted to show a profit in 1994.

Going worldwide, Federal Express quickly found, produced trouble that never seemed to go away. It took three years to get approval to fly from Memphis to Japan, four times a week. Then three days before that service was to begin in May 1988, Japan, showing concern about harming its own fledgling air cargo lines, notified FedEx that no package weighing over seventy pounds could be carried to Tokyo or passed through its airport. In a year's time that restriction cost Federal Express a million dollars.

In an interview Fred Smith said: "Not to our credit, we were very late doing what we did in Europe. . . . We are the clipper ships of the the computer age."

Assessing the expansion in a 1990 article, *Fortune* magazine said:

What happened next is a lesson for all managers with dreams of going global. A product that sells well in the U.S. carries no guarantee in alien markets. And while you're busy trying to make your domestic magic work overseas, your competitors may come charging in to steal customers from under your nose, as FedEx is finding out. . . . Flying Tigers has become an albatross around the Memphis company's neck.

Pilot unhappiness at Federal Express, at the height of the overseas crises, exploded. The handling of the seniority squabble left a bitter taste, and other unilateral actions by the company were galling.

Flight assignments became inflexible; no longer did pilots have easygoing options, permitted to choose when and where they would fly. FedEx captains were getting $125,000 to $150,00 a year—on a par with commercial airline seniors—but suddenly their pension plan was changed. Airline captains could look forward to a pension of about 75 percent of salary, but in Federal Express the retirement benefit was cut to slightly less than 50 percent.

Instead of poor-mouthing, FedEx pilots organized with the help of the Air Lines Pilots Association and forced the National Mediation Board to hold an election in 1989 on union representation.

The effort to unionize was defeated, getting only 709 votes from the company's 2,022 pilots. But the fight wasn't over. The ALPA launched another organizing campaign in 1991. Smith went around personally to his fliers, listening to their complaints, making some changes, and promising to do more to satisfy them.

Even so, when the second election was held in August 1991, pilots trying to unionize the company lost by only twenty-three votes.

Analysts who follow Federal Express interpreted that as a bad sign. "ALPA made a lot of inroads," said one. "Smith hasn't heard the last of this, by any means." Under federal labor law, however, the pilots could not petition for another election for at least a year.

Despite turmoil at Memphis headquarters, Smith felt that his customers were highly satisfied. He decided in January 1989 to go after the U.S. Department of Commerce's coveted Malcolm Baldrige National Quality Award in the service category. He organized a one-thousand-man team to begin the detailed investigation and evaluation required to file an application for the honor. Their findings shocked him, revealing that the company was not as good in customer service as he had thought. Immediately he began a crash improvement program to correct deficiencies and prepare for entering next year's competition.

New and higher standards for service and customer statisfaction were set, measured by a twelve-component "Service Quality Indicator" that more deeply involved the FedEx high-tech computer networks and senior executives in evaluating service not on average trends, but virtually on day-to-day charts of on-time performance.

When FedEx entered the Malcolm Baldrige competition in 1990, Department of Commerce examiners came to Memphis to spend days quizzing employees for the true picture of their efficiency. Identical surveys were conducted in company offices in Los Angeles and Chicago.

Federal Express won. In October 1990 the Department of Commerce awarded Smith the coveted trophy. One item in the citation was especially pleasing to him: in the previous five years 91 percent of its employees said they were "proud to work for Federal Express."

Aviation Week & Space Technology awarded Smith one of its 1990 "Laurels" for this achievement, coupled with FedEx having met its Civil Reserve Air Fleet commitment to the government by cutting loose four Boeing 747s and three McDonnell Douglas DC-10s for transporting military cargo in Operation Desert Storm. Said the magazine: "Thus, perhaps to the People-Service-Profit slogan of Federal Express, there should be added a fourth element—loyalty."

But the overseas gamble was draining profits. Expenses escalated. Business abroad was difficult, if not impossible, to generate in profitable terms. Often FedEx planes flew four-fifths empty to Tokyo because of the seventy-pound limit.

Although Fred Smith had poured $1.5 billion into expansion abroad, Federal Express was making just one of ten express deliveries in Europe, compared with one of two in the United States. Its planes often flew half-empty from Europe to New York, and within Europe its truck fleet largely carried not express, but unprofitable freight like toilet paper.

For the first time since going public in 1978, Federal Express reported in spring 1991 a quarterly operating loss—$105.6 million.

The hemorrhage in foreign operations triggered drastic action. Smith started pulling back. He had a major problem in Great Britain, where there was not nearly enough business to support his work force of eight thousand. Despite his "no layoff" pledge, he fired two thousand of them, taking a $121 million charge against earnings, which pushed nine-month losses to $201.4 million.

The Wall Street Journal bluntly reported: "The company's international operations, after almost a decade of expansion, fine-tuning, and promises of success, are on the ropes." The FedEx chairman put the best face he could on the calamity and promised, "I'm absolutely determined we're going to get that side of the business profitable."

But he couldn't do it.

By the end of 1991 Federal Express's overseas operating losses totaled $629 million for the preceding three years, dropping the company's net income from $185 million in fiscal year 1989 to just $6 million in fiscal year 1991. *Forbes* magazine called that "an almost invisible margin for a company with revenues of $7.7 billion."

Not unexpectedly, the overseas turmoil brought about upheavals at Memphis headquarters.

What was called "the deepest recession in at least ten years" prompted Smith and the board of directors in April 1991 to order a freeze on the pay of sixty top executives. At the same time they cut performance awards to $50, lowered retirement contributions, and increased salary deductions $20 a month to cover health insurance.

"We have not laid off any employees," said a company news release. Federal Express at that time employed about 18,000 in Memphis, 72,100 in the United States, and 93,000 workers worldwide.

Just how difficult it had become in Memphis was indicated by *The Wall Street Journal,* which reported: "Already, executives traveling on business must get personal approval from Mr. Smith or his second in command to fly a commercial airline rather than grab a jump seat on a Federal cargo plane."

Smith could not watch his profits disappear without getting worried—and angry, an anger he took out on his executives. The upshot was that several senior officers departed. It caught Memphis by surprise when chief financial officer David C. Anderson quit on September 9, 1991, and a month later the number two man, chief operating officer James L. Barksdale, also resigned. Both said they left for better-paying jobs; insiders suggested Smith had pushed them, but publicly he denied they were fired.

On Anderson's watch, Federal Express had trusted a flamboyant California con man with $100 million to handle their corporate tax payments, only to discover the FBI investigating him for embezzlement. FedEx had to set aside $32 million as a possible loss. The day this scandal broke, March 23, 1991, audit vice-president Jack Roberts resigned without explanation. Ironically, as chief quality officer, Roberts had played the major role in winning the Malcolm Baldrige trophy. Anderson, who earned about $325,000 a year at FedEx, went to Burlington Northern Inc., a railroad company based at Fort Worth, Texas, reportedly at a raise of $250,000.

Barksdale, in the company since the 1970s, made $531,000 a year as COO and owned about $4 million in FedEx stock; he resigned to go to McCaw Cellular Communications Inc. on promise of being made president.

Turnover at the Federal Express vice-presidential level had risen to 15 percent, Smith conceded in a January 1992 letter to company managers, a state of affairs he linked to the company's "extremely modest" executive compensation levels. Pay for forty vice-presidents in 1989 totaled $8.4 million, dropping the next year to $6.3 million for forty-seven vice-presidents. Compensation improved slightly in 1991, Smith wrote, with $7.4 million paid to forty-nine vice-presidents. Smith's own total cash compensation for 1990 was $662,491, which *Forbes* magazine listed at the bottom of publicly held companies of similar size. (IBM Corp. chairman John F. Akers led the list at $7.6 million.)

The departures hurt the company, in the opinion of David Guthrie. "The Federal Express pay scale for senior vice-presidents is not very high," he said. "They are in very high profile, and easy to pick off if they desire at all to move."

To replace departing senior staff, Smith reshuffled his top people. Only months after his being raised to senior vice-president for international operations, Thomas R. Oliver, fifty, was promoted to second in command, as executive vice-president. Similarly, Ted Weise, forty-seven, a pilot and bomber flight engineer who joined FedEx in Little Rock at $700 a month, was made senior vice-president of domestic ground operations at $341,900 a year. And a few months later he succeeded T. Allan McArtor as senior vice-president of air operations. This change took place three days before the second pilots' union vote, presumably because Weise was more popular with the flight crews. McArtor, one-time air force Thunderbird stunt pilot and for two years head of the Federal Aviation Administration, had lost favor with FedEx crews because it had fallen to him to adjust seniority lists to accommodate incoming Tiger pilots. His new company assignment was to launch a subsidiary dealing with aircraft overhaul, pilot training, and spare parts.

Smith's wrath appeared to fall, too, on Ron J. Ponder, forty-eight, another senior vice-president, who quit a professorship at Memphis State University in 1977 to become director of operations research and developed the use of bar codes to track packages in transit. In a surprise move Ponder jumped to Sprint/United Telecom in Kansas City as executive vice-president and chief information officer.

What Memphis insiders considered significant was that none of the reshuffling enhanced Federal Express's opportunity to win the global struggle. Rather, developments revealed that Smith was abandoning basic principles and policies of his original concept.

Gone, or going, was the axiom of FedEx maintaining total control of the package in transit—by flying it only on company planes, delivering it exclusively by FedEx couriers. Now FedEx considered taking on partners in places like Japan and Australia and even studied licensing local companies to take over parts of the domestic markets—under the Federal Express logo and technology. Tom Oliver was quoted: "We're prepared to be eclectic."

Despite this reversal of Smith's philosophy, *Jet Cargo News,* a leading trade journal, found reason for optimism:

> Federal Express is world-class contender at all levels. Market forces will ultimately determine how victorious FedEx will emerge in its global expansion. But the carrier is doing everything in its power—from the top commander on down to the trenches—to ensure its success into the twenty-first century as a worldwide distribution leader.

Smith's attempt to conquer Europe stumbled badly from the start. The invaders from Memphis, too brash for Europe's tradition-steeped business culture, compounded mistakes and miscalculations. They tried to set up a hub in Frankfurt, demanding the airport waive night flight curfews and some labor rules. When the Germans declined, Federal took the hub to Brussels. Lamented Smith's chief agent in France: "We thought it would be just like doing business in the U.S."

The engine that launched this global concept was the driving personality of Fred Smith; and it was his never-say-die ego that drove it forward despite snag after snag.

Wall Street analysts began voicing serious doubts about the ultimate success in Europe; big shareholders grumbled. Smith, whatever qualms he might experience, showed the world only a confident face. Further, his vision and actions were strongly endorsed by the FedEx board, especially directors Peter Willmott, Phillip Greer, John B. Tigrett, and his Memphis schoolmate J. R. "Pit" Hyde.

The steady flow of red ink from abroad did not seem to faze Smith or put him under personal strain. David Guthrie, seeing him three or four times a year, noted no change. "He looked just the same to me," said Pepper Rodgers, his erstwhile NFL franchise partner. "We play tennis about three times a week. Doubles—a social game. He is a very intense man. He walks out on the court, and one second later he's swinging as hard as he can. There's no finesse in the Smith game—he comes at you."

Coming at the global market remained the FedEx game as well. No quarter would be given in the attack to capture the continental market. Smith himself made that clear in sessions with Wall Street analysts in October 1990 and May 1991. However, with international operations showing a loss of $201 million in the nine months preceding the latter session, the FedEx chief said "fat" already was being cut but was vague and offered no timetable for a turnaround. He showed confidence in his judgment by announcing that international service would be expanded from 129 to 195 countries. But he gave a glimpse of his frustration by sharply criticizing unnamed analysts and reporters who persisted in "negativism" about FedEx's future.

To boost revenue, Federal opened "EXPRESSfreighter" routes to give shippers next-day and second-day delivery between the United States and Tokyo, Osaka, Singapore and Penang, Malaysia, Hong Kong, Taipei, Frankfurt, and London. The Asian flights stopped at the FedEx hub in Anchorage, Alaska, en route to Memphis.

Analysts did not think these flights attracted enough high-yield cargo to justify their operating costs. Smith claimed they increased "international priority volume" 30 percent.

Stubbornly trying to get a foothold on the continent, Smith seemed unwilling to concede that Europe's cozy boundaries were made to order for truck traffic and rendered an air system virtually useless except on certain long-range routes. Or that Europeans never warmed to the "move 'em out quick" philosophy that Federal Express employed in the United States and was putting in place in Asia.

Those were not mistakes made by chief rival United Parcel Service. It built to serve fifteen European countries a truck system, using 4,500 vehicles and 17,000 employees, that was largely on a par with its American delivery network. To that ground fleet was added an air hub at Cologne, with twenty flights, hauling five hundred thousand packages daily.

Worldwide, Fred Smith & Company came in a poor second to UPS's $15 billion revenue and $700 million profit, derived from 350 aircraft, 122,000 vehicles, and 252,000 employees moving 11 million packages daily. FedEx claimed 380 aircraft, 213 of which were small Cessna 208s, 34,200 vehicles, 93,000 employees, delivering approximately one million packages five days a week from 1,820 stations and service centers.

By the start of 1992 FedEx was on the ropes in Europe. Even Smith admitted failure. The debacle could be explained simply: not enough business at too much cost. Instead of diminishing, losses had feverishly escalated. FedEx was about to post a quarterly loss of almost $200 million, its highest ever.

Prompt drastic action was needed. Smith was ready to pull back. With his board he tried to develop a strategy to get out from under door-to-door service in Europe, but still keep his purple jets hauling cargo across the Atlantic.

As he summed it up: "Our domestic businesses in Europe have simply not provided the synergies with our international business. The operations needed to support our intra-European service have been extremely costly, and we have not generated adequate revenues to cover our costs. In addition, the market in Europe has not developed express traffic as quickly as we had expected it to."

In rapid moves, Federal Express unloaded virtually all its European courier operations, discharged 6,600 employees, closed its

Brussels hub, canceled leases on a dozen aircraft—and took a $254 million charge to cover the cost of the retreat.

In the United Kingdom, Securicor Omega Express Ltd. bought (for an estimated $12 million) FedEx's domestic customer base and agreed to pick up and deliver its international shipments. TNT Express Europe N.V. signed a similar deal for Sweden, Norway, Spain, Finland, Ireland, Northern Ireland, Portugal, Denmark, Greece, Turkey, and Austria. Part of the deal was that FedEx would deliver Securicor and TNT packages in the United States. TNT also took over FedEx facilities in France.

Tom Oliver explained: "It's important to understand what we are doing and what we are not doing. We will pick up a package in Rome, Georgia, and fly it to Paris, France. We still pick up a package in Paris, France, and fly it to Rome, Georgia. But we will not pick up a package in Paris, France, and fly it to Rome, Italy."

The retreat still left 2,600 Federal Express employees in sixteen key cities in seven European nations.

Analysts who follow Federal Express were critical of Smith. Paul Schlesinger said in our interview: "I think Fred's struggling to save his ultimate dream, a single worldwide small package delivery system. It's possible that the acquisition of Tigers was the fatal step along the way. Tigers was so expensive to acquire that it has zapped their balance sheet and their access to capital. It's clear in Europe they tried to do too much, they did not control well, poorly conceived, poorly implemented. . . ."

Schlesinger described as "troubling" the departure of so many Federal Express top executives, adding:

> It could be that they looked long and hard at the task and concluded it wasn't worth it . . . it couldn't be done . . . that they had lost faith in Fred. They were tired of Fred leading them off on what proved to be fool's errands, and that Fred was making the critical decisions and blaming others when it didn't work. Or just that they got tired of unsuccess.
>
> They've had pricing initiative problems. Sounds like they are a little bit out of control. There are personnel decisions in the lower ranks that are sort of bizarre. Serious pressures

with labor relations. The issue with the pilots is not settled yet; could wind up being unionized. Their international area—that just isn't working right.

One way or another, Fred's losing the faith of the troops. I don't know if that means the people driving the trucks, but the management in the field. You assume it is demoralizing to the whole organization. There seems to be some deep-seated internal problem. In other companies where the founding entrepreneur perhaps overstayed their ability to contribute . . . Look at Apple Computer and Compaq Computer. Fred is aware of these precedents; he doesn't want to lose control but doesn't want to take the thing into oblivion like the bombardier in *Dr. Strangelove*. Fred still has a twinkle in his eye, still charming, but he's obviously under some stress.

As a user domestically, one still has to be amazed that the thing works as well as it does. It's extraordinarily impressive still.

Robert Marcin, partner in the money management firm of Miller, Anderson & Sherwood, which "owns a few million FedEx shares for our clients," considered the retreat from Europe as positive.

"Most people I talk to are happy with what Federal Express is doing domestically," Marcin said. "It is a very small part of the company that is causing a lot of pain and grief. They kept saying they would never let it get out of hand; there was never any admission that the structure conceptually was wrong, or they were too late in the market, and they didn't have any competitive advantage, being number four in a three-man game.

"What they have now done is to admit to that, and Fred has shown his ability to be flexible, albeit after causing a lot of problems. I think the guy has changed and is willing to admit he made a big mistake."

Hometown analyst David Guthrie saw no likelihood that disenchanted investors would undertake to pressure the Federal Express board to remove Smith as chairman. "I don't think there is any heir apparent out there who could move up and take his job," Guthrie said. "In spite of all the problems they have had, Fred is still highly regarded by most of the employees. I don't think there are many out there who would vote to have somebody else running the company.

"I think this illustrates, more than anything else, that even a smart person only has one brilliant idea in their entire life. And Fred did, back in the early seventies. It is very unlikely that a person is going to have two or more brilliant ideas. So they've tried ZapMail, they've tried Europe . . . Still nothing can compare with the original idea."

Guthrie estimated the European restructuring would save Federal Express only $150 million a year but saw enough positive signs to change the negative position Morgan Keegan had taken on the stock for three years. "We finally put an accumulate rating on it. . . . It will take a while, but this is the best shot they've really had in five years to get turned around and back on track."

The clouds lifted a trifle at the end of June 1992. New York's Morgan Stanley & Co. analyst, Kevin Murphy, decided that Federal Express losses in fiscal 1993 would decline sharply and issued a "buy" recommendation, causing the stock to jump by almost $5 to $45.125 a share on the New York exchange.

Federal Express maintains a stringent and effective shield on leaks from corporate headquarters. In victory or defeat, Fred Smith has rarely exhibited his emotions. The *Journal of Commerce and Commercial* said accurately that the "ashes" of the European venture was a "bitter but necessary pill" for the FedEx chairman. Yet there was no official, or unofficial, word indicating Smith lost any of his corporate power—or his eagerness to take on new entrepreneurial challenges.

"Fred lives for competition," said Pepper Rodgers. "He likes to see who blinks first."

By the year 2000 Smith will be turning fifty-six, still young for a chief executive of a multibillion-dollar company. If his vision remains sharp, in any challenge down the road to his air cargo supremacy, who would dare risk betting that Fred Smith would be the first to blink?

NOTES AND ACKNOWLEDGMENTS

Frederick W. Smith's interest in having his biography written, by me or by anybody, is "absolutely, positively" nil. That was clear from the outset. In the spring of 1990, having finished my book on Sam Walton, I was casting about for another interesting and emerging personality in American business to write about. I was familiar with Federal Express but knew nothing of its founder. I made a small expedition into history and discovered the intimate linkage of the fabulous "transportation" Smiths—grandfather, father, and son— and became infatuated with their colorful story.

When I mentioned my prospective subject to people who know him, they immediately tried to discourage me: "He's a very private person. He won't help you at all. He'll fight you."

Fred Smith did not make any contribution to this book, nor did his company. He declined requests for interviews and ignored my efforts to establish any kind of "liaison for factual information" with his subordinates at Memphis FedEx headquarters. I have no quarrel with his attitude and, in fact, feel sympathetic about the awkward situations that have arisen in his life, which doubtless foster his disinclination to be the subject of personal history.

In Vietnam Fred Smith was a brave and gallant marine and a genuine hero of the war—lucky to come out of it alive. In America's business history he will go down as one of the foremost entrepreneurs of the century, and deservedly so. But his youthful adventures and his early and unremitting passionate drive for success, coupled with a few horrid instances of abysmal bad luck, have tarnished his otherwise white knight persona. I believe he ducked the opportunity to participate in this biography chiefly because of those embarrassments. However, if a fair, honest, and worthwhile biography is to be written of any public figure, especially one who may serve, as Fred Smith does, as an inspiration to oncoming generations, doors must not be closed on the bad episodes in a life and opened only on the spotless.

It required a year and a half to gather the facts and write Fred Smith's life story—up to now. That meant combing courthouse files in Arkansas, Tennessee, Kentucky, Missouri, and Illinois, usually in a musty basement vault, for records of births, marriages, wills, lawsuits, and so on. At the same time I did intense research in newspaper morgues, library archives, and cemeteries. But most of all I talked to people—about Fred Smith. In all, there were more than two hundred interviews.

None was more forthcoming or helpful than Smith's mother, Sally Hook, whom I first interviewed in her condominium on the western side of Little Rock, Arkansas, in the fall of 1990. Gracious and soft-spoken, she evokes the "southern lady" gentility of plantation days. She was pleased that I was writing a book about the family and spent many hours telling me of Smith family history: about her romance with big Fred Smith and their marriage, and her rush in 1944 over rural roads to reach the hospital at Marks, Mississippi, before her son Fred was born.

Sally Hook sat on her living room sofa and conversed with my wife and me as if we were kinfolk who had dropped by for a Sunday visit, and she volunteered—though she knew her son had declined to be interviewed—to try to talk him into meeting with us and her. She asked us to come back for other visits, and we have stayed in touch by phone. She was unable, however, to change Fred Smith's intransigence. Others in the immediate family also have been forthcoming in interviews, especially Smith's artistic half sister, Fredette Smith Eagle, who lives in a little mansion at McLean, Virginia, overlooking the Potomac River. She is an avid and keen student of family history and a raconteur of note and wit. For their input, my thanks also to Charlotte Smith of Fort Lauderdale, Florida, the second of big Fred's four wives, and mother of Fredette; Bryan Eagle III, Fredette's son, and her former husband, Bryan Eagle, both of Memphis; Laura Ann Rohm of Robstown, Texas, Fred Smith's adopted half sister; and his half brother Gary West, of Memphis. Also his mother-in-law, Kathleen Hammond Davis, and her son Buddy, both of Memphis; as well as several cousins (of varying degrees) including Joann Smith of Destin, Florida, Lindsey Smith Brady of West Palm Beach, Florida, Judge Carl Smith of Metropolis, Illinois, and Linn Smith of Bridgeport, Illinois; as well as Jewel Hook and Linda Reeves, both of Memphis; and a descendant of Captain Jim Buck's wife, William J. Windland of Memphis.

Among the former Federal Express executives interviewed were Michael J. Fitzgerald of Oxford, Maryland; J. Tucker Morse, Colonel Irby V. Tedder, and Lucien Taillac, all of Little Rock, Arkansas; Roger J. Frock of Annapolis, Maryland; Charles L. Lea, Jr., of New York City; Joe Golden of Mobile, Alabama; Richard C. Runyon of Los Angeles, California; and Art Bass, Francis X. Maguire, Charlotte Curtis Houser, William Arthur, and his wife, Jeanne, and Alvin J. Jeffrey, and his wife, Johnnie, all of Memphis.

Information on Fred Smith's tours in Vietnam came from the U.S. Marine Corps history section in Washington, D.C., where Lena Kaljot was of great assistance; and from interviews with Major General Carl A. Youngdale of Virginia Beach, Virginia, Lieutenant Colonel D. N. Rexroad of Tallahassee, Florida, Colonel H. A. Fritz Zander of Havelock, North Carolina, Lieutenant Colonel Billy Dee Bouldin of Twenty Nine Palms, California, Major Edward J. Murphy of Southern Pines, North Carolina, Colonel Stan Carpenter of the Marine Aviation Association at Quantico, Virginia, and his secretary, Nancy Campbell, and Jay Gourley and Peter Copeland of Washington, D.C.

Classmates who helped fill in the Yale years included Dennis Tippo of Andover, Massachussets, Michael Neal Waterman, Jr., of Dallas, Texas, Gilbert Watts Humphrey of Sewickey, Pennsylvania, and Bob Frame of San Mateo, California. Also interviewed were former Yale professors Roulon Welles of Salt Lake City, Utah,

George Pierson of New Haven, Connecticut, Robert S. Cohen of Boston, and Richard Corbin Porter of Ann Arbor, Michigan, along with Terry Holcomb of the Yale development office, and student Nicholas Gilhool, who did research.

For help on the history of the steamboat era I am indebted to Captain William Tippitt of Hernando, Mississippi, a renowned river authority and writer; Captain Tom Meanley of San Diego, California; Colonel Thomas Tappan of Memphis; Captain John Beatty of Warsaw, Kentucky; Kelly Horn of the Clarksville, Tennessee, *Leaf Chronicle;* and two invaluable reference books, *Way's Packet Directory 1848–1983,* compiled by Frederick Way, Jr. (Ohio University Press, Athens, 1983) and *Way's Steam Towboat Directory,* compiled by Frederick Way, Jr., with Joseph W. Rutter (Ohio University Press, Athens, 1990), through which volumes I was skillfully piloted at the Cincinnati Public Library by rare books researcher Melissa Kesterman.

Eyewitness accounts of the two fatal automobile accidents in which Fred Smith was involved were obtained from retired Tennessee State Trooper Melvin Holland of Parson, Tennessee, Milton Huggins of Michie, Tennessee, the Reverend Sam N. Clements of Westmoreland, Tennessee, and Dr. and Mrs. Eugene Gadberry of Memphis, in the Pickwick Lake incident; and from Detective Eugene Lee Milner and former prosecutor Reed L. Malkin, both of Memphis, and the Brantley Gillespie Funeral Home in Olive Branch, Mississippi, in the Memphis hit-run case.

Research into the bank fraud trial included obtaining the 447-page transcript and interviews with defense attorney Lucius Burch of Memphis (who was also a fount of data on other subjects), prosecutor W. H. "Sonny" Dillahunty of Little Rock, and Herbert Hall McAdams and Griffin Smith of the Union National Bank. At the Little Rock, Arkansas, *Gazette* (since closed) help was obtained from David Petty, managing editor, Joe Nabbefeld, business reporter, and Pat Patterson, photographer.

My considerable assistance at the *Memphis Commercial Appeal* came principally from Lionel Linder, editor; Joseph Williams, business manager; Frank Ahlgren and Gordon Hanna, retired editors; Colleen Conant, former managing editor; Walter Dawson, metro editor, now executive news editor; Ginny Everett, the librarian, and her assistants, Rosemary Nelms and Greg Paraham; Larry Coyne, photo director; and John Branston, Mary Alice Quinn, Debbie White, Jerome Wright, Jim Chisum, Jim Kingsley, the late Dan Henderson, Mike Fleming, former staffer Lewis Nolan, and retirees the late Alice Fulbright and Irma Merrill. At Nashville I was aided at the *Tennesseean* by John Seigenthaler, publisher, and Annette Morrison, librarian. In Paducah, Kentucky, I was helped at the *Sun* by Jim Paxton, editor, and Hazel Davis, librarian; at the Paducah Public Library by Patricia Powell; at the Jackson Purchase Museum by Charles Manchester, curator; by rivermen George Crounse and Louis Igert, Jr.; by Betty Boggess of Oak Grove Cemetery; and by James Craig of the Roth Funeral Home.

At the Memphis Public Library I am indebted to Patricia M. LaPointe, in the history section; at Memphis University School to Kathy Daniel Patterson and Cathy Evans; and at Memphis State University to Professors Wayne Podgorski, Herman Patterson, Charles Crawford, and Michele Fagan, librarian of special collections and her assistants, Ed Frank and Bobbette Walker. And also in Memphis to John T. Fisher, Colleen McCarthy, John S. King III, Lucia Doggrell, Shelby Foote, Dr. George Coors, Judge Wyeth Chandler, Lucia Outlan, James K. Dobbs III, P. K. Seidman, Clark Porteous, the late Arthur Halle, Norfleet Turner, Curt Norred, Frank H. Liberto, Ernest Williams III, Allan Wade, Bill Farris, and Forest Hill Mid-town Cemetery.

For his superbly researched book on Federal Express, *Absolutely, Positively Overnight!* (with Roger R. Easson, Memphis: St. Luke's Press, 1988), I salute the amiable Dr. Robert A. Sigafoos, formerly of Memphis State University, now retired to an Ozark mountain chalet at Eureka Springs, Arkansas, and thank him for our frank and open conversations and for his cogent and interesting observations on the entrepreneurship of Frederick Smith.

Dixie Greyhound Bus history was hard to come by, but some insight was provided by George Graveley of Dallas, Professor Carlton Jackson of Bowling Green, Kentucky, Howard Loring of Nashville, and Leroy Logsdon and Frank Maness of Memphis. Others to thank are Joe Rogers, Sr., of Atlanta; Mary Lindsey Dickinson of

Hernando, Mississippi; Tom Weber, editor of the *News* at Stuart, Florida; Elizabeth Beckerle Tolles of Summit, New Jersey; Evelyn Turner of Tutwiler, Mississippi; Vernon Giss, Mike Smith, Jon Jacoby, and the late "Mr. Witt" Stephens, all of Stephens, Inc., Little Rock; J. E. Furr, Jr., of Clarksdale, Mississippi; General Howell M. Estes of Bethesda, Maryland; Ken McAdams, Chappaqua, New York; Joann Julius of the *Professional Pilot* magazine of Alexandria, Virginia; and Tom McFarland of Boston, section head, Federal Reserve System.

▶ INDEX